D0875721

Elizabeth Murray

Elizabeth Murray

A Woman's Pursuit of Independence

in Eighteenth-Century America

PATRICIA CLEARY

University of Massachusetts Press   Amherst

LC 00-030277

ISBN 1-55849-263-1

Designed by Mary Mendell

Set in Baskerville by Keystone Typesetting, Inc.

Printed and bound by Sheridan Books, Inc.

Library of Congress Cataloging-in-Publication Data

Cleary, Patricia, 1962–

Elizabeth Murray : a woman's pursuit of independence in
eighteenth-century America / Patricia Cleary.

p.   cm.

Includes bibliographical references (p.   ) and index.

ISBN 1-55849-263-1 (cloth : alk. paper)

1. Murray, Elizabeth, 1726–1785.   2. Boston (Mass.) — History —
Revolution, 1775–1783.   3. Women — Massachusetts — Boston — Biography.
4. Businesswomen — Massachusetts — Boston — Biography.   5. United
States — History — Revolution, 1775–1783 — Women.   I. Murray,
Elizabeth, 1726–1785.   II. Title.

E73.44.C6 2000   974.4'6102'092 — dc21   [B]   00-030277

British Library Cataloguing in Publication data are available.

This book is published with the support and cooperation
of the University of Massachusetts Boston.

For my mother and in memory of my father,
Lorraine E. and Thomas G. Cleary
Thanks for everything M & P

Contents

ILLUSTRATIONS

ACKNOWLEDGMENTS

Many have lived through the process of this book with me. When Tim Breen first sent me to the basement of the Northwestern University library to read the advertisements of colonial shopkeepers, I wondered what I — never a fan of shopping — would find. I thank him for that initial excellent advice and for his ongoing encouragement. More than anyone else, Andrew Hurley deserves the title of reader extraordinaire. With unflagging enthusiasm, he has read and reread every word of this book, finding fascinating connections in the history of consumption between the eighteenth and twentieth centuries. In endless conversations, he has offered incisive criticism and useful suggestions. For his good ideas, bad jokes, and friendship, I thank him. Other colleagues and friends who volunteered — or graciously agreed — to read parts or all of this study merit special mention. Under time pressure, Carol Cleary-Schultz and Elizabeth Young read faster than I could revise and gave me the kind of intelligent commentary that every author would be lucky to have. Cornelia Hughes Dayton, June Namias, George Robb, Sharon Salinger, Sean Smith, and Peter Thompson have provided constructive feedback, various kinds of assistance, and welcome encouragement. For warm hospitality, sound advice, unstinting support, good wine, and delicious food, I am grateful to Kitty Cleary Adamovic, David Cressy, Claire Martin, Debi McGinnis, Tim Meeks, Pamela Roberts, David Shafer, Sharon Sievers, Anita Tien, and Kim Trimble. Margaret Howe Ewing has been most generous in allowing me to use her private collection of Murray family papers; she and her husband, Joe, graciously opened their home to me and shared their enthusiasm for Murray family history. For help in Scotland, I thank Stephen Busby for his time and assistance and Christina Cleary for her superlative and indispensable navigational skills. To the Library Café in Long Beach, I am indebted for steady currents of caffeine and electricity.

To my family and friends, who came to know the details of Elizabeth Murray's life too well, aren't you glad this book is finished? For suffering through deadlines and distracting me from them, I thank Tom and Karen Rabideau Cleary, Mike and Carol Lillian Cleary, and Greg Pepek. And to my mother, who asked, "How's Elizabeth?" as often as she inquired about the weather, thank you. I am very sorry that my father did not live to see this book in print, but at least he was able to read parts of it; he admitted that it helped him fall asleep several evenings.

A number of institutions and audiences facilitated the completion of this study. California State University, Long Beach, provided course reductions and summer stipends to enable me to pursue this project; I thank Dorothy Abrahamse especially for her support. My students inspired me to do my best to make the past alive. The Berkshire Conference of Women Historians made it possible for me to spend several months in Boston doing research. The Bunting Institute at Radcliffe gave me an office as big as my living room, a congenial group of fellow scholars, and the opportunity to present my findings before a group of brilliant critics; Bonnie Honig and Laurel Thatcher Ulrich asked probing questions that made me rethink parts of the study. As a summer fellow and regular visitor at the Massachusetts Historical Society (MHS), I enjoyed the privilege of conducting research at a wonderful facility. Conrad Wright, Peter Drummey, Virginia Smith, Ed Hanson, Donald Yacovone, and many other members of the staff generously gave their expertise and time to assist me. Audiences at the MHS and the Early Americanists seminar at the Huntington Library offered helpful criticism. I also thank the staff at the New-York Historical Society, the Museum of Fine Arts in Boston, the Historical Society of Pennsylvania, and the American Antiquarian Society. Some parts of this study have been published previously in different forms. For permission to use that material here, I thank the Massachusetts Historical Society, New York University Press, and the *Pennsylvania Magazine of History and Biography*. I also thank Paul Wright, my editor at the University of Massachusetts Press, and Nancy J. Raynor, for her careful copyediting of the manuscript.

P. C.

ELIZABETH MURRAY

Introduction:
An Extraordinary Ordinary Woman

I beg to know what else I am accused of. Be assured, Dear Sir, I will with pleasure account for every action that I remember since the year seventeen hundred & twenty six. — Elizabeth Murray Inman, 30 July 1775

If these words, simultaneously pleading and defiant, sound like those of someone on trial, in a sense they were. During the summer of 1775, when Elizabeth Murray Inman wrote these lines to her husband Ralph Inman, she was living on the family farm, trying to protect the year's harvest from scavenging colonial troops. When the countryside erupted in war in April 1775, Ralph chose refuge in the British-occupied town of Boston; Elizabeth did not. Despite his entreaties that she join him, Elizabeth stayed at their Cambridge estate. During this separation Ralph resolved to leave the colonies without Elizabeth, a decision that stunned her. Indignant at her husband's seeming lack of faith in the propriety of her actions and his apparent disinterest in her well-being, Elizabeth was hurt and insulted. As one who took pride in her judgment and abilities, she requested a hearing, proclaiming her willingness to explain her conduct from the year of her birth. Instead of doing so, she responded to Ralph's criticism with anger, questioning his character and reproaching his actions in a sarcastic tone, her frustration barely contained.

The historian can only wish that in lieu of launching a spousal counterattack, Elizabeth Murray Inman had sat down, "with pleasure," and written what she said she could: an account of her every action for the previous forty-nine years. Her compelling and eventful history would make such a record welcome. The sketchiest outlines demonstrate abundantly that her life was one of movement, incident, and adventure. During her youth, she undertook multiple ocean crossings as she journeyed throughout the British Empire, leaving her girlhood home in the Scottish borderlands for the disease-ridden and racially diverse setting of North Carolina, before traveling to the bustling metropolis of London. She finally planted herself in Boston in 1749. There, at the age of twenty-two, she decided to settle in New England's largest town, without friends or family, and to support herself as a shopkeeper. Over the next few decades, she practiced her chosen trade successfully and married three times, once to an elderly man who upon his death left her an extremely rich widow. Indeed, for a time Elizabeth Murray (her birth name) was undoubtedly one of the wealthiest women in colonial America.

Her Revolutionary War experiences captured central dramas of the period, from quartering soldiers and midnight rides to accusations of spying. Both British and American troops were stationed in buildings belonging to her spouses, rendering her position in the conflict perhaps unique among inhabitants of the colonies. In the late 1760s the redcoats took up residence in a sugarhouse run by her second husband; it was from this barracks that they sallied forth in 1770 to fire the shots that created the colonial martyrs of the Boston Massacre. Then, in the wake of the Battle of Lexington and Concord in 1775, the estate where she was living was seized by leaders of the Continental army, who transformed it into the first headquarters of that body and briefly took her prisoner. Both armies thus took shelter in properties that contemporaries associated with her and her family. Murray's own relationship to the troops was equally intense and complex. Loyalist by family association, she felt torn by her fondness for her adopted homeland. She counted both royal officials and high-ranking colonial officers among her friends. During the Battle of Bunker Hill in June 1775, rebel commander General Israel Putman assigned his son to escort Murray on a wild nighttime ride to another family estate far removed from the dangerous fray. Later on in the war, Elizabeth Murray found herself reviled by name in the Revolutionary press as a "masculine" woman and likely spy.

In the absence of a personal memoir recounting such events, the history of Elizabeth Murray could be like that of the overwhelming majority of colonists, its daily detail and texture permanently shrouded by time and a paucity of evidence. We know very little in depth about most eighteenth-century individuals, especially women; relatively few left records that make it possible to flesh out their existence. Moreover, not everyone, male or female, possessed literacy skills, nor did the literate automatically save their scribblings for posterity. And women were much less likely than men either to be literate or to have their papers preserved.[1] As a result, we simply lack much of the qualitative material necessary to reconstruct individual lives — the records of days, hopes, plans, and passions that sometimes emerge in personal writings, in diaries, and in letters.[2] Such evidence-driven difficulties involved in recapturing personal narratives stand out as one of the central challenges in writing the history of early American women.

Fortunately, Elizabeth Murray Campbell Smith Inman, whose history holds significant potential for enlarging our understanding of eighteenth-century colonial America and women's lives in that period in particular, left a comparative wealth of evidence documenting her existence. Her personal papers, my central source for this study, represent a rich and far from exhausted treasure of records, including commercial accounts and correspondence from the 1740s through the 1780s. In their letters, Elizabeth Murray and her friends, relatives, and business correspondents commented on subjects ranging from politics, education, and commerce to fashion, friendship, and marriage. As they migrated throughout the Anglo-American world, they communicated their joys and sorrows to absent friends.

The transatlantic and intercolonial nature of this correspondence provides a broad, comparative canvas for analyzing women's lives in the eighteenth century. Elizabeth Murray did not experience her life wholly within the context of colonial America's geographic boundaries. To the contrary, she maintained cultural, economic, and emotional contacts throughout the Anglo-American world and crossed the Atlantic repeatedly, undertaking hazardous voyages with surprisingly little hesitation to settle in new lands. Accordingly, in this book I endeavor to locate Elizabeth Murray and her associates within a world of permeable physical and cultural borders; as Nancy Cott puts it, "Once we leave behind the conception of history as the story of the past politics of nation states, there is no compelling reason why we should hold history within national boundaries."[3] This broader view makes particular sense for studying Elizabeth Murray, a woman who with apparent ease also crossed other kinds of symbolic borders based on political allegiance and expectations of appropriate behavior for a woman.

I first encountered Elizabeth Murray in the context of studying the work of "she Merchants" in colonial America, women shopkeepers who sold imported British goods.[4] In the late 1740s and 1750s, as she established herself as a purveyor of imported wares in Boston and advertised her stock, Elizabeth Murray, like hundreds of other colonial women, participated in commercial developments that transformed consumption in the eighteenth century.[5] The absence of such women of commerce from the historical record has been the result of oversight, not lack of importance.[6]

Shopkeepers linked colonial consumers to British manufacturers and to merchants on both sides of the Atlantic, performing a range of essential services in an expanding economy.[7] Although shopkeepers primarily retailed goods, some also sold merchandise wholesale and engaged in small-scale importing; such trading activities could blur distinctions between shopkeepers and merchants. Although business practices may have overlapped in individual cases and shopkeepers could be either male or female, merchants were typically and almost exclusively male.

Gender influenced Elizabeth Murray's entrance into and experience of this commercial world. Her choice of occupation, trials and successes, and later efforts to sponsor other women in retailing ventures suggest that women in the colonies found keeping shop a relatively accessible and rewarding trade. Selling imported merchandise did more than provide women like Elizabeth Murray with a livelihood. Their economic activities had political ramifications and personal implications that shaped their sense of identity and gender consciousness. Through keeping shop, women confronted the expectations governing their social, economic, and political roles. Occasionally, particularly as the Revolution approached, they encountered situations that enlarged their opportunities for independent thought and action.

On yellowed, fragile sheaves of paper, Elizabeth Murray's uneven scrawl and unpunctuated prose survive. So, too, does her voice. As in the epigraph that opens this introduction, Elizabeth Murray demands to be heard. Even as she addressed her husband formally, as was the custom, she prepared to challenge him. She chafed against the constraints of her role as a married woman, a position she had freely chosen, and against the restrictions she felt had been placed on her in a difficult political situation. She behaved according to her own best judgment and was shocked when her husband did not approve.

Although there is nothing innately significant about one woman's difference of opinion with her spouse over two hundred years ago, that disagreement provides a clue to understanding important themes in Elizabeth Murray's life. Acting in accordance with eighteenth-century dictates for womanly behavior — by marrying and trying to preserve her family's estate — Elizabeth Murray nonetheless found herself challenging social norms, in this case, the authority of husbands over wives. Throughout her life, as similar types of situations arose, Elizabeth Murray became a figurative as well as a literal border crosser, an individual who, ironically, transgressed contemporary mores while nominally fulfilling gender roles. In negotiating her way through these roles, Murray carved out a niche for herself and other women that existed at times in tension with accepted notions of feminine behavior. That tension illuminates the ways in which these mores were contested and in flux in the Anglo-American world of the mid— to late eighteenth century. Thus Elizabeth Murray's history can illustrate the constraints and choices colonial women encountered in their daily lives, how and why they chose particular paths, and what mattered most to them. She is at once a representative and a unique woman. Although such a statement appears at first glance to be contradictory, it captures the dynamics of Elizabeth Murray's life. Overall patterns of experience, woven out of the threads of family, migration, and marriage, for instance, bear similarities to those of other colonial women; it is the design that proves to be distinctive on closer examination.

Repeatedly, Elizabeth Murray attempted to preserve some control in situations that normally precluded women's autonomy. How and why she did so is a central focus of my work. In this book I ask how an eighteenth-century woman tried to make a place for herself — and for other women as well — in a society that did not help women to do so when their aspirations conflicted with expectations for their sex.

I follow one woman as she matured and grappled with her sense of self, with the ambiguities and ambivalence inherent in her experiences as a woman, wife, and political being. In each phase of her life, she acted very much within the context of familial ties and responsibilities; the story of one woman is at the same time the chronicle of a family.

Firmly grounded in the historical moment of the second half of the eighteenth century, this examination of Elizabeth Murray's life places her in the midst of critical developments of the period, exploring both how she understood them and how they affected her. In her life we can see vividly how an eighteenth-century woman negotiated commercial change and political upheaval, for example, and came to identify herself for a time as an American during a period of cultural Anglicization. I argue that it was her experience of economic self-sufficiency as a shopkeeper which imbued her with "a spirit of independence," a faith in her own abilities and in those of other women.

Nearly as rare as the extensive verbal testimony documenting Elizabeth Murray's life is the visual record. Remarkably, given how few colonial Americans had their portraits done, we know what she looked like. Her two-dimensional image, which graces the cover of this book, was painted by the preeminent colonial portraitist John Singleton Copley in the fall of 1769, when she was forty-three, and now belongs to the Museum of Fine Arts in Boston, where one may — or may not — see it. Over the course of the past several years, as I visited Boston to do the research for this biography, I discovered that the museum staff members were playing "musical walls" with her image; first she was in one room, the next time in a hallway, then she had no place to hang at all. When I went to see the 1995 Copley exhibition, hopeful that the painting might have been pulled out of a closet, I happily found Elizabeth Murray's likeness in a gallery with those of several of her contemporaries, although not with the major Copley show. When I returned a few weeks later, she was gone.

The mystery of the elusive figure that refused to be pinned down struck me as oddly analogous to the process of writing a biography — now you see your subject, now you don't — and therefore as needing an explanation, which Carol Troyen, the museum's very helpful curator of American paintings, provided. Confirming that the portrait was on view only sporadically, she employed a sports analogy to express the museum's policy, telling me that Elizabeth Murray's was a "B–level" portrait in its present condition which came out when the "A team" was elsewhere or outside the museum. That was why it was on view during the Copley exhibition. All the good Copleys joined the center-court show on the second floor, leaving room for Elizabeth Murray to get a shot at a first-floor gallery. When the Copleys not part of the traveling display returned to their rightful places, Elizabeth Murray went back into storage, the perennial benchwarmer. When I asked what made her portrait "B-level," Troyen explained: "She needs some conservation. She's dirty. The varnish has yellowed, it's grimy, the darks are sinking, [which means] for example, you can't see the pleats or folds in the dress." She added, "It's not as though it's a bad picture."[8]

The issue for the Museum of Fine Arts, in a sense, was competition: which paintings deserved the spotlight and why? The curator's explanation centered on the condition and quality of this portrait in comparison with that of other Copleys in their collection, such as the famous image of Revolutionary figure Paul Revere. Maybe, the curator concluded, some day, after cleaning, the portrait would "sing again." Artistically, Elizabeth Murray did not at that moment deserve the spotlight. Historically, however, I thought she did.

In composing this prose portrait, I have chosen to arrange the pieces in chronological order, with each chapter focusing on a distinctive phase of Elizabeth Murray's life. Each section is framed in terms of her movement through cycles of dependence and independence in familial, legal, economic, and political contexts. It is not a linear progress. In choosing this structure, I have emphasized major turning points in Elizabeth Murray's maturing sense of herself and her priorities. Each of the chapters also addresses important historical themes and developments — from migration, social mobility, and marriage to commerce, female friendship, and Revolutionary politics — that shaped her experiences throughout her life cycle.

The first chapter traces the arc of loss and mobility leading to Elizabeth Murray's first encounters with dependence and independence. It opens with her birth and youthful trials. Born in Scotland in 1726, she came to the colonies for the first time in the late 1730s, after both of her parents had died. In North Carolina, she lived with her oldest brother, James, acting as his housekeeper, a position of some responsibility, before they both returned to Scotland a couple of years later; there, he married a first cousin. When in 1749 James, his new wife and daughter, and Elizabeth all came back to America after residing for several years in Britain, they stopped in Boston on their way to North Carolina. There, Elizabeth Murray made the fateful decision not to go on to the south. Instead of accepting the status of dependent by returning to reside in her brother's home, she chose to establish herself as a shopkeeper in New England's largest port.

In this chapter I explore decisions to migrate and examine how the Murrays used geographic mobility as a strategy for achieving economic mobility. Family matters occupied their time, energy, and attention as they moved throughout the Atlantic world. Without a permanent, fixed locale, they were people in motion whose definitions of their responsibilities and loyalties underwent similar fluctuations. In this period of journeying from one setting to another, of making the transition from dependent girlhood to youthful independence, Elizabeth Murray sought to establish herself as a competent adult, capable of supporting herself.

The second chapter focuses on 1749–60, the period during which Elizabeth Murray kept shop. During these years she came into her own as a businesswoman and married for the first time. She kept shop before, during, and after that marriage, selling imported British fashions and even traveling to London once to select wares she thought would best suit the Boston market. Exploring her midcentury experiences as a shopkeeper, I address women's involvement in retailing enterprises and commercial differences between Boston and London. In comparison with other occupations open to colonial American women, shopkeeping held a distinctive appeal, one that Elizabeth Murray and other women acknowledged explicitly. Ongoing discussions among these individuals about trade and fashion provide insight into the cultural ties between Great Britain and America. In addition, I examine how the effort to achieve financial independence on Elizabeth Murray's part led to a redistribution of authority within her family network. Her successes enhanced her voice in family matters. At the same time, her mercantile activities influenced her attitudes toward a range of issues that would occupy her later years, including the education and social roles of women and the political conflict between the colonies and the mother country.

During the 1750s, Elizabeth Murray entered the first of her three marriages. In this union with Thomas Campbell she experienced the legal coverture that attended marriage for women — that is, marriage, which had both clear religious and legal components, assumed a unity of interests between spouses and the impossibility of a separate legal identity for the woman. Once married, a woman could no longer make contracts or write a will, sue, or keep any income she might earn. Instead, these rights and responsibilities belonged to her husband. When Thomas Campbell died before the decade's end, the new widow found herself in contention over the estate with her in-laws. By the end of the 1750s, having known various roles — single woman, wife, beleaguered widow, businesswoman — Elizabeth Murray Campbell faced difficult choices about her future.

Her decision to remarry and its repercussions form the subject of the third chapter, which covers the period 1760–69. Her second match transformed her life, largely because of her husband's age and finances. When they married, she was thirty-three, and James Smith, an extremely prosperous and childless widower, was seventy. Soon they both retired. Self-support was no longer a pressing concern for her; James Smith had signed a prenuptial agreement that largely canceled out the legal coverture of marriage and made her a wealthy woman. Thus Elizabeth Murray Smith gave up one kind of security — the full legal independence of widowhood — but gained financial security while retaining a measure of a separate legal identity. For the rest of the decade she spent much of her time caring for her frequently ill and feeble spouse. In 1769 the marriage ended with James Smith's death. Exhausted from caring for him and apparently not in good health herself, she decided to leave the colonies for a rest and returned to Great Britain to see her relatives. It was during preparations for that trip that she commissioned the Copley portrait.

The fourth chapter follows Elizabeth Murray's path from the independence of new widowhood to her resumption of the dependence of married life. Her sojourn abroad from 1769 to 1771 witnessed a rebirth of sorts. Despairing of her health when she left the colonies, she regained optimism and energy in Great Britain. A woman of means, she followed her own whims and wishes and took to directing the activities of others, particularly young women. In England she decided that two of her teenaged nieces had been educated improperly. They were trained in such decorative accomplishments as speaking French, dancing, and drawing, rather than in practical skills, like bookkeeping, that she had come to value through personal experience. Equally problematic, the girls did not have the wherewithal to support the appearance that their genteel education dictated. To solve these dilemmas, their aunt determined that they should leave their home, move to Boston, and become shopkeepers under her sponsorship. It would be good for them: "rouse their faculties," she declared.[9]

Given Elizabeth Murray Smith's wealth and resources—she was the only one in her family in a position to offer financial help—her siblings agreed with her plans. Accordingly, she sent her older niece to New England in 1770 and brought the younger with her when she returned in 1771. Under her auspices and thanks to her guidance and generous credit, Polly and Anne Murray became retailers. Thus, although she had achieved real financial independence through the not uncommon strategy of marrying well, Elizabeth Murray Smith sought to establish young women in positions of self-support through the means she had first pursued herself: shopkeeping. This chapter, then, addresses women's education and Elizabeth Murray Smith's efforts to instill in her nieces and several other young women a sense of industry and independence. Explicit discussions of the meaning of women's education among Elizabeth Murray Smith and her friends lend immediacy to contemporary debates over women's roles and their responsibilities in colonial society. She, as well as some of her friends and family members, saw a disjunction between the education and opportunities available to women on opposite sides of the Atlantic.

After making a number of negative pronouncements regarding the likelihood of ever remarrying, Elizabeth Murray Smith surprised nearly all her acquaintances by taking a third spouse almost immediately after her return to Boston. The fourth chapter closes with her new life in New England and her 1771 marriage to Ralph Inman, a widower whom she had known since her first years in Boston. Although marriage centered on intimate ties between individuals, it carried wider repercussions for family fortunes, finances, and relationships. Given the larger and public ramifications of this private act, it is not surprising that each of Elizabeth's decisions to marry involved balancing generational, personal, and pecuniary interests. Like James Smith, Ralph Inman signed a prenuptial agreement that guaranteed his wife the right to dispose of her property as she wished. Despite this contract, Elizabeth's family worried about the impact of her marriage on their financial situation. During the first few years of this marriage, Elizabeth juggled her various responsibilities to her new family and the nieces she had brought to America. This marriage, which lasted until Elizabeth Murray Inman's death in 1785, proved the most problematic of her three unions.

The fifth chapter opens with the spring of 1775 and traces women's Revolutionary political activities, experiences, and expressions during the war. At the outset of the hostilities, Elizabeth was at the center of the maelstrom, guarding the family property in Cambridge while her husband Ralph remained behind British lines in Boston. The separation between the two became the source of profound marital discord. In addition to her problems with her spouse, Elizabeth Murray Inman had to deal with the vulnerability of her position in the countryside. Briefly held prisoner by American troops, she saw her home transformed into the barracks for colonial soldiers in the summer of 1775.

During this period, Elizabeth Murray Inman and many of her friends were caught up in the tumult of rebellion. As residents in the Boston area, they found their daily routines charged with political connotations and themselves the occasional targets of patriotic mobs. These moments provided the impetus for heated conversations among women who once considered themselves nonparticipants in the realm of politics. Some assumed a political voice when their husband's loyalties met with public censure. At the center of this circle, Elizabeth Murray Inman tried to keep up the spirits of her friends, even as she wrangled with the recalcitrant Ralph. With members of her extended family supporting opposing sides, she was particularly well positioned to view the conflict as one with personal repercussions.

In the sixth chapter of the book I trace Elizabeth Murray Inman's final illness and the controversy that enveloped the settlement of her estate. Acting on her rights to draw up a will as specified by the terms of her prenuptial agreement with Ralph Inman, she bequeathed a relatively paltry legacy to her spouse. The struggles that followed over the executorship of her estate, as well as the accusations that flew between family members and across the Atlantic, reveal with clarity the difficulties that women encountered in attempting to determine their fates and distribute their property, even when they had the legal authority to do so.

In the "Note on Writing Biography" I consider several issues of interest to students of history and biographers regarding bias, point of view, and presentation of self in various texts. How does one interpret an individual's life, capturing it in all its nuanced vividness? In the end, some questions will remain. It is not possible to know fully the dynamics of Elizabeth Murray's relationships with each of her spouses, friends, and relatives. The attitudes that she ultimately embraced toward gender equality and political change remain somewhat obscured.

In contemplating Elizabeth Murray's experiences, the reader will come closer to discovering what it meant to be a woman in eighteenth-century America, what was within the realm of possibility for someone of her background. For Elizabeth Murray, the economic self-sufficiency she sought came partly as a result of familial assistance in her early life. Without it, she would have had to struggle greatly to eke out a living as a retailer. Her successes as a shopkeeper laid the basis for her views of the need for women to be self-supporting, her estimation of their abilities, and her desire for preserving elements of her own autonomy, even within the legally restrictive bonds of marriage. This narrative populates the colonial world with women and men who were vigorous, voluble, and occasionally volatile. Mobile and active, Elizabeth Murray, like her contemporary Benjamin Franklin, tried out different roles in her search for success. Immigrant, entrepreneur, wife, foster mother, political commentator, and devoted friend, Elizabeth Murray lived an adventure. Her story conveys a breathtaking sense of movement and excitement and an appreciation for the physical, cultural, and emotional forces shaping lives in a specific historical moment, when the ties between the personal and the political, the ephemeral and the epochal developments of the day called forth unsuspected autonomy and actions that rendered ordinary lives extraordinary.

1

Migration and Mobility

Men and women living in Britain's North American colonies in the eighteenth century did not have to look far to find sources of disruption in their lives. Although distant from the seat of empire, colonists found themselves caught up in its workings, suffering the repercussions of repeated European wars and political turmoil. For new immigrants, already uprooted, the advent of war further rent the fabric of daily life, bringing international conflicts home in an immediate and painful way. Such was the situation of Elizabeth Murray, fourteen years old, parentless and a newcomer to America, when one of the century's many contests over commercial and colonial territorial rights erupted. At odds over trade and the Spanish seizure of English vessels, Britain went to war in October 1739 and asked for colonial troops. The ensuing War of Jenkins' Ear, named for the mariner who years before had lost that bit of flesh — and preserved it — when his ship was attacked by the Spanish, led thousands of colonial volunteers to leave their home. Elizabeth's closest companion, her brother William, was one of those who joined the king's forces and sailed south to participate in the disastrous siege of Cartagena, the Spanish military outpost on the coast of present-day Colombia.[1] Then sixteen and preparing to embark on his first naval expedition, William was forced to confront the prospect that he might not survive long in his chosen profession. He wrote a will, leaving all he had to his younger sister. When he showed her the paper "and told her what it was," Betty, as she was then known, began to cry, the tears running "down her Cheeks like hail."[2] The document tangibly symbolized the possibility that their imminent parting might prove a permanent one.

Only recently settled in America, Elizabeth and William had good reason to dread the prospect of separation. Born and raised in the Scottish borderlands, the childhood companions were extremely attached to each other. In their young lives, they had already experienced a great deal of loss and upheaval. In 1728, when they were toddlers, their father had died; six years later they left the farm where they had been born, the only home they had known. Then, after their mother's death in 1737, Elizabeth and William were shuttled between relatives, with responsibility for the orphaned pair eventually devolving on their brother and guardian, James. Because he had emigrated to North Carolina several years earlier, James had to return to Scotland to settle his mother's affairs and retrieve his younger siblings, bringing them back with him to the colonies in 1739. Now, less than a year later, these young newcomers in a strange land prepared for another round of farewells, with the specter of death raised by the will that James insisted William prepare.

If there was continuity in Elizabeth Murray's childhood and youth, any element that was predictable, it was that she had repeatedly said good-bye to loved ones and homes, familiar faces and settings. Mobility and loss accompanied her early years like a refrain. Yet in moving often, Elizabeth Murray and her siblings were far from unusual. Indeed, they were like tens of thousands of other Scottish emigrants in the eighteenth century who crossed Scotland's boundaries and spread out across the British Empire. Journeying south to England or west to America, the Scots migrated in hopes of finding better opportunities, seeing an irresistible promise of upward economic mobility. Although there were various avenues for seeking advancement, such as through occupational change or educational training, migration was the most important and dramatic strategy the Murrays pursued. When they moved, they traded families, friends, and birthplace — the comfort and security of the known — for the prospect of starting over. Adrift in the empire, they had to forge new contacts, establish themselves in distant and sometimes exotic settings, and build from scratch lives that would sustain them economically and emotionally.

For Elizabeth, the experience of migration would have been marked by sharp social, cultural, and environmental contrasts between her native Scotland and the places she lived subsequently. Born on 7 July 1726, the third daughter and eighth child of Anne Bennet Murray and John Murray, Elizabeth spent her early childhood at

Unthank, a farm not far from Scotland's frontier with England. Taking its name from the ungrateful soil, Unthank sat in a beautiful valley.[3] From a house situated on a low ridge, Elizabeth would have gazed out upon two streams, the Ewes Water and Unthank Burn, which babbled and mingled in the marshy bottomland below, and along whose banks she and her brother William studied their hornbook and learned to read. Soaring hills such as Unthank Pikes — the tallest peak at sixteen hundred feet — which rose to define the sky in every direction.[4] The weather and topography were equally bracing. Unthank was a green bowl that glistened from the rain and sunshine and where clouds moved quickly, casting deep shadows across steep hillsides dotted with sheep. If Elizabeth had climbed an hour or more to the hilltops, she would have seen the larger world beyond. From one summit, she could have almost glimpsed the secluded castle of the Hermitage, the famed locale of Mary Queen of Scots's romantic rendezvous. From another, looking toward the south and west, she might have spotted silvery Solway Firth in the distance. If she had made such a trek, Elizabeth could scarcely have dreamed that she would one day not only see the Atlantic up close but also cross the ocean repeatedly.

With little arable land and rolling hills, the region where Unthank was located seemed better suited to sheep than people.[5] The Murrays' parish of Ewes, at the eastern end of Eskdale, probably came by its name on account of the woolly flocks that it supported.[6] In short, the area was isolated and pastoral, almost beautifully desolate in the eyes of some. The regular and plentiful rainfall, which provided too much moisture for the cultivation of many crops, kept the hills covered in green, except for small patches of purplish heath.[7] Decades after the Murrays and many of their compatriots and neighbors had emigrated, Dorothy Wordsworth, the poet's sister, penned an evocative description of the place, characterizing a Ewes vista as "melancholy and wild, but not dreary, though there was no tree nor shrub; the small streamlet glittered, the hills were populous with sheep; . . . the gentle bending of the valley, and the correspondent softness in the forms of the hills, were of themselves enough to delight the eye."[8] Wordsworth's description of the area could have applied to Unthank itself.

Sheep-raising was most likely the chief enterprise on the farm where Elizabeth was born, with agricultural endeavors relegated to a distant second place by the climate and terrain. If the Murrays had tenants, they were probably farmers who cultivated a range of crops important to the local economy, such as potatoes and barley, a grain used for porridge and fermented to produce beer and whiskey. Husbandmen, who pastured their herds of sheep along the banks of the waterways, would have helped generate the wool that was transformed into stockings, undergarments, and other items of clothing that provided welcome protection against sometimes viciously cold winter temperatures. The frigid and snowy winter of 1739, for example, was so severe that it was impossible for people to break the frozen ground enough the following spring to dig up the peat — chunks of organically rich and combustible earth — that they dried and used to heat their homes.[9]

Just as challenges from climate and topography influenced life in Eskdale, so too did proximity to England. Even the features of the landscape revealed the history of the English connection, with the Esk River deriving its name, which means "strife," and fame from the battles between the Scottish and English that took place along its banks.[10] The cultural legacy of these historic conflicts appeared in language and liturgy. Like other residents of the borderlands for generations, the Murrays spoke English, rather than the Gaelic increasingly relegated to the Highlands, and were Episcopalians, sharing religious convictions with their neighbors to the south.

For the Murrays, raising a growing family was undoubtedly complicated not only by the local terrain and economy but by the Scottish structure of landholding as well. Although related to Scotland's landed gentry, with knights and lairds dotting the family tree, John Murray did not own the Dumfries estate that he and his cousin Anne Bennet had occupied since they married and set up housekeeping in 1712. Instead, he leased the land from the Duke of Buccleuch.[11] One might assume that the Murrays possessed a lowly status because they were not landowners, but such was not the case. In Scotland, where land was concentrated in the hands of a few, tenancy described an economic relationship more than it did one's social status, and tenants had their own subtenants as well as servants.[12] Although the Murrays lacked great wealth, they were nonetheless well connected to the upper social stratum of the area, with direct ties to the titled Sir John Murray of Philipaugh.

Although tenancy of a particular piece of property in Scotland was not necessarily inheritable and therefore could foster geographic instability within a region, this transiency did not translate into severed family ties.[13] After her own marriage, Elizabeth's mother had remained close to her family in a neighboring county and become part of the elaborate network of Murray kin that had long populated southeastern Scotland. When she gave birth to her daughter Elizabeth, thirty-one-year-old Anne probably anticipated that the newborn, if she survived to adulthood, would marry and settle within easy reach. Why should the general course of her daughter's life differ from her own? The multiple migrations of Elizabeth and her siblings would have been difficult for their parents, as representatives of another, earlier generation, to foresee or understand.

If death had not disrupted Elizabeth's childhood so thoroughly, perhaps she never would have left Scotland. But such losses struck the Murray household repeatedly. In February 1728, John Murray died at the age of fifty-one. Two months later, Elizabeth's newly widowed mother gave birth for the last time, to a son, Andrew, who did not live long. Of the nine children Anne Bennet Murray had borne in just under sixteen years, only five yet survived: James, fifteen; Barbara, eleven; John, five; William, four; and Elizabeth, not quite two. These multiple deaths, which were not unusual in an age of high infant mortality rates and medical care which was spotty at best and which could even be life threatening, permanently changed the Murrays' future.

Widowhood for Anne signaled an alteration in the dynamics of family governance, with James, her oldest son, beginning to share authority with her over finances and decisions about how to raise the younger children. Until 1732, all the Murrays remained at Unthank. Then, when the lease was transferred, James left for London, while Anne and her four youngest, with the new landlords' permission, remained on the farm as subtenants. Despite his attachment to his mother and siblings, James left Scotland in search of better economic opportunities. With the assistance of relatives and family friends, he obtained an apprenticeship with the London merchant William Dunbar, who conducted trade in the West Indies. James's inheritance of one thousand pounds, although insufficient to enable him to acquire enough land locally to sustain a farming life, was adequate when coupled with his abundant family connections to provide him with options in commerce and the professions. His younger siblings would not set out in life with similar resources. Given their lesser legacies of one hundred pounds each, their support and eventual livelihoods required more creative and careful planning.

From the distance of London, James remained actively engaged in his family's life, establishing early on a pattern of involvement with and responsibility for younger relatives from which Elizabeth benefited and later emulated. Although busy with his work, James issued financial dictates to his mother in Scotland and did not hesitate to let her know when he did not approve of her plans. Cautious and always concerned with money, James at one point asked his mother to settle an account with him by selling off any extra furniture she had, hoping that others would not interpret his plan as an ungenerous attempt to extract funds from her.[14] Rather, he merely wanted to make sure that everything was completely clear in his account with her and the children. Another time, he tried to tell her how to invest her income. Although "Sensible" that she "could manage it as well as most of [her] Sex," James insisted that she should not venture it on a farm.[15] A less-than-ringing endorsement of his mother's managerial skills, this remark reveals James's growing sense of command within his family, as well as his view of men's superior business sense. In later years, perhaps as a result of Elizabeth's commercial successes, James would articulate different views of women's financial acumen. In the 1730s, however, his dealings with his mother suggest the economic struggles of widowed women and their children and their dependence on male relations.

The precarious economic future of the younger Murrays, aspirants to a genteel lifestyle who possessed limited resources, made their education a priority. From London, James tried to instruct his mother about their training, urging her to move to a town. The children were missing crucial opportunities by living in the countryside; their mother's "too strict" economizing could hurt them in the long run. Relocating to an urban setting would make it possible for the children to be appropriately educated, a legacy more valuable than any financial boon to be gained through their continued residence at Unthank.[16] It was clear to James that they had to be qualified for some profession, because it was through business that "the lads in particular" would "Earn their bread."[17] Their inheritances would be impractical for lengthy and costly apprenticeships in commerce. Though landless and fatherless, the Murray boys could search out economic opportunities as mobile professional men in the British Empire.

Shared familial responsibility, joint decision making regarding the rearing of children, and a willingness to embrace mobility for economic advancement — all practices and attitudes that shaped Elizabeth Murray's actions and decisions as an adult — influenced her life early on as her mother and brother James planned the family's future. While James did not speculate in detail about his sisters' future, perhaps assuming that their chief employment would be as wives and housekeepers, he carefully considered the training of his younger brothers, particularly that of John. A bright eleven-year-old with three years of Latin school under his belt, John would soon be ready to pursue a medical career through a several-year apprenticeship to a surgeon-apothecary in Edinburgh.[18] James offered to pay for John's training, if his mother would agree to reimburse him at her death. At once generous and self-interested, James believed this arrangement would enable him to help his brother without endangering his mother's finances or unduly compromising his own situation. Because physicians did not require a large sum of capital to invest in stock, John would enjoy "a very good chance of handsome bread almost anywhere" and be able to live "in a genteel way."[19] Gentility, that elusive and highly desirable quality of men and women of the middling ranks and upper classes, was at least partially connected to the possession of an income adequate to sustain a certain standard of consumption and display as well as carefully polished manners and behaviors.[20] Sought after and highly prized by the Murrays and scores of other individuals, gentility fueled educational and consumer agendas in the eighteenth-century Atlantic world.

The planning for John's medical training, which resulted in his long career as a physician, illuminates the differences in boys' and girls' education and opportunities, as well as the Murrays' esteem for genteel living and willingness to migrate. Anglicized in word and creed, the Murray children were culturally, if not necessarily economically, well prepared to venture out into the empire to find their niches. A career in medicine struck James as appropriate for a bookish lad with little capital. (In 1740, as surgeon's mate on a man-of-war, the *Tilbury*, John was part of the British expeditionary force in Jamaica that his brother William joined and was thereby reunited with his younger sibling; eventually John settled in England). For Barbara, already a young woman, and Elizabeth, still a child, the need for professional training was less clear. Presumably, they could learn what they needed to about household management, the probable future activity for women of their background, at their mother's side.

James likely assumed that his sisters would gain status and financial stability by marrying well. Given the importance of the marriage market, it is not surprising that James saw Barbara as more in need of advice about how to behave than help in choosing an occupation. Her comportment, not her career, would secure her a position as a wife — that is, rather than as a practitioner of some trade. From the distance of London, twenty-one-year-old James instructed his seventeen-year-old sister to behave with humility. Pointedly, James urged Barbara to be guided by the counsel of those more experienced than she instead of following her own will with a "perverse" obstinacy. Above all, she should love God and religion and display "an obliging behavior to the world in General," with particular deference to parents and relatives.[21] He urged submissiveness and dependence, virtues that were celebrated in the domestic and religious spheres but of little value in the competitive realm of business.

Young women's behavior and self-fashioning had financial and moral repercussions in the world of gentility. One measure of the genteel woman was her fashionable dress, yet Barbara Murray did not possess a fortune. Explicitly, James advised Barbara not to be fond of dressing in finer clothes than she could truly afford, insisting that she wear neat and clean attire that was "Suitable" to her "station."[22] In addressing the theme of consumption and feminine display, James articulated common concerns about women in the eighteenth century. Many contemporary critics saw women as predisposed toward dissipation, as seekers after luxury whose corrupt and sensual inclinations could impoverish a family.[23] Many railed against what they saw as women's expensive and self-indulgent habits, decrying, for example, the tendency of poor women to go off with the men who promised them fine dress and thus linking excessive consumption and immoral conduct. Consumers, particularly female ones, could endanger their family's financial security by making purchases beyond their means. As they did so, emulating the standards of the highest ranks of society, they aroused alarm in the elite, who targeted luxuriant dress among their inferiors as the usurpation of class position and privilege.[24] James's primary, practical worry was less that Barbara would offend her social superiors than that she would pursue a standard of dress that exceeded her income. Economic behavior and morality were connected; as James reminded Barbara, "The least breach" of modesty or chastity "tends to the utter ruin of your Sex."[25] On this point, satirists, moralists, and pundits agreed. For Barbara, as for other young women, immodest and unchaste conduct could ruin fortunes on the marriage market, destroying the chances of finding a spouse.

The solution to the Murray children's varied needs, for marrying well and finding livelihoods, proved to be migration. While in London, James had begun to plan his future, concluding that he could make the most of his patrimony by moving to the colonies. In so doing, he became the first in his family to embrace life on the far side of the Atlantic. Hopeful of gaining trade and land, James resolved to seek his fortune in North Carolina. He chose the Cape Fear region, near the colony's border with South Carolina and newly opened to Europeans. Before the 1730s, conflict with Native Americans had slowed European colonization of the area.

North Carolina became a popular destination for Scottish immigrants in part because of fundamental population shifts that took place in the early 1700s, when such indigenous groups as the Cape Fear and the Tuscarora were decimated through exposure to European diseases and warfare.[26] Conflict erupted in North Carolina in 1711, when the Tuscarora attacked plantations in retaliation for colonists' territorial expansion and acts of aggression, such as the kidnapping and enslaving of the Tuscarora. In response, South Carolina colonists came to their neighbors' rescue with fighters recruited from among the Yamasee and other Indian trading partners who were enemies of the Tuscarora. As a result, hundreds of Tuscaroras were killed or enslaved; another fifteen hundred fled, moving north to join the Iroquois.[27] Adding to the disruption in the indigenous population was the Yamasee War of 1715, after which the Cape Fear Indians, who had fought against North Carolina troops, basically disappeared from their homeland, some captives or casualties of war, others refugees to South Carolina.[28] The demographic effects of the Tuscarora and Yamasee Wars thus facilitated European occupation of North Carolina.[29] Yet the late 1710s found the most notable Europeans plying the North Carolina coast to be such infamous pirates as Blackbeard rather than settled colonists. Hearing such accounts of Cape Fear, replete with reports of Indian wars and pirate raids, could have only heightened the sense of the unfamiliar that immigrants like James Murray brought to their new Carolina homes.

Colonial settlement of the Cape Fear area developed rapidly in the 1720s. With the 1725 establishment of Brunswick, fourteen miles above the wide mouth of the Cape Fear River, North Carolina gained a deepwater port and direct access to trade with England.[30] White settlers from South Carolina moved to Cape Fear to produce naval stores and lumber.[31] Then in 1729, with the dissolution of the proprietary relationship, the Crown gained administrative control of North Carolina. Over the next few decades, the population of the colony grew rapidly, from roughly 4,370 white and 2,000 black inhabitants in 1720 to 30,000 white and 6,000 black inhabitants a decade later.[32] An expansion of town life accompanied these changes. In 1733, Wilmington, which soon outstripped Brunswick in population and commerce, was established sixteen miles upstream of the earlier town at the confluence of the river's two branches.[33]

As attractive as North Carolina's newly opened lands and towns would have been to such immigrants as James Murray, even more important was the appointment of a Scottish-born royal governor in 1734. Gabriel Johnston actively encouraged his compatriots to settle in the area, offering them various kinds of assistance. Lowland and Highland Scots alike flocked to North Carolina.[34] Soon after assuming his post, Johnston began to shape the area according to his own designs by favoring the town of Newton (soon incorporated as Wilmington) over the slightly older settlement at Brunswick, buying property near it and ordering the governor's council to meet there; he also directed port officials to maintain offices in Wilmington rather than Brunswick.[35] These actions fed acrimony in the Cape Fear region, as Johnston did not hesitate to alienate the local elite who had property holdings around the older town and interests in its continued growth.[36] Owing to his own close links with Johnston, James Murray found himself occasionally at odds with these leading citizens and others of his neighbors. Ultimately, Johnston's tenure in office was marked by charges of excessive favoritism, although patronage in itself did not trouble eighteenth-century colonists.[37] Aid that flowed through lines of kin, ethnicity, and similar religious background underpinned and facilitated economic transactions. In an age before computerized credit checks and instantaneous international communication, it made sense to do business with those whom one knew. Quakers, in particular, gained renown for their support of fellow sectarians,[38] while Scottish immigrants dealt closely with their compatriots both in the colonies and back in Scotland.[39]

For James Murray, Johnston's presence in North Carolina added substantially to his interest in the colony. When he first broached the idea of colonial settlement to his uncle, James went to great lengths to articulate the substantial benefits of emigration. He began by claiming that North Carolina possessed a climate as healthy as England's and that one could live there less expensively than anywhere in Scotland. (New England proved far healthier than the Carolinas, in general; to his sorrow, James would gain much personal experience of the unhealthiness of his chosen home.) More important than those advantages, however, were the possibilities for growing wealthy. With great confidence in the "Governor's interest" in supporting him and in his own abilities, James envisioned a "handsome plantation" and expansive trade. James argued that he had good grounds for anticipating success: patronage from the governor and the prospect of speculating profitably in land. A location isolated from foreign enemies and the promise of assistance from two trading partners, one in England and the other in the West Indies, cemented his case for migration. (James was almost as wrong about the safety of the area as he was about its healthiness; in the 1740s Spanish privateers sailed up the Cape Fear River and shelled Brunswick.) In short, aid from compatriots and mercantile associates, coupled with North Carolina's climate and opportunities, would promote James's economic endeavors (figure 1).[40]

James acted as though his move constituted a first step toward settling not only his own future in America but that of his younger siblings as well. As part of his colonial design, James decided to take his eighteen-year-old sister Barbara with him and asked his mother to send her to join him in London. Unfortunately, James's precise moti-

vations cannot be determined. He may have wanted his sister to come
with him to act as his housekeeper or he may have wanted to relieve
his mother of responsibility for her. Perhaps James thought Barbara
would encounter better marital opportunities in North Carolina.
While her dowry might be insufficient to attract a rich mate in Scotland, he may have reasoned, it would go further in a burgeoning colony, where land was comparatively available and inexpensive. Her
lack of wealth might also be simply less important in finding a spouse,
given that a skewed sex ratio tended to typify emigrant populations.
Indeed, North Carolina had a reputation for early marriages for
women, with some wedding as young as thirteen or fourteen.[41]

Barbara's feelings about leaving her home and family to move to
America with an older brother remain opaque. We can only imagine
her packing her belongings, saying her farewells, and preparing for
the long journey ahead. (Within two years of emigrating, Barbara had
achieved a kind of success, establishing her own household by marrying Thomas Clark, a North Carolina merchant about James's age.)
After bidding what turned out to be a final good-bye to her mother,
Barbara joined her brother aboard the *Catherine*, at the town of Gravesend, east of London on the Thames River. After several years' residence in the great metropolis, James might have been prepared for
the tumult of the scene; Barbara likely found it noisy, chaotic, and
altogether remarkable. At Gravesend, all seagoing vessels departing
from London dropped anchor and underwent final searches by customs officials. As each new ship joined the others at this point on the
river, a sentinel at the Gravesend blockhouse would fire his musket,
indicating in this manner that the pilot should prepare to stop. Those
who were too slow in complying found themselves warned with cannon fire. Occasionally, ships would attempt to avoid clearing customs,
taking advantage of especially foggy mornings to try to slip through
the crowded channel without being espied from the shore. Adding to
the bustle and excitement of this commercial port was the local ferry.
Huge, nearly incredible numbers of people came and went with every
tide, "by Night as by Day," between Gravesend and London.[42] Masses
of people were on the move, crossing rivers and oceans, as they passed
over natural and national borders, some hurrying to the great city,
others to new lives across the Atlantic Ocean.

When James and Barbara Murray sailed on 20 September 1735,

1   James Murray, from a portrait by John Singleton Copley.
Courtesy, North Carolina Collection, University of North Carolina
Library at Chapel Hill.

they carried with them an entourage of individuals interested in making a living in America. Traveling with the Murrays was a young kins-
woman, their cousin Jean Ker. In addition to the family contingent,
the Murray party included a lawyer, a female servant, and ten indentured laborers, each engaged to serve for several years.[43] Indentured
servitude, involving the promise of service, typically four to seven
years, in exchange for passage to the colonies, provided a common

means of financing immigration. Over the course of the colonial period, indentured servitude paid for the arrival of hundreds of thousands of individuals. The practice especially distinguished the populating of the Chesapeake colonies in the seventeenth century, accounting for roughly 70 to 80 percent of European newcomers.[44] By paying for the passage of his servants, James not only ensured that he would have a ready source of workers in a labor-scarce colony but also increased his landholdings. For each servant brought to the colonies, a master received a headright of fifty acres.[45] During the period in which North Carolina was a royal colony, this practice enabled immigrants to accumulate substantial but not enormous estates; most grants were less than six hundred acres.[46] (Tax records show James's midcentury holdings in North Carolina to have been substantial. He eventually acquired at least 1,680 acres of land, accumulated an estate valued at three thousand pounds, and owned twenty-eight slaves. He was a man of means; a royal councillor to the governor during most of his time in North Carolina, serving for a part of the 1740s, 1750s, and 1760s; and a justice of the peace.)[47]

The prospects and promises — of land, financial opportunities, and advancement — that drew the Murray family and their servants likewise captured the imagination of tens of thousands of Europeans over the course of the eighteenth century. Indeed, these voluntary migrants formed only a portion of what some historians describe as one of the most important transformations in the past five hundred years, as part of the "worlds in motion," the movement of peoples away from their original communities.[48] Exerting a powerful pull, the colonies drew a nearly constant stream of migrants along a number of sea-lanes, just as a magnet shapes iron files into repeated, predictable lines of attraction. Promoters of colonial ventures added to the call, extolling the virtues of economic independence that awaited the industrious individual willing to work the fertile soil of the American continent for its rewards.

Scottish migration was so substantial that it gained renown in the early eighteenth century. Writer Daniel Defoe, who criticized many Scots, celebrated the indentured servants among them for their willingness to migrate, declaring them models worthy of emulation. In England, he reported, corrupt individuals used the "scandalous Art of Kidnapping, making Drunk, Wheedling, Betraying, and the like" to secure servants for the colonies. By way of contrast, the "poor People" of Scotland offered themselves willingly, "thinking it to their Advantage to go." Defoe applauded their good judgment, noting that the Scots workers served out their time and became "diligent planters for themselves." Indeed, he opined, if the emigration of the Scottish continued for much longer, Virginia, where many of them went to work on tobacco plantations, would be "call'd a *Scots* [rather] than an *English* Plantation."[49] Defoe's perception was not far from the mark. Over the course of the colonial period, Scotland provided more of the European immigrant population than any other country save England.[50] Some historians argue that over time Scotland had developed a "migrant psychology," a centrifugal tradition and expansive mentality that turned it into "one of the greatest suppliers of emigrants to the Atlantic world in the eighteenth century."[51]

The domestic economy and political climate acted as strong inducements to Scottish migration. Coupled with poor land, high food costs, and undeveloped trade, unproductive agricultural practices translated into impoverishment. Limited opportunities at home inspired the desperate and the adventurous alike. Although the Scottish economy in the seventeenth century had gone through difficult periods of shortages and demographic crises, few options existed for seeking relief elsewhere. Before the eighteenth century, the Scots had been prohibited from moving freely throughout the colonial world controlled by England. All that changed with the 1707 Act of Union, which eliminated Scotland's own Parliament, merged its governance with that of England, and transformed its people into citizens of the British Empire. No longer possessed of a separate polity, the Scottish people agonized over what this new arrangement would mean — how it would affect their identity, culture, economy, and other aspects of national life. Although many debated the costs and benefits associated with the union, it is clear that the Scots gained much.

For many residents of Scotland, the primary opportunity of the union rested in the new freedom of movement it brought: the permission to migrate anywhere within the empire. Acting on their right to participate fully in the growing fields of government and military service, many Scots quickly moved up within the ranks of both, becoming so numerous as to inspire hostile reactions from the English.[52] When such men and women set sail, leaving homes and families in Great Britain, they knew that their fate rested first on the winds and weather as they crossed the Atlantic. They could not know whether their risk would translate into success or failure, into ease and independence, or into a life cut short by diseases endemic to the Americas. Deserting the familiar for the uncertain, they came despite the difficulties that would greet them in a new environment.

Like his countrymen, James Murray chose to migrate for a constellation of reasons, in the process making a single decision that profoundly changed his family's life. Because of his willingness to embrace an American adventure, none of his siblings would live out their lives in the land of their birth. Thus the nine-week journey that the Murray party undertook represented a turning point not only for James and Barbara but for their family fortunes in Scotland as well.

Making sense of migrants' decisions and their individual "migrant psychology," particularly in the cases of James and Barbara and later with regard to William and Elizabeth, depends on interpreting the papers such travelers left behind and extrapolating the motives of those who left no records of their hopes, dreams, and fears.[53] Among the literate, like the Murrays, letters to friends, family, and prospective business associates provide one level of explanation. These documents, such as James's presentation of his resolution to settle in America, reveal a host of push and pull factors that varied according to a migrant's background in terms of region, domestic political and economic situations, and religious concerns. Yet the overwhelming majority of immigrants did not leave such treatises for posterity. Understanding their determination to settle in the colonies requires more conjecture, with their actions alone providing a basis for speculation about their intent.

Given the relative paucity of records, distinguishing the factors that differentially induced men and women to migrate holds additional difficulties. With lower literacy rates than men, women less frequently penned accounts of their decision-making processes. Although Barbara and Elizabeth Murray could read and write, they, like most women immigrants, came as the wives, daughters, or sisters of men who chose to move to America. Thus women's input into decisions about migration and settlement in particular colonies remains largely hidden. No doubt many women greeted the possibility of permanent separation from a community of support with at least some trepidation; in an age when female friends and neighbors rather than male physicians controlled the domain of childbirth, the absence of kin could prove a keen hardship.[54]

While the wishes of the Murray females remain obscure, the reasons for James's decision to migrate emerge with clarity: possession of both years of experience in commercial affairs and an estate. In short, he moved in a world of male contacts and male knowledge of investment and financial opportunities. His actions—in comparison with those of his sisters—rested to a lesser extent on the approval or protection of family members and more on his own judgment and resources. In some regards he considered himself as the head of the family and acted accordingly. Arriving in North Carolina in the fall of 1735, he quickly set about establishing himself in trade.

To his disappointment, James's commercial aspirations did not meet with unmitigated success. Over the course of the next several years, he found his business plagued by difficulties. He had hoped that the shortage of artisans needed to supply colonists' needs would translate into a ready market for his supply of high-quality imported wares. Throughout the Anglo-American world, men and women were buying increasing quantities of manufactured items such as cloth and china. Despite increasing per capita consumption, the colonists' lack of hard currency rendered trade difficult for James, with the speedy collection of debts problematic at best. In James's first year of colonial trade, his investment in cloth, stockings, and other goods yielded little but debtors.[55] He complained that the people of North Carolina had the "South Carolina notion" that they were not obliged to pay for their goods in less than a year. Thus James was unable to make timely remittances to his own creditors abroad.[56] He learned only too well that colonial consumers could frustrate the careful business plans of anyone who engaged in trade.

Indeed, James experienced so much aggravation that he became ambivalent about a career in commerce and contemplated giving up trade completely. He considered devoting himself to running a plantation. The primary obstacle to that plan was the shortage of workers. Although James could afford some land, he could not "buy some negroes" until he could "turn some Money out of the country."[57] Until his customers settled their debts, James's acquisition of slaves would be delayed. His difficulty in establishing himself as a planter, then, stemmed from monetary woes rather than moral worries about participating in the brutally exploitive system of slavery. Despite the fact that his brother John ultimately penned an antislavery tract in England, at no time did James express any reticence about purchasing enslaved Africans or qualms about profiting from their labor. He was not alone in this regard. Throughout the Lower Cape Fear region, planters relied on bondsmen to provide the workforce for the cultivation of rice and the production of naval stores. By the 1750s and 1760s, slaves had grown to constitute over 60 percent of the Lower Cape Fear population, with distribution patterns resembling those of South Carolina's low country.[58]

While busy with his own financial affairs in North Carolina, James continued to monitor those of his siblings. He anticipated that his brothers would join him in America and sought an uncle's approval for investing in land for John and William. For fifty pounds each, he could purchase one thousand acres of good land in North Carolina. The money, he argued, "could not be better employed," especially as the colony would "probably be their place of residence."[59] Ironically, neither of his brothers made permanent homes in America, whereas both of his sisters did. Their similarly small legacies, when coupled with more circumscribed options in Britain—for finding spouses or supporting themselves—perhaps rendered the colonies more appealing to Barbara and Elizabeth; maybe they simply had less say in the matter than did their brothers.

James's plans for economic success in North Carolina had to be put on hold when he received word in the summer of 1737 of his mother's death. Her passing at the age of forty-two prompted James's first voyage back to Scotland. There, he had to settle the estate and make plans for William and Elizabeth, who had been living with their uncle Andrew Bennet since their mother's death. The financial responsibility for the two youngsters would fall to James; they would each receive only twenty pounds as a legacy from their mother's estate. James also had to decide whether the pair would live with him or with Barbara and her husband. Regardless, they would come back to America with him. Accordingly, in December 1738, James, William, and Elizabeth gathered in London in preparation for the Atlantic crossing.

While preparing to return to America, James undertook new efforts to invigorate his financial affairs in North Carolina. Rather than committing himself to the retired life of a planter, he decided to enlarge his commercial enterprises and go deeper into the Cape Fear trade than he or anyone else had attempted to do previously. Before leaving the world of trade for an agricultural sphere, James would give commerce one more chance. This time, he hoped to succeed by choosing the newest merchandise and targeting a market as quickly as possible. In London, he ordered over fifteen hundred pounds sterling of goods and chartered a ship that would go back to the colonies immediately with the best merchandise possible. If North Carolina consumers proved less than enthusiastic about purchasing his wares, James would take his business elsewhere. He could drop off William and Elizabeth with his sister and brother-in-law and hurry to South Carolina or Georgia, confident that his cargo would suit either place.[60] James's plan underlines his willingness to take commercial risks, his sense of regional variations in colonial tastes and fashions, and his assumption that he could dictate responsibility for the care of the younger children.[61]

Engaged in making plans to expand his commercial involvement, James also acted to invest William and Elizabeth's small legacies in the human capital of enslaved Africans. He sent their twenty pounds to a correspondent in South Carolina to use to buy slaves.[62] Throughout the colonial period, Charlestown, South Carolina, was the primary port of entry for Africans. Most of North Carolina's slave population came from other colonies—either overland, through coastal trade, or from the West Indies—rather than directly from Africa.[63] In deciding to purchase slaves for his siblings, James followed a not uncommon investment strategy. For colonists who could not afford land, buying slaves and then hiring them out became a way of generating additional income. This practice, especially common among southern white women in the late eighteenth and early nineteenth centuries, enabled slaveholders and nonslaveowners alike to profit from the labor of bondsmen.[64]

While their money traveled to America by one route, William and Elizabeth came by another. Younger than James and Barbara when they first made the voyage, Elizabeth likely embarked on the journey in a more somber frame of mind. At twelve, Elizabeth was leaving behind Scotland, a large circle of fond relatives, and the graves of both her parents. The image of her mother laid out as a corpse was one that remained vivid for Elizabeth decades later.[65] In the two years since that moment, Elizabeth had lived with her uncle's family and bid farewell to the members of that household. As 1738 drew to a close, she found herself in London, waiting to brave the Atlantic voyage in the company of her childhood companion, William, and her oldest brother, James, who had not been part of her life on a daily basis since she was six years old but who now assumed the role of guardian and father figure. Although it is impossible to know what Elizabeth thought about coming to America, we do know how she reacted physically. The rough crossing left her and nearly every other passenger seasick and in "Distress" for most of the voyage.[66]

Elizabeth's first views of her new home may have inspired a different kind of distress, or perhaps they sparked a combination of curiosity, excitement, and anxiety. Sailing along the North Carolina shoreline, she would have seen numerous islands, marshy coastal areas, and the shifting shoals that rendered entering the wide Cape Fear River a delicate and dangerous operation. Once the ship made its way safely into the river, Elizabeth would have passed freshwater and tidal marshes, dunes and beaches, longleaf pine forests that provided the raw material for the production of naval stores, and then the plantations of the area's earliest European colonists, who cultivated corn, rice, and indigo.[67] Unfamiliar vegetation, a flat landscape, heat unlike anything she had known in Scotland, and humidity would have greeted her as summer began. The Carolina climate and topography contributed to the flourishing of various species, some of which aroused Europeans' sense of wonder. Deer, wild turkeys, geese, and ducks abounded, as did enormous mosquitoes that swarmed ferociously and easily pierced buckskin gloves, coats, and jackets.[68] In the low-lying area where the Murrays settled, periodic floods and standing water attracted disease-carrying mosquitoes, whose presence made summer a time of particular discomfort, illness, and death. Although settlers had little understanding of malaria or yellow fever, they did recognize that people fell ill near bodies of stagnant water and that newcomers underwent a period of "seasoning," when they seemed especially susceptible to sickness.

In North Carolina, Elizabeth witnessed novel sights, encountering a world that differed dramatically from that she had known in Scotland or glimpsed briefly in London. The cold, damp, rainy winters and springs of the Scottish borderlands were replaced by the oppressive heat and humidity of the southern colonial coast. Although both Scotland and North Carolina enjoyed abundant rainfall, the coastal plain of the colony experienced both dry spells and hurricanes during summer and fall.[69] In place of the small streams that funneled through the steep valleys, like that at Unthank, slow-moving, broad tidal rivers cut through marshes that were home to such monstrous creatures as alligators. The contrasts between Eskdale and Cape Fear embraced social differences as well. Whereas Elizabeth's homeland possessed a homogenous population, with the signs of a nonindigenous group limited to traces of ancient Roman ruins and roads, North Carolina's inhabitants were far more diverse, including the dramatically reduced numbers of the Tuscarora and other Native American peoples, European colonists, and enslaved Africans.

Arriving in North Carolina in the late spring of 1739, Elizabeth would have been in America only a brief time before learning how different her new home was. A few months after her arrival, South Carolina witnessed the Stono Uprising, one of the biggest slave rebellions of the colonial period. In September 1739, dozens of slaves took up arms against their oppressors and killed a number of white colonists, not all of them slaveowners, before the rebellion was quashed. The slaves, most of them recent arrivals from Africa, had been trying to seek their freedom in Florida, a territory controlled by Spanish authorities quite hostile to their English neighbors to the north. In reaction to the insurrection, white South Carolinians enacted a highly restrictive and punitive slave code and stopped importing new slaves for a time.[70]

The uprising and subsequent fallout delayed the implementation of James's plan to invest his siblings' legacies in slaves. James instead put William's and Elizabeth's money into bonds paying 10 percent interest per annum.[71] Later, however, he did invest Elizabeth's money in human beings, three slaves whom he referred to as Glasgow, Kelso, and Berwick. These names, derived from Scottish towns near the Murrays' home, represent a common ethnocentric and racist gesture: ignoring Africans' identity and personal history by imposing new monikers.[72] After considering how best to invest William's whole fortune of one hundred pounds—a commission, land, or slaves—James eventually decided on a commission, setting William on the career path that began with his participation in the War of Jenkins' Ear. Thereafter, William spent much of his adulthood engaging in campaigns that kept him on the move.

Just before William left North Carolina to begin his military life, Elizabeth also found a position, assuming management of James's household. Beginning to fulfill the duties of that "station" in September 1740, when she was fourteen, Elizabeth acted as her brother's sole housekeeper, a post of some status and responsibility.[73] There were myriad tasks associated with running a home, including keeping accounts with local merchants and vendors, selecting and purchasing the items needed for household consumption, overseeing the work of any servants, and performing numerous chores associated with housecleaning and preparing food and clothing. Given James's involvement in trade, it is unlikely that Elizabeth had to make many purchases herself. Nonetheless, she did have duties to perform. In overseeing James's house, Elizabeth took care of one of the finest structures in Wilmington. The house contained a large room, twenty-two by sixteen feet, "the most airy of any in the Country," as well as two "lodging" rooms, a closet and garret above the first floor, and a cellar below divided into a kitchen and a storage space for food and drink. Split into two distinct spaces, the structure contained the Murrays' living quarters as well as James's business chambers, with a store cellar, a store and countinghouse on the first floor, and four rough rooms above.[74] The proximity of work space and family apartments was not unusual. It made possible the involvement of family members in running a business and provided ample opportunities for the informal training of both boys and girls in a host of enterprises, from craft production to commercial exchange.

Although the fall of 1740 began auspiciously for Elizabeth, with her assumption of the role of housekeeper, any certainty and security in her circumstances proved illusory. First, William left in November to join the war effort. Then James's affairs brought instability and more mobility to Elizabeth's life. In the summer of 1741 she lost both her housekeeping post and her place of residence when a friend of James's arrived in the province with his family. James invited them to stay in his house, explaining that he could easily send his "little Sis-

ter" to his sister and brother-in-law's home. After his friend accepted
the offer, James proceeded "to Discard" his family and disband his
household. One of those discarded, Elizabeth moved to Barbara
Murray Clark's home. Although still with a member of her immediate family, Elizabeth's situation was not necessarily a comfortable
one. Barbara had her own young family and was pregnant with her
second child. Although it is impossible to know whether Barbara
found her younger sister a help or a burden, it certainly could not
have eased her cares when Elizabeth fell ill around the time of Barbara's due date. While Barbara "bravely recovered" from her delivery
of a son, Elizabeth came down with "the fever & Ague," a common
description of malarial symptoms.[75] A sick sibling and an infant addition to her family no doubt temporarily increased Barbara's worries.

James's dismantling of his household, which anticipated another
transatlantic voyage, highlights the remarkable mobility of the Murray family. Travel posed financial burdens and at least temporarily
dissolved familial bonds. Yet the Murrays undertook long, arduous
journeys with surprising readiness. After crossing the ocean at least
three times in the 1730s, James sailed again for the British Isles in
September 1741. Staying once more at his uncle Andrew Bennet's
home, where he had resided while settling his mother's estate, James
became engaged to his first cousin Barbara Bennet. When he returned to the colonies in February 1743, he planned to go "home"
again soon to Scotland to get married. Back in North Carolina barely
long enough to arrange his affairs, he collected Elizabeth, now seventeen, and sailed with her to the United Kingdom in February 1744.

With the marriage of James and Barbara, Elizabeth gained a sister
and lost a job. Thus evaporated permanently the possibility of her
position as housekeeper. Yet she continued, for a time, to count
herself a member of James's household. Although her activities during the early years of her brother's marriage are unknown, we can
piece together some facts of her existence. During the first five years
of James's marriage, he, Barbara, and Elizabeth remained in Great
Britain, during part of which time they lived in London. James and
Barbara's first daughter, Dorothy (or Dolly, as the family called her),
was born there in 1745.

For Elizabeth, this second and more extended experience of life in
London presented yet another stark contrast to her previous situa-

tions. From a farm in Scotland to a small town in North Carolina and then the bustling metropolis of London, she had moved from the hinterlands of the empire to its periphery and now its very center. Over the previous two centuries, London had grown exponentially, with 10 percent of the nation's population, or 675,000 people, residing there in 1750. Expanding more rapidly than other European capitals, London grew primarily owing to migration, as men and women hurried to the economic hub of the kingdom.[76] Indeed, migration was substantial enough to counteract high mortality rates spawned by overcrowding and poor sanitation; supplying the capital with new inhabitants was, in the words of one historian, "the country's biggest business."[77] In addition to fueling rapid and sustained population growth, the scores of workers who had migrated to the capital for better wages contributed to the city's economic development. They required all kinds of produce, both foodstuffs and manufactured goods. Ready to respond to this expanding demand, producers of food and manufactured goods alike specialized, developing shops and showrooms for the London market.[78]

On street after street crowded with small shops, many of them run by women, Elizabeth would have encountered the fruits of colonialism and early industrialization. Imported and domestically produced fabrics, fine laces, and ceramics of dizzying variety were attractively displayed and sold at prices that made them increasingly available to consumers.[79] At the same time that the kinds and quantities of goods were proliferating, so too were the numbers of men and women able to afford them. Perhaps even more important than periods of residence in major urban areas was simply the exposure to the latest fashions that took place in hamlets and great houses throughout Great Britain.[80] The common practice of mistresses paying their female servants part of their wages in cast-off clothing helped to transform the laboring poor in at least a small degree into consumers of the newest goods. In addition, high rates of job mobility translated into greater communication between town and country, increasing the likelihood that servants knew something firsthand of life in one of the nation's burgeoning ports. These towns funneled the riches of the empire to the colonies, acting as the way stations for the tea and taffeta consumed by Britons and others from Massachusetts to Jamaica.

Cosmopolitan London, with its opulent and exotic material culture, public attractions, and hustle and bustle made a deep impression on visitors. Enthralled by its variety and vivacity, contemporaries were appalled by the noise, filth, and stench that rendered many of its streets unpleasant and unhealthy. Gin consumption, poverty, disease, and crime were just as much a part of London as its elegant assemblies and entertainments. For Elizabeth, residence in London provided her with the opportunity to observe the most populous, congested, and economically and politically vital city in the nation. Throughout her life, Elizabeth maintained affection for what she described as the pleasing diversions that the great metropolis had to offer.[81]

Elizabeth's London sojourn was interrupted when Barbara Murray Clark's husband died. As on previous occasions, family responsibilities dictated that the Murrays relocate. Although James had planned to return to North Carolina, he did so when the death of his brother-in-law prompted his journey. Sailing back to the colonies to assist his sister and her family, James was accompanied by his wife, young daughter, and Elizabeth. Rather than traveling directly to North Carolina, the Murrays stopped in Boston, the largest city in New England and one of the oldest settlements in the colonies.

Sailing into Boston harbor beyond the defensive fortifications of Castle William, seeing the town's hills and steeples, and feeling the bracing chill of a New England spring, Elizabeth might have immediately noted the points of contrast with both Wilmington and London. As opposed to the relatively sparsely inhabited lands of the Cape Fear region, Boston would have presented a rather more populated and settled vista. Elizabeth would have seen a harbor full of ocean-going vessels, a lighthouse, several tall hills, and, beyond them, the spires of the town's numerous meetinghouses (figure 2). Clearly more commercially advanced than Wilmington, Boston had numerous wharves, the largest of them, Long Wharf, extending twenty-one hundred feet into the harbor. Merchants' warehouses lined the wharves, providing ready storage for the influx of British wares. Once on land, she might have been impressed, as a visitor the previous year was, by the way the town was "conveniently laid into Streets which are paved with Stone," an improvement that Bostonians had undertaken long before many in England.[82] Although Boston's population of

2   View of Boston harbor, engraving by James Turner, 1745.
Courtesy, American Antiquarian Society.

little over fifteen thousand was only a fraction of that of London, it still conveyed a more diverse and distinctively urban aspect than did Wilmington. Disembarking directly on Long Wharf, Elizabeth would have walked past the warehouses lining the wharf before reaching land. At the corner of the first two streets—King Street, which was the extension of the wharf, and Mackrell Lane—stood the Bunch-of-Grapes Tavern. Directly ahead on King Street, at the intersection with Cornhill, was the impressive brick Town House, the center of an area where elegant structures stood, replacing those destroyed by a disastrous fire in 1711.[83] Nearby Faneuil Hall and Market, one hundred feet long, forty feet wide, and two stories high, had opened in 1742 as the new town market; there was also the 1739 Workhouse, another solid structure of brick, two stories tall and 125 feet long.[84]

While James sailed on to North Carolina, Elizabeth, Barbara, and four-year-old Dolly stayed on in Boston, perhaps because the southern climate was considered to be hard on newcomers, especially during the summer, or perhaps because James had no established household after a long absence. Another factor contributing to the planned separation may have been news from North Carolina, which had recently suffered from Spanish incursions. In the summer of 1747, a number of craft carrying armed men from Florida had prowled along the coast, raiding settlements, taking slaves, and killing cattle and hogs. Cape Fear witnessed one of the worst attacks in September 1748, when two Spanish ships sailed up the river as far as Brunswick and opened fire on the town. With the settlement being shelled and overrun by Spanish troops who had landed downstream, the inhabitants fled, deserting their homes and surrendering their property to the plundering invaders. While the Spanish met with substantial losses in lives and stolen goods when one of their privateers caught fire and exploded, the Brunswick residents suffered heavy property damages and some injuries.[85] Certainly the reports of such blatant acts of aggression and danger only a few miles below Wilmington and the Murray property on Cape Fear's northwest branch could not have increased Barbara's enthusiasm for seeing her new home.

Possibly adding to the impetus for the women to remain in the north was Barbara's new pregnancy. At the time of James's departure for North Carolina on June 5, Barbara was probably in her first trimester, when a lengthy and nausea-inducing coastal journey would have appeared extremely unappealing. Besides, Barbara had a pronounced aversion to travel. The family's delay in coming back to America had stemmed in part from her dread of making the trip.

The grueling journey that James undertook as he sailed south confirmed the wisdom of the Murrays' travel plans. Despite the hazards that attended oceanic journeys, the Atlantic crossing was less fraught with peril than was coastal travel. A colonist sailing from New England to southern ports confronted a range of dangers. Shoals, breakers, and uncooperative tides confounded many a pilot, while anxiety attended both those who traveled and those who remained behind. Reports of ruined hulls and lost lives dotted colonial newspapers and peppered conversations in coffeehouses. Arriving in North Carolina after one such very difficult and dangerous trip, James soon found his wife's absence a palpable source of sorrow and tried to hurry her to join him. Although he did not want her to come until September, when the season of sickness had passed, he longed for her terribly. His happiness, he declared, depended on her presence. Pining for his wife, James regretted that his life required that she be "tossed" around the world.[86]

While neither Barbara nor Elizabeth showed much enthusiasm

about leaving Boston for North Carolina, Barbara had limited choice in the matter. As a married woman, a *feme covert*, she had no legal identity separate from her spouse, no command over resources, and no property of her own. In effect, she herself was property, obligated to do her husband's will and bidding. Barbara did, nonetheless, delay the move as long as possible, staying in Boston a year and a half. During that period, in December 1749, she gave birth to a daughter, who did not survive. Ultimately, Barbara had no choice but to join James in the southern colony he had chosen.

Whereas Barbara Bennet Murray, as a married woman, had to go to North Carolina to be with her spouse, Elizabeth Murray faced no similar compunction to change her place of residence. She had seen North Carolina and decided to make her way elsewhere. Indeed, within weeks of arriving in Boston, she had decided that she would live there. Informing their brother John of this remarkable news, James began, "Sister Bettzy seems inclin'd to stay" and then crossed out "stay." He wrote instead that Elizabeth intended to "try the Millenary business at Boston," suggesting that he viewed her plan as perhaps a temporary one.[87] In England, milliners were dressmakers who possessed greater skills than mantua-makers, who specialized in loose-fitting, unconstructed apparel; in contrast, milliners made more elaborate clothing to order.[88] Apparently Elizabeth resolved to try her hand at this line of work only after seeing the New England town.

What did Boston have to offer a young woman? How would Elizabeth have compared it with London or with her memories of the North Carolina home she had not seen in several years? In 1749 the Puritan capital of Boston was New England's largest city, with a colonial urban population exceeded only by New York and Philadelphia. Unlike those two cities, its economic situation was not thriving. The poor were becoming more numerous, with women especially conspicuous among the ranks of the impoverished. Partly as a result of wars that left many women widowed, the poor female population of Boston reached high levels in the 1740s.[89] Nor could the port match London's commercial hubbub. Yet Boston may well have appeared preferable to North Carolina. Arriving in the spring, Elizabeth would have first encountered the town in bloom, its wharves busy with the seasonal trade, its warehouses and shops full of goods newly arrived from the mother country. With numerous churches and many other fine buildings, Boston may have been very appealing to one who had developed a liking for London's cosmopolitan diversions.

At the time that Elizabeth made her decision to stay in New England, she was just a few weeks shy of her twenty-third birthday. She had resided in Boston only a short time and was, for all practical purposes, on her own. Uprooted, with no permanent base in Scotland, England, or America, she faced some difficult choices as she considered her prospects and evaluated her options. Should she stay with her brother and sister-in-law and go to North Carolina where her sister Barbara still lived with her children? Or should she try to make a go of it on her own in Massachusetts? Elizabeth had to consider how to support herself and where she could best accomplish that goal.

Knowledge of the possibilities that awaited young women in Great Britain no doubt informed Elizabeth's appraisal of the colonial economy. She would have known that if she were not a dependent in a household — that is, if her lot in life involved self-support outside her immediate family circle — she would have to seek economic opportunities. In eighteenth-century Britain and America, some jobs simply were not available to women. Women did not fill the ranks of soldiers and seamen. Nor were the professions of law and medicine open to them, although women took care of nursing duties and less formally administered medical care. Clearly, then, the career paths that her brothers William and John had pursued were closed to Elizabeth. In addition, many of the skilled trades that required lengthy apprenticeships did not welcome women.

Women did work in many arenas, their options for employment varying with their assets as well as their marital status. Married women on both sides of the Atlantic engaged in a wide range of income-generating and unpaid labor to support their families. Although small in comparison with those of James, Elizabeth's resources, combined with her family connections, meant that she would not have to keep herself through domestic service, the most typical employment for women in eighteenth-century England. Indeed, the proportion of servants who were female increased over time, drawing women from the countryside into such cities as London and contributing to the shift in the population of that town to one increasingly dominated by women.[90] Colonial women of European descent also labored as servants, but they did so in smaller numbers than did women on the other side of the Atlantic. Women represented only a small portion of contract servants. Over time, indentured servitude opportunities decreased for women. In the eighteenth century, colonists' needs for skilled laborers, especially artisans, constricted the demand for female servants.[91] Inhabitants of the ports of Philadelphia and New York, which readily absorbed male indentured laborers into their labor pools, had less use for unskilled female servants. In addition to service, agricultural labor and manufacturing drew large numbers of female workers in Britain. While women had long been employed in the fields, the early stages of industrialization initiated a new phase of women's wage-earning experiences.

For women like Elizabeth, work in retailing would have presented an appealing option. In Europe women traders were neither unprecedented nor rare phenomena.[92] Scotland had its own traditions of women in commerce. In Edinburgh, many women were petty shopkeepers who vended goods in several areas, including the Luckenbooths. These small wooden stalls (locked booths, or "Luckenbooths"), where the front wall folded down to make a counter, were constructed in the fifteenth century. Abutting the massive church of St. Giles, the Luckenbooths provided Edinburgh consumers with regular access to haberdashery and clothing until their destruction in the nineteenth century.[93] In addition, the city had women milliners, often catering to a genteel clientele, whose participation in trade was protected by law, if not guaranteed under freedom of the burgh stipulations that protected many traders and artisans.[94] In millinery shops, women produced and retailed fine attire, cloth, and notions. In England, too, there were some skilled trades practiced by large numbers of women, particularly those related to dress. Informally, women made clothes to order for individual customers, sewed piecework at home, or found positions as journeywomen in milliners' shops. Seasonal changes in demand, however, could render making a genteel living in the needle trades difficult in such places as London, where fashionable folks left town during the summer.[95] Moreover, the prerequisites for pursuing a millinery career in London, for instance, may have exceeded Elizabeth's grasp. Apprenticeships with well-established dressmakers could be very expensive. On the other hand, a whole range of other choices awaited a young, single female immigrant in eighteenth-century colonial America.

The port towns of New England and the middle colonies, in effect the most developed urban areas of eighteenth-century colonial America, offered women with skills or assets a range of employments not to be found in the countryside. In these settings, women held positions in various trades, ranging from schoolmistress to drawing teacher to milliner. Although many women supported themselves in Boston, remaining tax lists and disbursements for the poor reveal the relative poverty of many. So numerous were these poor widows that the overseers of the poor initiated a workhouse/factory where they could be employed making cloth. The linen factory proved less than successful, however, with few women willing to leave the household setting for these positions.[96]

Women's skilled wage labor was not restricted to northern ports; southern cities such as Charlestown counted many women of trade among their artisans and shopkeepers. Colonial newspapers reveal a great variety in women's employment in the South.[97] Keeping school, teaching needlework, acting as midwives, running taverns, and selling and making millinery wares were but a few of the occupations pursued by colonial women. Numerous widowed women also appeared among the ranks of shoemakers, gunsmiths, and shipwrights, typically continuing businesses established by deceased spouses.[98] For any woman, following a particular calling depended on a variety of intersecting forces, ranging from age, marital status, and family responsibilities to training, possession of capital, and community norms.

Although Elizabeth left no record of her musings on the subject of employment options, her actions, both in the late 1740s, when she settled in Boston, and in later years, when she helped establish other women in trade, provide some basis for conjecture. Life in the southern colonies was not unknown to Elizabeth. With her brother married, however, her station as housekeeper had dissolved. She knew one possibility that awaited her in North Carolina: dependency as a spinster in her brother's home. An unmarried woman did not live alone; social mores and religious sensibilities precluded that path. Yet the need for self-support remained. In Boston, Elizabeth would have had to find lodgings and become a boarder in someone else's home. She would not, however, be a dependent in the same way; she would be free from the direct supervision of both male and female relations. Perhaps that position had some appeal.

By 1749 Elizabeth had also had some exposure to the conduct of commerce. Over the previous few years, she had occasionally acted as James's scribe, helping him keep up with his business correspondence. Moreover, she had seen how his retail efforts in the South had foundered. By the time Elizabeth decided to try her hand at commerce, James, who had initially envisioned his life in the colonies as involving trading ventures, had largely given up that endeavor for running his plantation, Point Repose. Perhaps his lack of mercantile success in North Carolina contributed to her resolution to settle in Boston. Given James's overall lack of achievement in commerce, however, the decision Elizabeth made to pursue the same general line of business appears somewhat surprising. She sought a livelihood in a trade that had brought her brother nothing but difficulties and failure.

Elizabeth's decisions about where to settle and how to support herself were informed by her geographic mobility in the dozen years since her mother's death. During that time, Elizabeth's repeated relocations and long journeys had provided her with ample opportunity to observe places and people, to consider the economic and emotional ramifications of migration, and to develop a certain flexibility when it came to domestic arrangements. She had lived with her uncle Andrew in Scotland, her sister Barbara in North Carolina, her brother James in North Carolina and in England, and her sister-in-law and a Scottish landlord, Mrs. Mackay, in Boston. She had crossed the Atlantic three times: at thirteen, seventeen, and twenty-two.

Such mobility may have weakened Elizabeth's attachments to any particular spot. She had lived in several different towns and countries, yet belonged to none. She had siblings and nieces and nephews, but no spouse or children of her own. Now an adult, she could determine for herself what place she would call "home." With ambition, optimism, some skills and financial resources, and the all important support — both financial and emotional — of James, Elizabeth decided to try her fortunes in Boston.

2

A "SHE MERCHANT" IN BOSTON

As the summer of 1749 began, Elizabeth committed herself to trying her luck in Boston, notwithstanding her brother's wishes to the contrary. Despite a lack of enthusiasm, James supported Elizabeth in her plan to become a milliner and shopkeeper largely because she persuaded him that she might make more money by doing so than she could earn in another setting. Just as James had listed the financial benefits behind his decision to settle in North Carolina the previous decade, Elizabeth now successfully advanced the same argument with him with regard to Massachusetts. And although James knew he would miss his sister, he was "far from desiring" her presence in Cape Fear if there was a chance of her "doing better" elsewhere.[1] Economic opportunities thus overrode emotional considerations once again, as the Murray siblings parted company to pursue their livelihoods in different colonies. On her own in Boston, Elizabeth spent the next decade trying to build a viable business and a satisfying personal life. As she worked toward establishing her shop, she undertook steps that offer one model of "how to succeed in business" as a female trader in eighteenth-century America.

By seeking to support herself as a shopkeeper, Elizabeth Murray was far from unique. Around her were numerous examples of successful women of business. These women ran specialty shops and general stores, maintained themselves and their families, and were respected members of their communities. Alice Quick, for example, had been in business for at least seventeen years when Elizabeth arrived in Boston. Widow Quick, who continued in retail until her death in 1761, was acknowledged as a "Noted Shopkeeper" who acquired a "considerable Fortune" in trade.[2] Henrietta Maria East, a retailer who set up business a decade after Quick, came to Boston in 1743 with the intention of keeping shop. Armed with fifty pounds sterling and a stock of goods she brought from London, East informed town authorities that she "desired Liberty" to open a millinery shop in Marlborough Street. Given East's capital and stock, it is not surprising that they readily approved her request.[3] Over the next decade, she regularly placed large advertisements describing her varied millinery wares and fan-making business in the pages of the *Boston Evening-Post*.

In addition to Elizabeth Murray, Alice Quick, and Henrietta Maria East, many other women in Boston pursued commercial endeavors. At least ninety women kept shop between 1740 and the Revolution.[4] Other colonial seaports, such as New York and Philadelphia, had substantial numbers of female vendors as well.[5] Estimates as to the percentage of eighteenth-century colonial shopkeepers who were women vary widely. Although figures based heavily on advertisements in colonial newspapers have ranged between 2 and 10 percent, such sources as merchants' account books, probate documents, and tax lists indicate far greater numbers of women in trade. In Philadelphia, for example, the 1756 tax list noted thirty-eight women, or 42 percent of the town's assessed retailers, keeping shop; these women traders represented nearly two-thirds of the women who were ascribed occupations.[6]

Despite the accolades accorded some women of trade, such as Alice Quick, female retailers were not universally respected figures in colonial towns. In 1733 Peter Zenger made them the subject of satire in his *New York Weekly Journal*. These "she Merchants" supposedly met and submitted an angry letter to the editor. Widows all, these women decried their unfair treatment at the hands of local authorities. Although housekeepers and taxpayers who carried on trade, they contributed to the support of the government but received neither recognition nor benefit. In contrast, the complainants declared, the husbands of their neighborhood were "daily invited to Dine at Court."[7] Regardless of its authorship, the piece highlights women's commercial activities and economic roles, suggesting as well that such contributions might be construed by women as conveying certain rights and privileges, despite their sex. Subsequent issues of the paper carried equally satiric essays that responded to the "she Merchants" and described the plight of other distressed New Yorkers, including unmarried women who bemoaned the fact that men were more interested in politics than in courting and bachelors who accused these maidens of turning a deaf ear to all but rich men.

Benjamin Franklin similarly targeted women in trade in a series of essays in the *Pennsylvania Gazette* in 1730. Sharply critical of shopkeepers, Franklin described the experience of a man who bargained with a woman retailer for some item. After the two agreed on a price, the shopkeeper informed her customer that she was losing money because people "were grown very hard" and that she could hope to make only occasional small profits. Her business was complicated by the presence of many competitors; consumers knew how to exploit that situation to get good deals. Franklin's point was that shopkeepers were dishonest traders who sought to take advantage of their clients. "Some of them have a Saying, that 'tis a Pity Lying is a Sin, it is so useful in Trade," he reported.[8] Shortly after penning this essay on lying shopkeepers, Franklin published answering letters to the editor, presumably equally invented. In one a male merchant complained that shopkeepers lied to wholesalers as well as customers: "I believe they think Lying full as convenient and beneficial in buying their Goods as selling them." In the other Franklin's fictional "Betty Diligent" declared herself to be the Philadelphia shopkeeper attacked in the earlier issue of the paper. Diligent found the essay biased against retailers because the author ignored the deceptions practiced by shoppers. They tried to manipulate the terms of sale, she insisted, by boldly lying that they had purchased similar merchandise much cheaper elsewhere. Consumers told "a hundred Lies to undervalue our Goods, and make our Demands appear extravagant," she complained; therefore, they should bear "the Blame of all the Lying." Indeed, it was because of such manipulative customers that shopkeepers were forced to "strain the Truth a little now and then."[9]

While Franklin may have been intimating that women in trade were more precariously positioned economically and therefore more likely to find deceptive practices a necessity, he offered a general depiction of shopkeepers' problems that applied equally well to women and men. Based on negotiation, commercial exchanges inherently involved conflict. While Franklin's satiric letters reveal his pessimistic view of human nature — the greediness of all who sell and buy — they also highlight the intrinsic difficulties of trade.[10] To make a living, a shopkeeper had to acquire sufficient credit to deal with merchant wholesalers, select fashionable stock that appealed to colonial consumers, and compete successfully for increasingly well-informed customers familiar with the shops of other retailers. An additional important ingredient to achieving success was the possession of a good reputation, hence Betty Diligent's round rejoinder to Franklin's insinuations. Bad press could hurt business.

Like Betty Diligent, Elizabeth Murray had to acquire credit, merchandise, and clients before she could support herself as a woman of trade. Presumably she would not have even considered becoming a milliner if she had not already possessed the ability to do fine needlework and make clothes to order, as well as at least some rudimentary knowledge of arithmetic and bookkeeping. Most likely, Elizabeth learned to sew and to keep accounts at home. Such aptitudes, while essential for a milliner, were similarly important for a housekeeper; a woman needed competence in these areas to handle her domestic responsibilities for maintaining her family's clothing and dealing effectively with traders from whom she bought goods for the household.

Elizabeth's venture into shopkeeping, like her earlier relocations, depended in no small degree on James. Without her brother's early and ongoing assistance and involvement, Elizabeth would not have flourished in commerce as soon or as fully as she did. The financial independence she sought through millinery work thus was based initially on familial aid. Shortly after he returned to Wilmington, North Carolina, in September 1749, James started to pursue business contacts for Elizabeth. Springing into action on her behalf, he enlisted the cooperation of the Mackays, the Boston mercantile family with whom Elizabeth was boarding, begging them to give her the advice she would "want" so badly, "having a mind . . . to commence Milliner."[11] To Elizabeth herself and to associates in Britain, James outlined strategies for getting started in trade. Although he provided his sister with financial aid, advice, and ready-made contacts, all in generous quantities, James made it clear that Elizabeth would bear ultimate responsibility for making decisions about her business affairs.

The first hurdle Elizabeth faced involved establishing credit. In an era of slower transmission of currency, communication, and shipping, traders who engaged in overseas commerce needed to develop sound relationships with the merchants who supplied them. Often colonial merchants acquired goods from English mercantile houses, generally on one year's credit, and then offered these items to local traders on credit for shorter terms of several months.[12] Although merchants tended to be generous about extending credit, retailers with substantial resources and a good reputation would fare better in seeking such arrangements. Elizabeth did have some resources when she went into business: the men she held in bondage. During the 1740s, while she was living in the United Kingdom, Elizabeth continued to benefit from the labor of the three men whom her brother had purchased with her patrimony at the beginning of the decade. These men had remained in North Carolina, where they were hired out. As soon as it was clear that Elizabeth had definitely "fixed" upon her "Scheme" of shopkeeping, James set about liquidating her assets—the enslaved men—to provide security for wholesalers who would consider supplying her.[13] Thus Elizabeth's pursuit of economic independence depended in part on the absolute lack of freedom of others. Nor did she end her involvement with the institution of slavery once she began her career in commerce. She purchased a woman slave, Hannah, for £250 old tenor (the paper currency floating throughout the colonies which functioned as legal tender and had set rates of exchange with British pounds sterling), half of that sum in goods.[14]

Making Elizabeth's financial situation appear sound and attractive to potential business contacts required several steps, involving bills of exchange, advertising and selling the enslaved men, cash transactions, and promises of credit. First, the North Carolina man who had hired the bondsmen agreed to deliver up bills of exchange for their value, drawn from a London mercantile firm, that totaled £145 sterling; to add to the security of these pieces of paper, James endorsed them as well. The sum covered the slaves' labor for three years and "the value of one" who had died in the intervening period. Advertising them for sale for pitch, tar, gold, silver, deerskins, or bills of exchange, James hoped that their sale would generate eighty to ninety pounds that he could send to a London mercantile house. In addition to handling the details regarding Elizabeth's capital in slaves, James pledged his own resources to help her get started. He promised one hundred pounds sterling of his own credit and urged their brother John to put up another hundred. Together, these various sources of support would enable Elizabeth to acquire "a fine Cargo" of imported wares. Perhaps anticipating that John might hesitate to risk money on Elizabeth's behalf, James expressed confidence in the appropriateness of providing her with fraternal support. He knew her "to be deserving" of such aid and felt certain that she would be "very Diligent," although presumably not in Franklin's sense.[15]

With Elizabeth's basic credit arrangements laid out, James next took it on himself to lay out a plan for her possible contacts with overseas correspondents. Recommending that she establish business relations with the London mercantile firm Messieurs Richard Oswald and Company, as well as with two women of trade, James outlined a division of responsibilities and spheres distinctive to men and women of commerce. In recognition for some service she had rendered, a Miss Edminstone, a milliner, would be employed. A skilled needlewoman, Edminstone could be hired to make up some finery. Another woman, Anne Elliot, would have a more significant role, selecting Elizabeth's stock by carefully searching out "cheap and fashionable" goods.[16] In turn, Oswald and Company would work directly with Elliot, letting her order "all or so many of the goods" that she thought "proper" for Elizabeth's new shop.[17]

Both the male merchants and the female shopkeeper would expect commissions for their transatlantic participation in Elizabeth's business. To ensure that they would all do their best to procure "goods of the newest fashion and best kinds" for her, Elizabeth offered liberal commission terms. From his experience in trading in North Carolina, James knew that consumers could be picky and needed to be enticed with the most fashionable stock possible. If Elizabeth were going to compete, she would need Elliot's and Oswald and Company's cooperation. Once the merchants agreed to do business on the terms James outlined to them, the business would become a reality. The merchants would insure the goods Anne Elliot selected and send them to Elizabeth on the first ship sailing to Boston in the spring of 1750.[18]

Splitting the responsibilities between a large mercantile firm and a small shopkeeper provided Elizabeth, in James's view at least, with an ideal combination of personalized attention and financial stability. Thus, while encouraging Elizabeth to do business with Anne Elliot,

James cautioned his sister not to rely on the woman trader too heavily. Although he considered having Anne Elliot handle all Elizabeth's overseas finances, he quickly dismissed the idea, deciding to send a letter of credit to Oswald and Company instead. James's doubts about Anne Elliot's capabilities stemmed from her sex and marital situation: she was "a single Woman, lately set up, & exposed to a great many accidents." Giving the entire disposal of her money to an unwed and newly established woman retailer would be "a greater trust" than Elizabeth "in prudence" should consider.[19] A woman in Anne Elliot's position did not have the years of experience, position, or familiarity with the law and commerce that the merchants — or James for that matter — did.

The traits that marked Anne Elliot as a business risk were ones that Elizabeth shared. New to trade, unmarried, and on her own describes her situation perfectly in 1749 and 1750. Given these similarities between the two women, it is not surprising that while James was willing to pledge some of his own credit and income to support his sister's venture, he did not view the endeavor as a guaranteed success. When he asked Oswald and Company to begin a correspondence with Elizabeth, he promised his own security, hoping that the participation of Anne Elliot would prove agreeable and that the credit he promised would be enough to induce the company to accept his sister's business. James offered the firm the best terms he could on his own, refusing to enlist the assistance of a well-to-do Scottish relation. James would not solicit patronage or risk the goodwill of his relative for the sake of a young woman's business enterprise.[20]

Even though James planned and suggested most of Elizabeth's initial business arrangements, he did not dictate to her how to proceed but deferred to her judgment, directing others to do so as well. For instance, instead of sending the bills of exchange for the enslaved men directly to London, he waited for several weeks in order to give Elizabeth time to send him instructions about making changes in the plan.[21] When ordering goods, James requested that Oswald and Company inform Elizabeth, rather than him, if any alterations needed to be made; they should write her "so that she may govern herself accordingly."[22]

This telling admonition reveals the dynamics of the relationship between Elizabeth and James as she began her life alone in Boston.

At the moment she took up retailing, her survival in trade appeared precarious, her independence fragile and rooted in her brother's support. In some regards, Elizabeth continued to rely on James as a stand-in parent, one who provided tangible financial assistance and guidance. He saw himself in the same light, as "not only a Brother but a sort of Parent."[23] Years before, when their mother's death left them parentless, James stepped fully into the role he had begun to assume from a distance after their father's death. Now, although the years of their coresidence had come to an end, James continued to offer his sister counsel from afar.

Over the course of the 1750s, however, Elizabeth began to reconfigure that relationship, asserting her own judgment in professional as well as personal matters. As she gained skill as a shopkeeper, she acted with increasing confidence in setting the terms of her business and her existence. She struggled to make a success of her trade and to define for herself how she would construct a family. These efforts, central to her life during the decade after she first arrived in Boston, brought her a sense of independence and competence on her own as a woman of business and vis-à-vis her siblings as a contributing, adult member of her family.

While supportive of Elizabeth's economic ambitions, her brothers did not, in the early 1750s, envision her achieving great success and continued to suggest other options to her. Both James and John repeatedly invited her to become a member of their households. Well before Elizabeth received her first shipment of stock, James suggested that she might again find shelter and a home with his family.[24] Clearly, James was not very enthusiastic about Elizabeth living on her own so far away from him. He urged her, if she revised her views of the potential "advantage and Satisfaction" to be found through keeping shop in Boston, to abandon that plan quickly and take the first opportunity to come south. There, she would find herself as welcome to him as ever "and more if possible," and he would do all in his power to make her life agreeable to her.[25] From England, where he had settled, John issued a similar offer, inviting Elizabeth to join him and become his housekeeper. In case John married, his wife would take her place as housekeeper, and Elizabeth could "do something" else in the area "to acquire a handsome livelihood." If Elizabeth did not choose to support herself, she would "be ever Welcome" in

John's family.[26] This generous but qualified offer underlines the precarious position of the unmarried woman. Elizabeth could be John's housekeeper for as long as it suited him and then, once it no longer did, support herself in some other way or accept the status of dependent. Elizabeth had lived through this scenario the previous decade when James married. Now, too, she refused her brothers' offers to pass her adulthood under a fraternal roof. (In later years, the tables turned as Elizabeth grew wealthy. In the 1760s, James accepted an offer of housing and occupation from her, and in the 1770s, John came to depend on her for financial support.)

In turning a deaf ear to James's entreaties to come to North Carolina, Elizabeth was not alone; Barbara likewise resisted his insistent pleas. In 1749 and 1750, while James was simultaneously helping Elizabeth to get her business going and inviting her to rejoin him, Barbara Bennet Murray remained in Boston, to the tremendous frustration of her distant spouse. Barbara was hesitant to journey to Cape Fear partly, it appears, because of the negative descriptions of the country she had heard, possibly from Elizabeth, who by settling on her own avoided returning to the South. Regardless of the origin of her disinclination, Barbara was unwilling to leave a moment sooner than necessary and stalled, even after she gave birth at the end of 1749.[27] Although he did not want to leave his business and spend time and money to travel to escort his wife to her new home, James finally stewed long enough to realize he would have to do just that if he ever wanted to see her.[28]

Arriving in May 1750, nearly a year after he left, James stayed in Boston with Elizabeth, Barbara, and Dolly until the end of August, thereby spending three of North Carolina's "most disagreeable Months" in "that poor Healthy Place New England" instead. When he and Barbara finally went home, James exulted that he had "at last" gotten his wife from Boston "to help to plant this New Country."[29] For her part, Barbara's prejudice against North Carolina dissipated quickly. A year after arriving, she liked the area "very well," according to James's take on the situation, and thought it had been "much misrepresented to her."[30] The positive outlook of the pair was not warranted by their subsequent life in Cape Fear. Indeed, it seems tragically ironic that the first description James gave of his wife joining him in North Carolina coupled praise for Boston's salubrity with a declaration of his intention to set down roots and people their new home. Before the end of the decade, his and Barbara's efforts to build a life would have failed utterly, with five of their seven children dead and Barbara falling prey to a fatal illness likely contracted as a result of exposure to disease in the local environment.

Well before Barbara sailed south, Elizabeth had begun a campaign to keep some of her family with her in Boston. During her first summer there, before her business got under way, Elizabeth launched an effort to persuade Barbara and James to leave their daughter, Dolly, with her. James was willing to part from his firstborn and defer to his wife's judgment; "whatever way" Barbara and Elizabeth decided, he would be "satisfied." Indeed, he promised that if Elizabeth enjoyed the arrangement and did not find it too costly, he might be able to send her more progeny in the future.[31] (Although Elizabeth did not immediately achieve her goal of building a family with parts of her brother's, she continued to press the plan and eventually succeeded. When Dolly finally joined her aunt's household a few years later, Elizabeth added the role of substitute mother to that of breadwinner.)

While James and Barbara spent the first half of 1750 negotiating over the date of Barbara's departure, Elizabeth put down roots in Boston and set up her business. That summer, Elizabeth received her first cargo of merchandise from Oswald and Company. Although the goods, valued at £118 sterling, arrived safely, Elizabeth was not entirely satisfied. The items were "out of season," an undesirable circumstance given the abundant competition from other retailers.[32] Over time, the repetition of this first frustration with unseasonable merchandise would inspire Elizabeth to take more control over the selection of her stock and eventually to travel to London herself to supervise the process.

Before embracing transatlantic journeys as a means of gaining a business edge, Elizabeth turned to the important and more immediate task of finding customers. In a port town, regular shipments of goods provided consumers with ready access to the newest fashionable merchandise offered by manufacturers and merchants in the mother country. Boston's Long Wharf was crowded with warehouses where such goods were stored; shops abounded in the winding lanes and alleys near the waterfront. In Cornhill, the central commercial district where Elizabeth's shop was located, a passerby could have peeked into many retailers' outlets to see the wide range of consumer goods that Britain was producing in ever increasing quantity and variety. For any aspirant to a career in retailing, finding patrons in such a competitive marketplace involved offering wares that appealed to current tastes and needs at a competitive price and making one's shop known.

Elizabeth decided to publicize her presence among the ranks of Boston's shopkeepers with a flashy broadside. Printed to order and then posted and distributed in the streets, such flyers were used for a variety of purposes, including announcing sales, presenting political views, and selling new songs. Elizabeth's served the important function of letting potential customers know where to find her. In Boston, where churches, drinking establishments, artisans' workshops, retail outlets, and private residences stood side by side and residents could walk the length of the city in a few hours, local landmarks took the place of street numbers and directions. Thus, Elizabeth directed consumers to her shop across the street from the Brazen Head. From the Brazen Head, Mary Jackson, a regular advertiser in the *Boston Evening-Post*, sold a wide range of metal goods, from imported steel, cutlery, and saddlery to teakettles, coffeepots, and baking pans, which she made.[33]

Elizabeth designed her broadside to appeal to fashion-conscious Bostonians and let them know her precise terms of trade (see figure 3).[34] Headed with the phrase "Imported from LONDON, by Elizabeth Murray" in large, decorative type, the flyer established her as a cosmopolitan woman with metropolitan connections, someone ideally suited to serve those who wished to adorn themselves with the newest goods available to consumers in Great Britain. Announcing that she would sell "by Wholesale or Retale," Elizabeth promised to cater both to clients who bought in quantity, perhaps for resale in their own shops, and to those customers who shopped strictly for themselves. Both could find good deals if they eschewed credit, for her wares were "Cheap for the Cash."

Elizabeth's broadside revealed the tempting array of merchandise to be discovered in her shop. While, like any good milliner, she carried many different kinds of cloth and trimmings, she also offered a range of luxurious and specialized goods that could outfit the fashionable consumer from head to toe in a variety of situations.[35] The

Imported from *L O N D O N,*

By *Elizabeth Murray,*

And to be Sold by Wholesale or Retale, at her Shop oppofite to the Brazen Head in Cornhill *Bofton,* Cheap for the Cafh.

Capuchins, flower'd Velvet and Capuchin Silks, black Fringes, Bone Lace, a variety of brocaded ftriped and crofs'd bar'd Stuffs and Poplins for Winter Gowns, FeatherSwan and Ermine Muffs and Tippets, brown Padufay and black ditto, ftriped and enam'd Mantuas, Luteftring ditto, Sattins of all Colours, Sattin Perfian & Stuff quilted Petticoats, the neweft fafhion'd Hoops, Caps, Ruffles, Stomachers, Tipets, and a variety of Gauze and Paris-Nets, Trimmings of all Sorts, black Pink and ... k Mitts, Kid Lamb and Sattin Gloves and Mittens, Stone ... d Flofs Necklaces and Earings, Silver and Flofs Flowers ..., Shoes and Golofhoes, neat Englifh Stays, Shades and Lorains, Womens Hatts and Heives of all Sorts, Silver Girdles, Twitchers, Spangles and Bugles, Umbrilloes, Millinet, flower'd and plain Lawns, flower'd Border'd Aprons, Ruffies. Canvas, Flofs, fine Shade Silk, Slacks and Crewells, Pound Silks, Silk Lacing, Ferret, Mourning Crapes and Hatbands, Galloom and Worfted Binding, Cotton Leifle, Flanders and Scots Threads, Tape and Bobin, Silver Lace for Shoes, Everlaftings, Ebony, Ivory, Bamboo, Church and Leather mount Fanns, Waddin for Caupachins, Silver and Gold Thread, Cord, Flat and Plate for Embroidery, Macklin, Bruffels, Flanders, Millenet, Dott, Trally and Englifh Cap Lace, Lappets and Lappet Heads, a variety of fafhionable Ribands, fmelling Bottles, Hungary and Honey Water, Bagg Hollands, Long Lawns, Cambrick and Muflin, Silk and Guaze Handkerchiefs, Fans Mounts &c. &c. &c.

3   Trade bill of Elizabeth Murray, ca. 1749. Courtesy, Massachusetts Historical Society, Boston.

curious shopper could find swan feather and ermine muffs on her shelves, as well as satin gloves, mourning hatbands, leather-mounted fans, shoes, "goloshoes," necklaces, and earrings. Although dry goods and attire made up the bulk of Elizabeth's stock, she sold merchandise designed to meet other needs, such as smelling bottles and Hungary water, a tonic that carried a royal cachet. Initially prepared for a Hungarian queen, the liquid, made from distilled wine and rosemary flowers, was thought to cure skin problems.[36]

Elizabeth supplemented her attention-getting broadside with advertisements in the local press. Her notices, like those of other retailers, reveal the increasing variety of consumer goods available after midcentury.[37] As the quantities of imports grew, merchants and retailers began to promote their stock in novel ways. Rather than simply announcing the arrival of new shipments of goods, they employed fancy type, illustrations, and borders to attract notice. Shopkeepers proclaimed "Superfine Dutch Hollands, and choice Irish Linens" and "All sorts of the Newest Fashion Millinery" imported from London.[38] Like many other traders, Elizabeth resorted to this strategy, touting her wares regularly in the pages of the *Boston Evening-Post*.

From 1750 to 1755, in large advertisements, Elizabeth declared that her goods were "just imported." During the summer of 1750, when Elizabeth placed her first notice, only two other women, Mary Jackson and Henrietta Maria [East] Caine, placed advertisements in the pages of the *Boston Evening-Post*. Both noted that they carried imported wares. In several prominent notices in June, Jackson informed customers of her various metallic merchandise available at the Brazen Head in Cornhill, while Caine announced her goods for sale "at the Sign of the FAN" in the South End.[39] In the issue for Monday, 20 August, when Elizabeth's first advertisement appeared, hers was the only notice by a woman. Topped by her name in large type, with eye-catching placement at the head of the second column of the paper's second page, Elizabeth's advertisement informed customers that her goods were "imported in the Last Ship from LONDON" and available "at the most reasonable Rates." Clearly, the London connection mattered to those conscious of metropolitan fashions.

The summer of 1750 witnessed other Boston entrepreneurs attempting to capitalize on cosmopolitan connections. In the issue in which Elizabeth first advertised, peruke-makers Murray (no relation) and Commings, "lately arrived from London," offered to dress "Gentleman and Ladies Hair, after the newest and neatest Fashion at present used in London," either in their shop or at their customers' home.[40] The physical embodiments of London — as recent denizens of the great city — Murray and Commings offered to do the hair of people likely to frequent a shop like Elizabeth's. From the distance of America such individuals sought to participate in the sophistication and material culture of the capital. One form of entertainment available in Boston that summer, a camera obscura, a prephotography device, provided curious viewers with the opportunity the see the sights famed on the other side of the Atlantic, "many of the Royal Palaces in Europe, with other handsome Buildings, Gardens, Parks, &c. represented to the Life," the very features that distinguished such places as London from provincial ports.[41]

Elizabeth's newspaper notices make it clear that while she invested most of her resources, efforts, and hopes in her shopkeeping enterprise, she sought to earn income through teaching as well. In March 1751 she announced her willingness to take on pupils who wished to study Dresden and other kinds of needlework.[42] Elizabeth was the first woman in America to advertise lessons in this style of embroidery, which used the stitching threads to pull the background fabric into a design, most commonly white thread on white linen cloth.[43] As a skilled needlewoman herself, Elizabeth could provide instruction in the stylish stitches of the day to the young ladies who were expected to display their knowledge of such fine sewing in decorative works of embroidery, which their families might frame and hang. Elizabeth also offered to accommodate her students in her home as half or full boarders at reasonable prices. This diversification of Elizabeth's business interests made good sense. In addition to selling goods, she could sell her skills to the daughters of the genteel families most likely to buy expensive millinery wares and, at the same time, gain some income from taking in boarders. Over the next few years, Elizabeth continued to advertise her shop wares regularly, but she did not solicit pupils again until the spring of 1753. Shopkeeping likely occupied the bulk of her time and attention.

Like Elizabeth Murray, most of Boston's women shopkeepers tended to offer dry goods such as cloth, lace, and millinery wares. Out of eighty women whose merchandise could be determined, forty-nine sold primarily dry goods, as well as such assorted wares as sealing wax, shoe buckles, and French paste earrings. Twenty-five women stocked imported seeds, groceries, spices, tea, olive oil, cheeses, and wine. Although retailers tended to carry large quantities of particular types of goods, shopkeeping was not fully specialized. As a result, a consumer could find a diverse range of items in the typical shop. Women traders not involved primarily in the dry goods or grocery trades sold merchandise ranging from cutlery and tools to spectacles and ointments. Others combined the sale of goods and services, advertising items like soap and candles along with horse-shoeing, for example.

Although increasing numbers of women traders advertised with each passing decade, few shopkeepers had regular recourse to print. The names of many shopkeepers appeared in the press only after their death, when their executors asked debtors and creditors to settle their accounts. Other retailers advertised only to announce a change in business operations or relocation. Indeed, other than the seed vendors who placed annual spring notices in the papers, the shopkeeper who advertised repeatedly and regularly was the exception. Elizabeth advertised more than most. The many who never advertised had to rely on local reputation, word of mouth, and the custom of friends and passersby.

The presence of these women traders suggests that in such colonial ports as Boston, retailing was an accessible occupation for some women.[44] To describe shopkeeping in these terms is not to suggest unlimited opportunity or a sure promise of riches. Rather, many women found shopkeeping a more attainable trade than were others. The comparatively limited skills required — literacy and simple math — coupled with easily obtained credit and rising consumer demand, made commercial endeavors attractive to those who needed to support themselves and who had enough assets to escape domestic service or dependent status in another's household. Despite economic instability, some women shopkeepers conducted business for extended periods. Twenty-five Boston women retailers kept shop for ten years or more; eight ran businesses for over twenty years.[45] Nine other women engaged in commerce for six to ten years, and twenty-one for at least two to five years. It should be noted that the longer a woman kept shop, the more likely it is that her work left some evidence. Thus, women who engaged in trade for very short periods would be more difficult to discern. Because of feme covert property laws, married women who ran businesses on their own or with the minimal involvement of their husbands are much more rarely noted in the historical record. The majority of Boston's women shopkeepers were widows, most of whom continued businesses established by spouses. Of sixty-three shopkeepers whose marital status could be determined, almost two-thirds were widows. A little under one-third were spinsters. At least two women began to keep shop while single and continued to do so after their marriages. Jane Eustis and Henrietta Maria [East] Caine were either divorced or separated during most of their business careers.[46] Eustis, a shopkeeper by 1755, had married Joshua Eustis, a tinplate worker in Boston, in September 1748. Before the end of 1749, he had deserted her, sailed to Barbados, and married another woman. On the grounds of his "basely and adulterously" violating the marriage, Jane Eustis successfully petitioned the court for the dissolution of their union in June 1760.[47]

As widows and spinsters, these female traders carved a niche for themselves, seeking economic independence, supporting their families, and occasionally raising their daughters to take their places behind the counter. Shopkeeper Abigail Whitney, for example, was married to a yeoman who died in 1749.[48] Her nineteen-year-old daughter Abigail, the oldest of her five children, became her partner in retailing. The two sold various goods, including cloth, combs, looking glasses, and shoes, from a shop in Union Street. When the company of Abigail Whitney and Daughter was dissolved by the former's death in 1768, the younger Abigail received legal acknowledgment of her work. In her will, Abigail Whitney named her daughter the executor of her estate and consigned the family business to her as well, despite the fact that she had an adult son.[49] Retailer Hannah Newman, who also had a shop in Union Street, acknowledged the assistance of her partner and daughter, Susannah, even more explicitly. In her will Newman gave her two sons only paltry sums while bequeathing the rest of her estate, both real and personal, to her daughter. Newman declared that her daughter had been "a great Comfort" and support to her in her advanced age and had "taken Care" of her business, contributing greatly by her "Diligence and Industry."[50] The business survived the dissolution of the partnership; after her mother's death, Susannah continued to sell imported seeds and foodstuffs.[51] Like Hannah Newman and Abigail Whitney, Elizabeth Murray supported other women shopkeepers both during and after the period in which she engaged in trade, forming and participating in personal and professional networks.

   Although Elizabeth eventually gained enough financial security to
set up other women in business, she found her own early economic
efforts to be quite challenging. Beginning to trade while unmarried
and without family networks in place, Elizabeth's marital status and
isolation likely contributed to her as well as her brothers' misgivings
about her enterprise. Although Elizabeth rejected both James's and
John's offers to join their households when she was first setting up
her shop, in the early 1750s she was not absolutely committed to
permanent residence in Boston. As long as James remained in North
Carolina, she would stay put; if he decided to return to Great Britain
for good, however, she was willing and ready to abandon Boston and
follow his lead.[52] As late as the fall of 1753, Elizabeth still considered
her fate and place of residence as linked to and somewhat dependent
on James's choices.

   Elizabeth's ambivalence may have stemmed from difficulties she
encountered in making the shop a success. Her fortunes changed
dramatically from one moment to the next. After a year in business,
she felt satisfied with her lot. By July 1751 she was making "both ends
meet" and thought "her Life more Comfortable than it could be" in
North Carolina, an assessment that James did not share.[53] Before the
summer was out, however, she had run into problems because of her
overseas correspondents. The woman who selected haberdashery
and millinery wares for her, presumably still Anne Elliot, had not
procured the best prices possible. Thus Elizabeth carried overpriced
stock and accordingly "suffered considerably both in reputation and
Interest."[54] If consumers doubted that a shopkeeper offered goods at
a competitive price, there would be little to tempt them to enter a
shop when other retailers carried similar wares. This unfortunate
experience led Elizabeth to adopt new business arrangements, with
James once again acting as intermediary. Promising to offer security
for her for goods worth two hundred pounds sterling, James asked
merchant Edward Bridgen to accept Elizabeth's business and insure
any goods before shipping. James assured the wholesaler that he had
no concerns about his sister's skills and was certain that she would
not mismanage the business in any way.[55]

   Problems with debt and stock may have undermined whatever confidence other members of Boston's trading community had in Elizabeth's business acumen. In early 1753 she found her commercial

skills ridiculed and herself embarrassed. Some Bostonians began to call her "the broken shop keeper," apparently for running out of stock. After finding herself with a rather bare-looking shop, she decided to protect herself from such derision in the future by ordering a gross of boxes that she planned to label with "letters & numbers on them & set them on the shelves."[56] She would appear well stocked regardless of the reality. This emphasis on maintaining the appearance of success calls to mind another contemporary entrepreneur, Benjamin Franklin, who self-consciously crafted his public persona. "In order to secure my Credit and Character as a Tradesman," he recalled, "I took care not only to be in *Reality* Industrious & frugal, but to avoid all *Appearances* to the Contrary."[57] Customers, he believed, would have more faith in him as a businessman and consequently patronize him more. Similarly, Elizabeth tried both to be successful and to maintain the illusion that she was.

While she could have borrowed more to keep her shop fully stocked instead of disguising her limited inventory, Elizabeth was wary of that solution. Having "suffer'd already" from problems with debt, she chose instead to keep herself financially clear rather than obtain goods on credit.[58] Whether proffered by a wholesale merchant supplier or given by retailers to consumers short of cash, credit rendered a shopkeeper dependent on others.

For women shopkeepers, marriage could present an additional difficulty in handling credit arrangements and indebtedness. Indeed, Henrietta Maria [East] Caine found her ability to carry on her business seriously threatened by a recalcitrant spouse. Four years after settling in Boston, she had married Hugh Caine, a man who turned out to have a wife, whom he had married in Ireland many years before, still living in London. Within a few years of their marriage, during which he "treated her with great Violence," Hugh Caine had "dissipated a great part of her Estate and carried away the remainder" in 1751. Nine years later, no one had heard from or of him again. Although free of his presence, Henrietta Maria Caine was constrained by the continuance of their marriage contract. As long as she remained legally and financially bound to this man, traders refused to supply her with the goods she needed to carry on her business. In 1754 she tried to resolve some of her financial problems by selling all her goods at public auction.[59] Several years later, still hoping for relief, she petitioned the court to dissolve her marriage.[60] Although the council that heard her case in 1760 was willing to approve her petition, the lieutenant governor was not. Within two years, her career as a shopkeeper had drawn to a close. Declared mentally incompetent by the court, she was under the care of nurses and attendants. Her remaining shop goods, valued at over £350, were sold at public auction.[61] In the time between Hugh's desertion and the court's pronouncement that Henrietta was a person non compos mentis, she suffered from the economic vulnerability that married women experienced as the result of laws that prohibited them from possessing independent control over property and income. Another retailer's financial difficulties made a strong impression on Elizabeth. Deeply in debt, the woman had to sell all her goods to satisfy her creditors and ended up financially imperiled and "a great many hundreds worse than nothing." This example troubled Elizabeth, inspiring her to double her diligence to keep herself "as clear as is possible in this place."[62]

Financial dependence of any kind weighed on Elizabeth. In particular, James's credit being entangled with hers gave her "great uneasyness."[63] Concerned that James would be ruined if her finances failed, Elizabeth proposed switching her business to two merchants who would supply her without a letter of credit from James. That Elizabeth contemplated this arrangement suggests that British merchants willingly gave credit directly to shopkeepers, small traders who lacked the backing of the sort that merchants — by definition men — enjoyed. Elizabeth's desire to make the change also emphasizes the precariousness of commercial endeavors; the financial ruin of one individual could destroy a family's well-being in an age when business ties frequently followed family lines.

Elizabeth's difficulties in early 1753 may have prompted her to diversify her business activities to emphasize teaching once again. For three consecutive weeks in March, she placed advertisements in the *Boston Evening-Post*, noting that she taught fine needlework and was willing to take in boarders. At her location, still "Next Door to Deacon Boutineau's in Cornhill," she taught "Dresden and Embroidery on Gauze," as well as "all sorts of coloured Work."[64] She also listed a variety of millinery goods for sale. This teaching advertisement may have inspired the Trumbull family to enroll their ten-year-old daugh-

4   Needlework overmantel, embroidery by Faith Trumbull, ca. 1754.
Courtesy, The Connecticut Historical Society, Hartford.

ter, Faith, as a pupil with Elizabeth that summer.[65] Faith created elaborate pictorial embroideries on silk, which survive today and were
most likely completed under Elizabeth's tutelage in the early 1750s
(figure 4). The Trumbulls paid Elizabeth over sixty pounds for tui-
tion and other expenses.[66]

In the early 1750s, while Elizabeth was struggling to make her business succeed, she relegated familial obligations and relationships to a
lower priority than financial concerns, weighing the potential impact
of her personal decisions on her shop. After careful thought, for example, she determined that a 1753 visit to North Carolina would have
to take place in the winter, when business was very slow, so that she
could be back in Boston by the beginning of April, when the spring
shipments arrived. Rather suddenly, Elizabeth canceled her trip to
see her family, deciding instead to travel to London on business.

Given her announced intention to stay in the colonies or leave
them depending on James's actions — a declaration she made in October 1753 — Elizabeth may have surprised herself as well as her family when she made arrangements two months later to sail to England
to lay in a stock of goods. This journey represents a turning point in
her reliance on familial guidance and dictates and indeed marks the
beginning of her maturation into an individual to whom the rest of
the family would look for advice and financial support. Well aware of
the dramatic step she was undertaking, Elizabeth suspected that her
family would "be very much surprised" when they learned of the
changes in her plans. She would sail long before any of her siblings

received word of her trip, to be able "to return early in the spring with the newest fashions."[67]

This journey is remarkable not just for the haste and ease with which Elizabeth undertook it but also for the independent judgment with which she planned it. Rather than soliciting James's advice, she made up her own mind and told her brother that her Boston friends deemed her plan a good one. Everybody thought her "going home" would prove a "very great advantage" to her because she could choose the goods that would "suit" Boston.[68] Her knowledge of the local market, combined with the financial wherewithal and willingness to travel, would give her an advantage over her competitors. Seeking neither permission nor counsel from family, Elizabeth acted as a mature woman of affairs. Yet while Elizabeth did not request her brother's approval of her plans, she continued to treat him deferentially, declaring her affection for him and gratitude for his generosity toward her. Over the next several decades, variations on this scene were replayed numerous times, only with the roles of the actors shifting, as Elizabeth and her growing economic power assumed increasing importance within the Murray family circle.

Elizabeth's trip to London also marks a transition in her career as a shopkeeper. In undertaking the journey, she attempted to improve her position and gain an edge over her commercial rivals. Always aware of the consumer, she strove to capitalize on what she knew of Bostonians' tastes by selecting the merchandise herself. A careful observer of purchasing behavior, Elizabeth was critical of the suppliers who sent her items that were unlikely to sell. The fall 1753 shipments had arrived with goods suited to summer. Doubtful of her ability to get a good return on these wares, Elizabeth decided to advertise her imminent departure for London, trying to entice consumers with the possibility of good prices in the shop of someone trying to clear the shelves. The strategy proved successful.[69]

Before embarking for England, Elizabeth made careful arrangements for her home, business, and property. After marking prices on all the goods in her shop, Elizabeth enlisted the assistance of a widowed woman who would stay in her house free of charge and earn a commission of one shilling per pound on any merchandise sold during her absence.[70] When she took an inventory of every article in her shop, Elizabeth discovered that she had stock worth seven hundred pounds sterling in addition to the shop furniture. That substantial sum was free of encumbrances other than the financial obligations she still had to James. Appreciative of all of James's assistance, Elizabeth tried to express her debt to "the best of Brothers," begging him, if any accident befell her during her trip, to accept all that belonged to her and do so with a conviction of her feelings. "Believe that it comes," she told him, "from a sister that owes it all to you," one who would always acknowledge what she owed with the sincerest gratitude "that every mortall was capable of."[71]

Arriving in London in February 1754 after a passage of six weeks, Elizabeth pursued business single-mindedly. The financial considerations that motivated her to undertake the trip also governed her behavior abroad. In England she concentrated purely on her mercantile mission, neglecting the opportunity to visit relatives on that side of the Atlantic, despite their insistence that she travel to Scotland. Economic "interest" triumphed over emotional "inclination," and she did not visit any of her family other than her brother John. Instead, upon her arrival in London, Elizabeth went directly to the home of Edward Bridgen, the merchant from whom she had already received some goods. During her stay, Bridgen taught her a "short method of bookkeeping" that she found "very easy." "A most generous friend," he also insisted that Elizabeth stay with his family and accompanied her on her rounds while she chose "a very ne[a]t assortment of goods" that would "suit the Boston market very well."[72]

Although Elizabeth may have possessed astute judgment about the tastes of New England's consumers, she did not yet have enough credit in her own right to act on her purchasing decisions. Rather than ask James for additional support and perhaps desirous of lessening her dependence on him, Elizabeth planned to use a "very handsome letter of Credit" given to her by Ralph Inman, a substantial man of commerce in Boston, to obtain as many goods as she wanted. Bridgen, however, discouraged her from involving herself in this way with a nonrelative, suggesting that James would probably give her a larger letter of credit if she asked and agreeing to provide her with goods on that basis. Having intended to use Ralph Inman's letter, Elizabeth had left America without discussing an extension of credit with James. Given the time constraints — she wanted to be back in Boston in the spring — Elizabeth went ahead and promised James's secu-

rity, feeling "very much ashamed" about doing so without his knowledge.[73] In short, Elizabeth continued her financial dependence on
her brother and deepened her own involvement with Bridgen and his
partner, James Waller, but she did so primarily because she chose to
reject another kind of dependence, represented by offers of credit
from other potential lenders. Ralph Inman's willingness to extend
credit to Elizabeth, a young, unmarried shopkeeper, hints at friendly
relations between the two and admiration for her skills. (Nearly
twenty years later, that esteem found more tangible expression when
the two wed; Ralph's wife died in 1761, shortly after Elizabeth married her second spouse. When they married a decade later, after she
had been widowed for the second time, her financial situation was so
dramatically improved that their roles had reversed. Ralph would
look to her for support and income, ultimately prompting her relatives to charge him with being after her money.)

Returning to New England in the spring of 1754, Elizabeth threw
herself into her life in Boston, doing well in her business, creating a
family, and achieving a degree of autonomy. She continued to teach
embroidery and remitted large sums to Bridgen and Waller well
within the nine to twelve months allotted for payment. Her success in
doing so no doubt contributed to Bridgen's promise to oversee the
selection of her stock himself. Determined to remain "as Clear as is
possible" in her finances, Elizabeth kept the prompt payments of
debts high on her list of business priorities.[74] When an investment
she made turned sour, Elizabeth vowed to be even more cautious,
putting her money into a lawyer's hands and deciding to buy bills
from only one man, Colonel Royall, no matter how attractive the
return offered by others appeared.[75] Meanwhile, her efforts to persuade James and Barbara to part with Dolly finally succeeded. At the
age of ten, Dolly, after saying what turned out to be a final farewell to
her mother, sailed north to be educated. Her parents entrusted her
to Elizabeth's care, motivated by a belief that Boston offered superior
educational opportunities and confident that Dolly would receive
"better breeding" there under her aunt's direction than North Carolina could afford.[76]

In 1755 Elizabeth Murray got married. In wedding Thomas Campbell, a ship's captain and trader, she exchanged the legal independence of her single life as head of household for the coverture

of wedlock. At a distance from both their families, Elizabeth and Thomas conducted their courtship free from the interested eyes of loved ones. Long before the couple cemented their ties in Boston, their families had been well acquainted in North Carolina. It is likely that the connection of their youth lay the basis for them becoming better acquainted as adults. A regular traveler between the two colonies, Thomas served as a courier of Murray correspondence after Elizabeth settled in Boston, conveying James's letters to Elizabeth and spending evenings visiting with her when he did so.

While she clearly decided to marry Thomas on her own, Elizabeth nonetheless went through the motions of seeking James's approval, as the oldest male and titular head of the family, before giving her suitor a final answer. James thought it fitting that Elizabeth ask his "Approbation" of the match and readily assented. Always one to indulge her, James had "never had Occasion to refuse any thing" Elizabeth asked. Of greater weight, however, was Thomas's character. A young man of "Sobriety, Industry & Integrity," Thomas possessed qualities "not always to be met with in this part of the world."[77]

After living in America for twenty years, James had come to the conclusion that the country offered better economic opportunities for men than women because of a rather poor marriage market. In North Carolina a boy could gain enough property to become the equivalent of a lord, whereas a girl would find little hope of advancement through matrimony. James saw colonial men as so singularly lacking that he was at a loss about how to plan for his own daughters' futures. Given that the colonies had "no nunnerys" and "but an uncultivated indolent set of Men," James had no idea what to do for them and could only hope that "the men & Country" would "be much Improv'd" by the time they came to the marriage "market."[78] The shortage of men of good character made James certain that Elizabeth had accepted the best matrimonial offer possible: she had good judgment. Moreover, delay would not increase her chances of good proposals, "considering she had not much time to wait for further Choice."[79] At twenty-nine, Elizabeth was getting older, which narrowed the marriage field. James guessed — incorrectly, as it turned out — that Elizabeth was facing her last, best chance to get married.

Thomas Campbell possessed numerous traits that made him a

good prospective husband. In addition to his sobriety, industry, and integrity — qualities equally valuable in successful business dealings and marriages — Thomas had much in common with the Murray family. Of Scottish descent, Thomas was also well connected in the ancestral homeland, related to a professor at St. Andrews. His father, who had recently died, had been a householder in Wilmington, North Carolina, and thus a neighbor of James's. As a result, James had known Thomas since "his infancy."[80] Now that he was an adult, Thomas occasionally met with James in North Carolina when he visited there in the course of business. Engaged in coastal trade and bred to the sea, Thomas had commanded several small vessels based in Wilmington. Thus Thomas Campbell shared ethnicity and commercial enterprise with his new spouse and her family.

These ethnic and economic commonalities, together with personal characteristics, boded well for the match. When she learned of their marriage, Barbara Murray Clark congratulated her younger sister on being "so happily" married. Barbara, who had formed a good opinion of Thomas as a boy, hoped not to be disappointed now that their connection was so much closer than that of neighbors.[81] Altogether, she felt "much pleased" that her sister had made "so good a Choice" and anticipated the mutual satisfaction of the newlyweds. "I hope you will be happy in each other," she told Thomas, "for I know her to be of a good natural temper."[82]

In marrying, Elizabeth and Thomas linked their fates to each other's, legally and financially, with Elizabeth giving up the autonomy of the single woman and Thomas apparently giving up his line of business to be with his new wife in Boston. Barbara suggested that Thomas had switched his profession to suit Elizabeth, asserting that he had given her a proof of his affection "in Changing his way of Life." In acknowledging this act, Barbara asked her sister what business Thomas intended to follow, adding, "All your friends is desirous to know."[83] Unfortunately, the paucity of evidence on this point makes it impossible to determine whether this colonial man gave up his career to accommodate his wife's — if he chose to reside in Boston for economic gain (perhaps Elizabeth's business was more successful than his), for emotional desires, or for some other reason. Nor do the records from the brief period of their union supply enough detail to test Barbara's predictions of marital happiness. It seems equally plausible that Elizabeth's business had more potential for profit and expansion than her husband's did at the time and it was practical for him to join her venture or that he foresaw the possibility of continuing to engage in shipping ventures with Boston as his new home base.

Elizabeth's commercial successes, coupled with the fact of her marriage, led to a dramatic restructuring in her financial arrangements. Legally, the property she brought into her marriage now belonged to her husband. In the absence of prenuptial agreements, women in the colonies had very limited rights over their estates, with control of property they brought into marriage automatically devolving on their spouses. Given that Thomas gained legal authority over Elizabeth's finances as well as responsibility for her debts, it is not surprising that James moved quickly to remove himself from involvement in her business. He asked Bridgen and Waller to release him from his earlier bond. Several years before, when she was unmarried and struggling, Elizabeth had been, in James's eyes at least, partly his responsibility. It had been his duty to stake his fortune "to encourage and support the Laudable spirit of Industry which she shewd." Now, with Elizabeth in possession of "a good Capital and a good Husband," James thought it right for his "former Obligations" to cease. James's decision to remove himself from Elizabeth's business affairs may have triggered some concerns on the part of her contacts in England. While Bridgen and Waller had conducted trade with Elizabeth for years with the security of her brother's bond, now they would be dealing with her unknown spouse. James provided the merchants with a positive assessment of Thomas's assets. In addition to his good character, Thomas also possessed a "not inconsiderable" fortune as a result of his father's recent death.[84] The couple were doing so well financially that no one would suffer for giving them credit; the risk of giving credit to Thomas was much less than that attending "bolder Traders with thrice his fortune."[85] A cautious pair, then, Elizabeth and Thomas merited the merchants' confidence and credit.

Elizabeth and Thomas's joint involvement in her establishment proved successful. In 1757 James described Elizabeth as continuing "in very good Business under her Husband's directions."[86] They each dealt with different aspects of the enterprise. Thomas appears to have assumed responsibility for handling the commercial correspondence, writing about trade to his brother-in-law James and responding to Bridgen and Waller's letters. For her part, Elizabeth continued to take care of the shop; letters addressed to her described her as a "Milliner in Boston."[87] Legally, their arrangement made sense. Married women in Massachusetts did not have the right to make contracts or hold property in their own name. Unlike Pennsylvania and South Carolina, Massachusetts did not have *feme sole* trader statutes that recognized and protected the business and property rights of married women in business. Given law and custom, Elizabeth's suppliers would have assumed that Thomas would exercise authority over financial and business decisions.

This division of responsibilities between Elizabeth and her husband highlights one of the reasons that historians have had difficulty finding evidence of women's commercial endeavors in the colonies. Because of the legal coverture that attended marriage, women who kept shop while married are sometimes obscured by the records of merchants, for example, who headed accounts in their ledgers with the names of the husbands rather than the wives who may have selected the goods and run the shops. When a woman kept shop before marriage and continued to do so afterward, as did Elizabeth [Murray] Campbell or Henrietta Maria [East] Caine, she was more likely to appear in the historical record. Largely as a result of married women's historical invisibility, widows make up the majority of known shopkeepers. Many of these women undoubtedly worked alongside their spouses in family enterprises and made a mark in records only after a spouse's death. Other married women kept shops while their husbands — the legal heads of the businesses — engaged in other occupations or aspects of trade, thus explaining both the absence of such women from records as well as the striking levels of acceptance and success they enjoyed while trading on their own after a spouse's death.[88] Twelve of Boston's women shopkeepers ran businesses directly related to their spouse's work; five other widows had been married to men connected with trade as either ship captains or mariners. In advertising for the first time after her mariner husband's death, Ann Domett may have been fairly typical. She announced that she sold wine, brandy, and rum as usual and shortly thereafter applied for her own license to retail liquor, "the decease of her husband having made such an application necessary within the Year." In approving her request, Boston's town leaders imposed the condition that she sell only "in the manner she had done in the life time of her deceased husband."[89] While many widows did continue familial enterprises, at least one third of the widowed shopkeepers had no connection to their husband's occupations; these eight women were married to men who followed trades ranging from physician to wig-maker.

Although historically invisible, women shopkeepers — whether widowed, married, or single — undoubtedly had a visible presence in Boston, taking part in burgeoning consumer experiences as members of commercial and neighborhood networks. Visiting merchants' warehouses, advertising their wares in the press, enlisting their daughters in their businesses, and inviting consumers into their shops and dwellings — these "she Merchants" were recognizable within Boston's trading community. The presence of other women engaged in other enterprises, from running a boardinghouse to teaching school, and the interactions among them suggest that these workingwomen had familiarity with and supported each other's economic activities.

Elizabeth participated in this community of women as both a retailer of goods and consumer of services offered by other women, particularly teachers. She enlisted other women to instruct Dolly in the various skills James and Barbara hoped their daughter would acquire. Given that legal and social support for education in Massachusetts exceeded that in the South, they were right to assume that their daughter would encounter good educational opportunities in Boston. Laws in the Puritan colony required towns of over one hundred families to establish schools; Latin schools were required by the 1730s. Yet statutory endorsements for schools did not necessarily translate into uniform approval of female education.[90] While some communities provided funds as early as the 1760s for teaching girls basic literacy skills, others, including Boston, did not do so until decades later.[91] Yet Boston did offer a variety of educational possibilities for the training of boys and girls. In dame schools, or informal schools in the homes of women, youngsters of either sex could learn the rudiments of reading and writing. In grammar schools, boys who possessed a solid background in English studied Latin and Greek in preparation for college. Informal training in sewing and a range of other skills could be procured through individual instructors who advertised their services.

Initially, Elizabeth attempted to train and educate her niece primarily at home but found that her business made it impossible to do so. She tried to instruct and oversee Dolly's progress as a seamstress, "but people coming out & in so much to the shop" took her away from her work too much.[92] It is not clear whether Dolly was simply distracted by the parade of customers or interrupted her needlework to act as her aunt's assistant in the shop. Regardless, the busyness of the shop necessitated that Elizabeth send Dolly elsewhere to acquire the desired skills. Reading and sewing schools came to the rescue. If she picked up an issue of the *Boston Evening-Post*, Elizabeth could have scanned the announcements of a number of teachers and masters.

Among those willing to take on pupils was Eleanor Purcell, a schoolmistress in Milk Street. For several years, between 1751 and 1755, Eleanor and her sister Mary kept school together, offering instruction in needlework. When the Purcell sisters dissolved their partnership in 1755, Mary went into business with divorced retailer Jane Eustis, whereas Eleanor continued to advertise on her own. In the *Boston Evening-Post* for 21 April 1755, Eleanor announced that she taught "after the neatest and newest Manner" all sorts of "embroidering in Gold and Silver," as well as "Japanning, and Coats of Arms, and all Sorts of Flowers in Shell-Work." Sewing coats of arms, typically with silk thread against a black silk background, was a specialty taught by several women in Boston in the 1750s and 1760s.[93] In short, Eleanor had the skill "and all the Materials for the Work" that "any young Lady" might wish to do.[94] Dolly studied with a Miss Purcell, very likely Eleanor, and also received training from a Miss Reed.[95]

Elizabeth shifted her patronage in 1757 to Jannette Day, her close friend and protégé. That year, Elizabeth sent Dolly to study needlework with "Mrs. Day," who had recently emigrated from Scotland and taught "all sorts of fine work."[96] With a failed love affair in her past, Jannette Day had arrived in Boston in 1756 with a young daughter, few resources, and no self-confidence. Elizabeth stepped in and befriended the newcomer. Jannette later declared that Elizabeth alone had faith in her when she had lost all standing in the world, even in her own eyes. Perhaps reflecting on her own travails in starting life in a foreign port, Elizabeth took pity on the pair and helped her countrywoman set herself up as a teacher in Cornhill. Like her mentor, Jannette announced herself in the Boston press. For over a

decade, Jannette ran a school, took in boarders, advertised her establishment in newspapers as far away as Newport, and found students
among New England's well-to-do.[97]

As partners or patrons of one another's businesses, Boston's workingwomen shared personal and professional ties. For those who
never married, friendships may have provided the social and emo
tional support that marriage might otherwise have offered. Mary
Purcell, for example, who worked first with her sister Eleanor and
then with Jane Eustis, formed a third partnership with retailer Sarah
Todd by 1759, which lasted until the latter's death in mid-1777.[98]
Purcell's switch from teaching to shopkeeping points to her confidence in the potential financial reward of retailing and her familiarity with the commercial enterprises of other women. Her business
relationship and friendship with Todd lasted almost twenty years.
When Todd died, she bequeathed everything to her "dearly beloved
friend."[99]

Advertisements offer further evidence of both women's relationships and the prominence of some women's businesses. In March
1759, after an announcement appeared stating that "Mrs. Jane Day"
was opening a school "where Mrs. Campbell now dwells," William
Townshend placed a notice in the paper saying that no one had the
power to rent out the property except him and that he had done so
to "Mrs Sarah Todd," at whose "desire" he informed the public of
the confusion. Apparently, Elizabeth had planned to move her business to a nearby shop recently occupied by merchant Gilbert Deblois
and had suggested that Jannette take over her premises. Without
clearing the plan with the landlord, who had made other arrangements for the prime spot, Jannette had advertised her new location.
The difficulties were not fully resolved until that August, when Todd
and Purcell advertised that they had moved their shop, "notwithstanding the ill-natur'd Opposition they have met with, though not
from the Landlord," to the house "lately occupied by Mrs. Elizabeth
Campbell."[100]

This trading network and Elizabeth's success in participating in
it inspired various members of the Murray family, including Elizabeth, to consider careers in retailing as possibilities for other young
women. Demonstrating a dramatic change in attitude, James in 1757
suggested that Annie Clark, Barbara's daughter, should learn to keep

shop under Elizabeth's supervision. He proposed that Elizabeth take
Annie into her home "to Instruct her in her Business."[101] Tutelage
under Elizabeth's auspices appealed to the Murrays, whether it involved apprenticeship to shopkeeping or other kinds of study. Annie
Clark, her cousin Dolly, and eventually Betsy, Dolly's younger sister,
all received training in their aunt's household.

The Murrays' practice of placing the girls of the family under their
aunt's care led to formation of deep bonds between Elizabeth and
her nieces and also set the pattern for Elizabeth's lifelong commitment to assisting and training other women. Over time, Dolly and
Elizabeth became so close that James characterized his sister's affection for his daughter as "more like a Mamas than an aunts."[102] Indeed, even after James and Barbara named a daughter after Elizabeth, she declared that her loyalties belonged to Dolly. "Obliged" to
her brother for the honor of a namesake, Elizabeth doubted the newborn would supplant Dolly: "I do not imagin I shall like her half so
well as my Doll," she declared possessively.[103] Under Elizabeth's auspices Dolly attended dancing and writing schools, except in winter,
when the cold weather imposed a burden.[104] Wherever she developed her writing abilities, Dolly eventually achieved a much more
regular and elegant hand than her aunt ever produced.[105] Thomas
Campbell thought Dolly had "a genius more for an Accomptant than
a Seemstriss" but hoped nonetheless that she would perfect both
skills before leaving Boston.[106] Dolly's training in arithmetic and accounting may have had two purposes: to prepare her either for
household management or for commercial endeavor. The relationship between Elizabeth and Dolly became so close that Elizabeth
even resisted requests to return her niece to the parental hearth. In
January 1758 Elizabeth admonished her sister-in-law in a rather pos-
sessive tone, "As you commit my Dolls Education wholly to my care
you must Concent to her staying time enough to learn."[107] Indeed,
she told Barbara not even to consider Dolly's return for another two
years; the youngster would "learn more in that time than She [had]
done yet."[108] Barbara, ill at the time, may have wished for her daughter's presence at her side, or perhaps she and James simply needed
reassurance about the merits of the long separation from their eldest
child.

The discussion surrounding Dolly's future education and Barbara's and Elizabeth's conflicting desires was interrupted abruptly in early 1758, when death cut a wide path through the family. Barbara died in North Carolina on February 17 after a lingering illness. The events of that month proved with finality that James's early positive assessment of North Carolina's climate was gravely wrong. Fevers and illness, sickness and death had already taken a number of his and Barbara's children. Although they had lost four children by 1755, James at that point had still been sanguine about the future, noting that his two surviving daughters were "very healthy and hearty" and that Barbara had not suffered "an Hours sickness since she [had] been in the Province."[109] Just as the Murray children succumbed to disease, so eventually did Barbara Bennet Murray.

James's heart-wrenching account of Barbara's final illness and death captures both the level of medical knowledge at the time and the more poignant, personal tragedy of a man who buried five of seven children and his wife.[110] From his description, malaria appears a likely culprit. The summer of 1757 had been marked by stagnant water standing in low-lying areas for long periods. When the water drained in September, "the Vapours from the Swamps made the Inhabitants near the low Grounds very sickly."[111] Of course, if Barbara did have malaria it was not vapors but one of two species of malaria-carrying mosquitoes that caused her illness.[112] Yet James believed that the swamps were to blame. Following popular practice, the Murrays traveled to the seaside for a cure. There, Barbara recovered quickly and was "impatient to be home" so that James would be free to attend to business. Their sense of relief and confidence in her full recuperation was short-lived, however; once they returned home, Barbara relapsed into intermittent fevers "attended with Swellings." A return trip to the sound the following month failed to provide her with "equal benefit."[113]

Compounding Barbara's mortal illness was her seventh and final pregnancy. In malarial areas in colonial America, women between ages fifteen and forty-five suffered a noticeably higher death rate than elsewhere; pregnancy may have acted to nullify whatever immunities to malaria a woman might have possessed.[114] When she first contracted the disease that presumably killed her, Barbara was probably about two months pregnant. The pregnancy lasted until 17 February, when Barbara delivered "a Daughter in the 8th Month"; two days later, Barbara died.[115] The unnamed infant survived only two weeks, with Jeany, the Murrays' four-year-old, following her mother and sister to the grave on 23 March. "In a very short time," James grieved, it had "pleased God" to make "a wide breach" in his family.[116]

Barbara Bennet Murray's death tore apart her household and precipitated rearrangements in Elizabeth's, with James requesting that Dolly return to take her mother's place as his housekeeper. His needs overrode Elizabeth's program for her niece's education. "As soon as you think her fit to be housekeeper for me she must be dismiss'd for that end," he insisted.[117] Until Dolly arrived, James employed a woman, Bell McNeil, to help care for the house and two-year-old Betsy, whose apparent good health gave little comfort to the bereft husband and father. With resignation, James acknowledged that she seemed to thrive, "but so did the rest at her age."[118] Doubting that his daughter would survive long, he also anticipated an early demise for himself. Despite his grief and understanding of his wife's disease, James did not condemn his Carolina homeland. "I am not out of humour with the Country," he declared, persuaded that he enjoyed better health there that he "could have any where else."[119] Perhaps he could not bear to admit that he had brought his wife to a fatal shore.

In the months that followed Barbara's death, James began to pressure Dolly to hurry home. He urged Dolly to prepare herself for coming to North Carolina to be a mother to her younger sister as soon as she was ready. "It behooves you," he told her in December 1758, "now you are coming to the most critical part of your Life, to be very serious & Industrious, to mind the Lessons & Example your Aunt will give." If she failed to do so, all his labor and hopes might be lost, as well as her "own future peace in this Life and happiness in the next." To add substance to these admonitions, James sent his daughter the prescriptive pamphlet "Thoughts on Education," a treatise printed in Boston during his 1749 stay there.[120]

While Elizabeth readied herself to say good-bye to the niece who had become like a daughter, she was preparing for the arrival of her own firstborn. In December 1758, James congratulated his brother-in-law about the tidings. A close family friend had reported "the agreeable News" that Thomas was "soon to be a father." Longing to have the information confirmed under Thomas's "own hand" and delighting in the prospect, James wished Thomas and Elizabeth "all health and happiness" on their imminent parenthood.[121]

The following months brought news not of health, happiness, or motherhood but of disease, loss, and widowhood wreaking destruction in Elizabeth's life. In early 1759 measles struck the colonies. In New England, Massachusetts was especially hard hit, with the first cases appearing in Boston in January.[122] Elizabeth's husband was among those who were afflicted and died, although mortality rates were relatively low in this outbreak. The *Boston Gazette* for 12 February reported that "Thomas Campbell, Merchant, a Gentleman very well respected," had died of the measles.[123] Elizabeth either miscarried or bore a soon-deceased child whose brief existence left no mark in the historical record. Unfortunately, a gap exists in the letters between Elizabeth and James until May 1760.

Whereas Barbara's death left James emotionally distraught, Thomas's death brought the additional burdens of financial and legal upheaval to Elizabeth's life. Twenty-nine when she first married and busy with her shop, Elizabeth at thirty-two found herself widowed, with two minors—Dolly and Samuel, her husband's younger brother who had been living with them—on her hands, and beset by demands and accusations from her dead husband's family. In this context she first experienced the financial and legal wrangling that could attend widowhood. Her former husband's family questioned her handling of his estate, doubting her integrity as well as her care of Samuel Campbell. One in-law warned another kinsman to observe how Elizabeth acted as Samuel's guardian, to make sure that she kept him in school. He also suggested that caution and oversight might be in order regarding the settling of Thomas's estate. By assisting Elizabeth and making themselves as "Acquainted with her Circumstances as much as possible," the Campbells hoped "to assist her in paying her Just debts." Elizabeth's male in-laws seemed to doubt her competence and possibly her cooperation and honesty. One relation, William MacKenzie, hypothesized that she would in the future "do justice" to Thomas's brothers, although it might "not be in her power at present."[124] They apparently considered it possible that Elizabeth was entangled in settling debts and too involved to pay them their due or that she was withholding the estate. Figuring out various payments for her brothers-in-law and settling accounts, Eliza-

[But *Two* Blanks to a Prize.]
IMPORTED in the laſt Ships, and to be Sold by
Elizabeth Campbell,
*Who has removed her Shop, from the next Door to Dea-
con Beauteneau's in Cornhill, to the Shop lately oc-
cupied by Mr. Gilbert Deblois, at the Corner of
Queen-Street, viz.*

BRocades, ſtriped, figur'd, enameled & plain Mantuas, brocaded and plain Sattins, plain, ſtriped
and changeable Luteſtrings, black and brown Paduſoys,
Taffities, Damaſks, black and crimſon Corduſoy for
Mens Waiſtcoats, black and colour'd Cardinals, Capu-
chines, Polaneſe, Dauphineſſes and Cloaks, Silks and
Hatts for ditto, Bonnetts, Umbrellas, Hollands, Gar-
lix, yard-wide, 7,8 & 3,4 Iriſh Linnens, Sheeting ditto,
Doulaſs, flower'd Minionett and plain Lawns, a Variety
of Cap Lace, white and colour'd Blond Lace, Ribbons,
Necklaces and Earings, brocaded & ſattin Shoes, Clogs,
Silk, Thread and Cotton Stockings, quilted and Hoop
Petticoats, Silver Lace, with a Variety of other Arti-
cles, to be Sold cheap for Caſh or ſhort Credit.

5   Advertisement of Elizabeth Campbell, *Boston
Gazette and Country Journal*, 30 April 1759.
Courtesy, American Antiquarian Society.

beth relied on James. "Next month," she wrote her brother in January 1760, "I must settle with the judge and then I shall let you know
how things will turn out and write you as soon as possible." She asked
that James see to Campbell property in North Carolina, try to settle
outstanding accounts, and "procure an exact inventory of all Mr.
Campbells estate, real and personal."[125]

Elizabeth found her in-laws' attitude toward and treatment of her
unsatisfactory and painful. While she preserved a "very high opinion" of her brother-in-law Billy, she was not confident of continued
good relations. "Did I think he could use me as I see the others
would," she declared somewhat bitterly, "I can serve him in the
same manner." With some exasperation, she described the Campbell brothers' behavior as ungenerous, especially given that Thomas
would have given her his entire estate "if [she] had desired it," other
than a portion for his mother during her lifetime. "How unlike him
does some of them act," she opined.[126] Clearly, then, she believed
that her husband would have willingly and legally given her full control and ownership of his estate if she had asked — and apparently she
wished she had. The legacy of Thomas's death on Elizabeth's life was
acrimony with and distrust of his family.

Elizabeth Murray Campbell, now a thirty-three-year-old widow, had

IMPORTED in the laſt Ships and to be Sold

By *Elizabeth Campbell,*

Who has removed her Shop from the next Door to Deacon *Boutineau's* in Cornhill, to the Shop lately occupied by Mr. *Gilbert Deblois,* at the Corner of Queen-ſtreet, *Boſton,* viz.

BRocades, ſtriped, figured, enameled and plain Mantua's, brocaded and plain Sattins, plain, ſtriped and changeable Luteſtrings, black and brown paduſoys, Taffitys, Damaſks, black and crimſon Corduſoys for Mens Waiſtcoats, black and coloured Cardinals, Capuchins, Polanſſes, Dauphineſſes and Cloaks, Silks and Hats for Ditto, Bonnetts, Umbrellas, Hollands, Garlix, yard wide, 7 8th and 3 4th Iriſh Linens, ſheeting Ditto, Dowlaſs, flowered Minionet and plain Lawns, a variety of Cap Lace, white and colour'd blond Lace, Ribbons, Necklaces and Earings, brocaded and ſattin Shoes, Clogs, ſilk, thread and cotton Stockings, quilted and Hoop Petticoats, ſilver Lace, with a variety of other Articles to be ſold cheap for the Caſh or ſhort Credit.

Mrs. Jane Day,

Oppoſite the Brazen Head in Cornhill, Boſton,

HAS opened School, and teaches in the neateſt and neweſt Manner, Embroidering in Gold and Silver, and all Sorts of ſhaded Work in Colours, Dreſden and plain Work, &c. where alſo Ladies may be boarded or half boarded as may be moſt convenient for Town or Country, and can ſupply her Scholars with Materials for Work.

N. B. Makes in the neweſt Faſhion all Sorts of Millinary Work.

JUST IMPORTED, and to be Sold

By *Ralph Inman,*

At his Warehouſe on *Green's* Wharf,

HOgsheads of Stone Ware well ſorted, London and Briſtol Pipes, blue, red and drab colour'd Duffills, blue Broad Cloths, Kerſeys, red and blue Bays, green and drab colour'd Ratteens, Ironing-Cloths, ſtrip'd and ſpotted Swanſkins, Oznabrigs, Ticklinburg, Ruſſia Duck, Thickſett, Mahogany Plank, Block Tin, Sheet Copper, with Caps and Bottoms for Stills, &c. &c. &c.

6   Advertisements of Elizabeth Campbell, Jane Day,
and Ralph Inman, *Boston Evening-Post,* 14 May 1759.
Courtesy, American Antiquarian Society.

over a decade's worth of Boston experience behind her. She had done what she had set out to do: establish a shop and make it work on her own. Elizabeth took up the trade as a single woman and continued it during her first marriage in the 1750s. A few months after she became a widow, she changed the location of her shop, announcing in May 1759 that she was taking over the shop space recently occupied by Gilbert Deblois, a merchant friend of hers, at the corner of Queen Street (figures 5 and 6). There she continued to sell newly imported wares.[127] Elizabeth still carried basically the same kind of goods: cloth, bonnets, lace, stockings, and similar items. In some regards Elizabeth's commercial efforts seem less fraught with peril than her marital venture. Marriage had complicated her personal life and finances without bringing the family she anticipated. As the 1750s drew to a close, Elizabeth found herself a childless widow, beleaguered by legal and economic difficulties with her deceased spouse's family, and responsible for the care of two young people until Samuel returned to North Carolina to rejoin his mother and brothers in late 1760. She faced a host of challenges about what to do with her life similar to those she had encountered in 1749. But a kind of resolution took place quickly. In March 1760 Elizabeth married again, this time an elderly man whose immense wealth and indifferent health changed her own fortunes dramatically and permanently.

3

The Bonds of Marriage and Benevolence

March 1760 transformed both Boston and Elizabeth Murray Campbell's life. On 13 March she signed an elaborate prenuptial agreement. Before her wedding could take place, however, Boston had gone up in flames. Minor fires on the seventeenth and eighteenth were followed on the twentieth by the Great Fire, which started near Elizabeth's home and shop. The blaze began at two o'clock in the morning in the Brazen Head, the Cornhill shop belonging to Mary Jackson and her son. Within moments, the fire had spread to adjacent structures, sweeping through Pudding Lane, Water Street, and Quaker Lane and consuming everything in its path. As strong winds came up, much of Boston ignited. Despite the efforts of residents to remove the powder from the South Battery, the racing flames reached remnants of the stores, adding powerful explosions to the terrors of the glowing night. Although no one had died, before the last embers were extinguished, 349 buildings had been destroyed, more than a thousand people had lost their homes, and huge property losses had been sustained.[1] This conflagration was but the first of many challenges Bostonians encountered in the 1760s. Over the course of the next several years, they endured one ordeal after another, rebuilding after repeated fires, fleeing from smallpox epidemics, protesting against parliamentary legislation, and confronting occupation by British troops. By the time political turmoil brought the decade to a close with its own kind of brewing firestorm, Boston's difficulties had become common knowledge beyond Massachusetts, matters of concern to colonists throughout America.[2]

As the townspeople reeled from the catastrophe of the Great Fire and several women retailers who had been Elizabeth's neighbors contemplated the ashes of their former businesses, Elizabeth married, taking a step that constituted a similarly dramatic break with the past.[3] In an issue devoted largely to the devastation, the *Boston Evening-Post* noted the wedding of "Mrs. Elizabeth Campbell, of this town," to "Mr. James Smith sugar refiner."[4] This marriage, a newsworthy event that linked the fortunes and fates of two well-known residents and commercial figures, altered Elizabeth's life and future in unanticipated ways. In marrying, she followed the most typical feminine path to wealth and moved toward more financial security than she had ever experienced. Yet the ease she sought eluded her. For Elizabeth, as for her neighbors, the happenings of March prefigured a decade of difficulty, upheaval, and uncertainty.

Although the evolving political situation of the 1760s impinged on Elizabeth's life, marriage and its myriad repercussions influenced her more profoundly and with greater immediacy. With resources at her disposal and freedom from the responsibility of running a business, Elizabeth probably envisioned a steady improvement both in her own circumstances and in the lives of those whom she hoped to assist even more directly. Yet rather than setting her "above the cares of the World," her second marriage brought new constraints and new kinds of dependence into her life. As Mrs. James Smith, Elizabeth took on substantial tasks. At the same time, the marriages of close female friends and relatives tore at the emotional fabric of her life when their weddings precipitated relocations to distant shores. She came to experience, painfully, the ways that the bonds of wedlock could take precedence over other ties, particularly her relationships with other women.[5] The acts of generosity that her marriage made possible also had unsettling effects. Largely as the unintended consequence of her successful effort to persuade her brother James to join her in Boston and accept her patronage, she found her family at the center of the emerging political tempest. In short, she was buffeted about by the crises of marriage and politics in the 1760s, by the new responsibilities she had acquired, and by the disorder overtaking the Puritan capital. Her struggles—to find economic security through marriage, to manage the duties that attended her new position, and to clarify her own loyalties—reveal the negotiations and compromises that women endured and the gradual process of politicization that affected them.

As the decade began, the Widow Campbell likely looked at the prospect of remarrying with a somewhat wary eye. After ten years as a shopkeeper and a year as a beleaguered widow, she had known both the financial and legal independence of single life as well as the dependence of marriage. She knew only too well that a woman who lost control over her income and legal identity risked problems. Given the harassment of her in-laws over the settlement of her first husband's estate, Elizabeth might well have been hesitant to marry again. Yet the prospect presented itself soon. In the year following Thomas's death, while she would have been mourning the sudden loss of her husband, grieving over her miscarriage, and dealing with her avaricious and suspicious in-laws, Elizabeth found herself courted by a long-time neighbor who sought to win her affections and hand. James Smith, a Scotsman who had settled in Boston by the 1720s, was an elderly, childless widower. A prominent and wealthy sugar refiner, he had a house on Queen Street and a sugarhouse on Brattle Street, was a patron of the newly constructed Anglican King's Chapel, and acted as a churchwarden.[6]

Initially, Elizabeth resisted her suitor's entreaties. Yet by early 1760 James had persuaded her to accept him, despite the rather large difference in their ages. When they married that March, days after the Great Fire, she was still thirty-three; he had seen his seventieth birthday come and go. She had already buried one spouse and could well anticipate outliving her second husband. Why, then, did she so soon undertake a match seemingly destined to similar brevity and loss?

Money apparently played an important role in motivating Elizabeth to remarry. Thrilled by the financial aspects of the match, Elizabeth's family welcomed her new husband into their sphere not only because he was good tempered but also because he was very liberal with his riches. James Murray considered his brother-in-law's "Wealth and generosity" to Elizabeth to be an "essential part of the Story" behind the marriage.[7] Indeed, when he offered marriage, the elderly sugar merchant promised to make Widow Campbell a very rich woman. Throughout her life, Elizabeth was highly conscious of monetary matters—the fiscal aspects of marriage, the profitability of commercial enterprises, the advantages of women possessing financial independence—and always considered her own interests in this regard very carefully. As Elizabeth's friend Christian Barnes once told her, "I dont know any body better calculated to turn a Penny then your Self."[8]

Elizabeth gained much more with this marriage because she and James, unlike nearly all their colonial contemporaries, entered the married state with a prenuptial agreement.[9] Such arrangements were especially uncommon in Massachusetts, where Puritan leaders adapted English law in ways that discouraged separate estates and married women's ability to control property.[10] Indeed, the colony had no legal tradition regarding married women's trusts; no court had clear jurisdiction over such arrangements.[11] Under English common-law traditions, marriage typically signaled the obliteration of a separate legal identity for a woman. Ceasing to possess a distinct legal status apart from her husband, a wife had few rights and could, for example, neither sue nor be sued, keep any income she earned, or make a will and bequeath property. With religious roots in the biblical subordination of Eve to Adam and civil origins in the medieval hierarchical relations between lords and their vassals, marriage for women was a "crisis" that placed them in a legally disadvantaged and vulnerable state.[12] With the protections for married women eliminated in New England, custom and contemporary mores meant that few challenged this system or found a way around it. Yet, remarkably, James Smith and Elizabeth Murray Campbell did so.

Under the terms of the 13 March 1760 settlement, titled the "Indenture of James Smith to Elizabeth Campbell," the groom promised to foreswear the legal and financial control that accompanied marriage and largely effaced women's legal identity and property rights. Because James was willing to bind himself to grant his new bride rare legal autonomy, Elizabeth gained numerous privileges. Their contract combined elements of a separate estate, which allowed a woman to retain control over the property she brought into a marriage, and a jointure, which dictated exactly what a woman received as a widow, in lieu of dower rights; jointures were not especially common in America and were most likely in England to be found among the wealthy.[13] James acted to make his new wife independently wealthy, settling one-third of the thirty thousand pounds sterling of his estimated estate on Elizabeth should he predecease her. If she did not survive him, she would nonetheless enjoy the power to dispose of a smaller gift sum of two thousand pounds by her own will. In addition, James gave Elizabeth other articles valued at one thousand pounds and agreed to allow her to retain full control of her own fortune. That stipulation of the prenuptial contract freed her from the coverture and dependence that almost all married women in colonial America experienced. By subscribing to an agreement that eliminated this marital control, James and Elizabeth entered marriage on terms of equality shared by very few colonists.[14] In short, Elizabeth Murray Campbell Smith was in a better position than most married women: she had power over her own purse as well as a promise of additional riches.

This prenuptial contract underscores the complex negotiations that marriage entailed for women who sought both the security of the institution and the independence it undermined. As a survivor of a marriage that had no financial protections, Elizabeth was apparently willing to marry again only with such an agreement in place. In general, widows were more likely than women marrying the first time to have marriage settlements.[15] After suffering through the veiled insinuations from her in-laws that she was cheating them out of their rightful portion of her first husband's estate, Elizabeth might have been careful about putting herself in the same position again. James's promises to grant her legal power and retention of her own fortune precluded such acrimony and confusion and thus removed one obstacle. Clearly she gained financially. But other issues may have played a role in her deliberations.

Given James's advanced years, as well as his childlessness, Elizabeth may have believed that marrying him would dim her chances of having a family of her own. Perhaps she had reason to believe that she could not bear children. And the family life in which she was most intimately involved, that of her brother James, had not been entirely joyful, given the early deaths of his wife and five children. If she had reflected on her own disappointments and her brother's in this regard, Elizabeth might have given consideration to other possible advantages of marriage.

In marrying again, Elizabeth's goals were like those of many other colonial women: she sought to secure herself from want, to help

those whom she loved, and to do good. For her, self-interest and benevolence seem to have been equally powerful motivators. Not only
did her family tradition contain a strong element of shared responsibility for younger members, but she also conducted herself according to ideals of femininity that celebrated the charitable neighbor
whose good deeds benefited the less fortunate.[16] In James Smith—
specifically in his wealth and willingness to share it—Elizabeth found
the means to fulfill her desires for physical comfort, financial independence, and extensive munificence. Her brother James thought
her a fortunate woman, "in the best Circumstances of any of her sex
here." She was not only well off but also "vastly beloved for her frank-
ness of temper and continual Endeavors to do good Offices" for the
unfortunate.[17] In her new situation she had gained "a freer Scope" to
practice the acts of generosity in which she delighted.[18]

The one apparent drawback to the match, James Smith's advanced
years, did not automatically preclude a successful marriage. James
Murray thought his sister had made a fair trade in exchanging her
relative youth for security; the "liberal settlement" his brother-in-law
made "attone[d] for the disparity of the Match."[19] Although separated by decades in age, the two enjoyed a companionable union.
Elizabeth's family rejoiced that "the old Gentleman" was "very affa-
ble and good natured" and that "a perfect good Understanding"
united the pair.[20] Still residing with her aunt, Dolly considered James
Smith her "good and old Uncle."[21] A year after the two had wed, they
apparently both enjoyed "a happiness . . . rarely met with in a match
of such disparity."[22] The septuagenarian clearly delighted in Elizabeth's company, describing her as "the Wife of my Bosume."[23]
Whether Elizabeth felt the same way is not known.

What is clear is that this marriage brought multiple changes to
Elizabeth's life, signaling not only a dramatic improvement in her
economic status but a cessation of her career and a relocation to the
countryside as well. Both she and James gave up the active pursuit of
business. How she ended her business, whether by vending her stock
at public auction, by selling it to other retailers, or by some other
means, is unknown. With James's retirement as a sugar baker in June
1761, the couple moved to Brush Hill, a farm he had earlier acquired
in Milton, a small community eight miles outside Boston. Although

they maintained quarters in the Queen Street townhouse, which had survived the previous year's fire, Elizabeth and James spent most of their time in the country.

The Brush Hill farm and its care presented striking contrasts to Elizabeth's Boston home and shop. From the bustle and hurry of the town, she moved to the relative isolation of the countryside around Milton. The three-hundred-acre estate, with gardens, orchards, and a rivulet that ran into the bay, presented a pastoral ideal that inspired visitors to rhapsodize about its beauty. From the house one could see a distant lighthouse and look out over the surrounding countryside. James Murray thought Brush Hill possessed one of the most pleasant situations imaginable.[24] Of course, James had always longed for the life of the country planter and may have been more appreciative of Brush Hill's quiet charms than was Elizabeth, who had chosen Boston over his Cape Fear plantation years before. Although the distance of eight miles did not prevent Elizabeth from seeing friends in town, it probably contributed to quotidian quietude. Her tasks, as well as her daily routine, circle of acquaintance, and sphere of activities, underwent a dramatic transformation.

In place of shop shelves stacked with imported British wares for sale, Elizabeth was surrounded at Brush Hill by richly appointed rooms full of objects that conveyed their owners' refined tastes, consumer aspirations, and wealth.[25] Spending money on such wares marked the purchaser as a genteel man or woman, one who established and maintained metropolitan cultural connections and loyalties in part through material goods. These consumer ambitions, styles, and standards would have been abundantly clear to visitors. A guest at Brush Hill might have dined on a black walnut table, sat on a mahogany chair, or been served a meal from one of the dozens of blue and white china plates, custard cups, or sweetmeat saucers. In the well-stocked kitchen, specialized utensils abounded, including myriad ladles, stew pans, skimmers, fish kettles, tongs, Dutch ovens, gridirons for broiling meat, frying pans, and chafing dishes. Five dozen glasses ensured that guests would not go thirsty for want of a tumbler. Two cases of ivory knives and forks completed the tableware. With such supplies and surroundings, Elizabeth could entertain on a lavish scale and occasionally did so. For a Commencement Day party in 1767, she had thirty-five guests for dinner. The possession of abundant chinaware, tables, chairs, and flatware reveals the thoroughly genteel material culture of the Smith residence; gentility regulated dining through the use of individual dishes and utensils and specialized furniture.[26]

Like other colonists for whom tea became all the rage, Elizabeth and James had ample objects for that singularly important beverage. By the middle of the eighteenth century tea drinking had become so widespread that colonists of every class and region sipped the stimulant. Even those dependent on public assistance asserted their right to the imported luxury. In Philadelphia two inhabitants of the almshouse, Mary Marrot and her daughter, petitioned the Overseers of the Poor for the addition of "pretty" substances, such as tea, coffee, and chocolate, to their diet; brought up in a "delicate" way, they found their current provisions "generally too gross for their nice Stomachs."[27] When even the indigent demanded inclusion in the consumer experiences transforming daily life, it is not surprising that well-to-do aspirants to gentility such as James and Elizabeth would devote substantial sums to the proper accoutrements for drinking tea. Their house held three tea tables designed especially for the purpose of holding all the tea equipage, as well as new and improved dishes manufactured for the purpose, including a set of "new fashion burnt China" with matching teapot, cups, and saucers. In addition to three burnt china teapots and other dishware of the same make, there were dozens of china dishes and pewter plates.[28]

As the mistress of Brush Hill and therefore the consumer rather than the purveyor of such imported objects, Elizabeth took on new responsibilities, not only for maintaining these wares but also for taking care of the house and running the farm, tasks that involved a staff of workers, both enslaved and free. As perhaps an indication of the depth of his admiration for Great Britain's culture, James Smith sought the services of a gardener from abroad. Gardens, common at great houses after the 1720s, acted as extensions of the parlors inhabited by ladies and gentlemen and echoed English styles; at the same time, servants could reflect and magnify the gentility of the master who endeavored to embrace a refined lifestyle.[29] Accordingly, James enlisted Elizabeth's brothers' aid in finding someone who would come to America under indenture or contract for three years and be willing to act as coachman and groom as well. As part of the job, the

British gardener would train a male slave to assist him.[30] In Massachu-setts, as in North Carolina, Elizabeth thus benefited either directly or indirectly from the labor of slaves, coming into a position of super-vision at Brush Hill over the bondsmen and bondswomen owned by her husband.

The biggest shift in Elizabeth's life revolved around the new set of duties she assumed as wife to a man who suffered from poor health. In marrying James, she exchanged caring for her shop and waiting on and interacting with customers for tending primarily to one per-son's needs. With her clientele reduced to one, Elizabeth found her-self acting as companion, housekeeper, and, increasingly as the years passed, nurse. Although James was well when they married, his condi-tion began to deteriorate within a year.

Before the end of 1761, James's failing health led Elizabeth to consider what she would do after his death. Anticipating a life of charity and celibacy, she announced that she would never remarry. Such a decision could well have had its sources in her experience of marriage up to this point. With her first union cut short by Thomas's sudden illness and death and her second marriage apparently head-ing toward an identical outcome only a few years later, Elizabeth had reason to eschew the institution and its attendant heartache and troubles. Moreover, she would have no financial incentive, as she had in 1760, for linking her fate to that of another.

In imagining her widowhood, Elizabeth envisioned herself as ben-efactor to her siblings' numerous children. Because of her prenup-tial agreement she would have the financial wherewithal to maintain herself very comfortably without working or marrying again. Equally important to her aspirations for fostering independence among the younger generation of Murrays, she would have enough income left over to provide for her ever-growing number of nieces and nephews, all of whom could benefit from her largesse. In addition to James' two surviving children and Barbara's four, there were John's children in England. Elizabeth's brother John and his wife regularly added to their brood and had ten children before the decade's end. When John learned that his brother-in-law Smith was in "decline" and that Elizabeth had announced a "Resolution to keep single after his de-cease, and to bestow the greatest Share of her Fortune on the most deserving," he knew that his sister had him and his large family in mind.[31] Who could be more deserving than the many young children of a struggling physician with an income insufficient to support them?

As she contemplated how best to help her family, Elizabeth invited her brother John and his family to immigrate to Massachusetts. Although grateful for the offer, John found himself disturbed by its mercenary aspects, especially when his brother James intimated that John should move his family to Boston to be close enough to support Elizabeth's "generous Intentions." The presence of family would serve as an immediate and tangible reminder of financial promises and make Elizabeth less likely to waver from her projected program. While John considered the plan seriously, he ultimately declined it, declaring that he would never want his "living near her or with her, to keep her from marrying." The very possibility would keep him from doing so. John refused to value Elizabeth's riches above her heart's future marital desires. "Having enjoyed much Happiness in that State," he insisted that no "pecuniary or other self Interest" could tempt him to stand in the way of any friend's marital prospects.[32] (In later years, when Elizabeth did marry again, John found ample reason to rue his words. By that time he had come to depend on the money she regularly sent and found himself inconvenienced by the financial complications that arose with her third marriage.)

Elizabeth's plans for her imminent future as a widow of means notwithstanding, her husband recovered. Indeed, James confounded all expectations regarding his mortality, neither dying in 1761 nor soon thereafter. He regained enough strength to live for years, surviving until after his eightieth birthday in 1769. His health, however, remained precarious throughout the decade, with bouts of illness that periodically rendered him an invalid. Although Elizabeth spent much of her time and energy caring for her spouse, her days were not confined to the sickroom or limited to nursing tasks.

Part of what filled Elizabeth's time was her exercise of benevolence. Although she did not succeed in persuading her brother John to relocate to Boston, where she could have assisted him more directly, she did find numerous other willing recipients of her generosity and attention, particularly women. She sought to educate them and support them in undertaking business ventures. In doing so, Elizabeth strove to provide young women with the training and re-

7   Dorothy Murray, portrait by John Singleton Copley,
ca. 1759–ca. 1761. Courtesy, Fogg Art Museum, Harvard University
Art Museums, Gift of Mrs. David Simmons.

sources they needed to maintain themselves and be competent and
independent individuals — that is, to follow her own example. She
seemed to derive much satisfaction both from raising her nieces, to
whom she was attached by ties of blood and family affection, and
from providing advice and aid to other women, whom circumstances
had left in need of friendship and financial help. Over the course of
the 1760s, Elizabeth actively directed the education of her nieces

Dolly Murray, Betsy Murray, and Annie Clark; sponsored the mercantile career of the Cuming sisters; and continued to help her friend
Jannette Day.

In supervising the education of her nieces, Elizabeth tried to foster
accomplishments she thought valuable and appropriate for young
women. Dolly, the first to join Elizabeth's household, studied reading, rudimentary accounting, dancing, sewing, and fine needlework
(figure 7). In 1760, after five years in Boston, Dolly had made progress in all the branches of her education, including writing, acquiring
training that blended the practical skills necessary to a competent
household manager with the decorative accomplishments of a genteel young woman. Some of these talents are apparent in the portrait
of Dolly painted around this time, which presents her as an elegantly
attired young woman displaying a garland she has artfully arranged.[33]
Although generally positive about Dolly's improvement under his
sister's tutelage, James was not entirely satisfied with his daughter.
When he visited Boston that summer James was displeased "to see the
indolent way in which she and the young Ladies of this place generally live." On a typical day fifteen-year-old Dolly slept late, did not
finish breakfast until ten, and then engaged in "a little reading or
work till 12." James claimed he did the young ladies of Boston "great
Justice in allowing that they employ to some good purpose two hours
of the twenty four." After taking two hours to dress for dinner, Dolly
usually passed the afternoon "in making or receiving visits or going
about the Shops." The dissipation of young girls — their wasting time
in self-indulgent activities — continued unabated until tea, supper,
and chat closed "the day and their eyes" about eleven.[34]

What is striking about James's critique of Dolly's habits is its emphasis on gendered activities and socializing.[35] Given Dolly's exposure to Elizabeth's shop and that of her friend Jannette Day, as well as
the appeal of fashionable goods directed at female consumers, Dolly
and Elizabeth may have considered shopping excursions perfectly
reasonable and harmless diversions. When she shopped, Dolly occasionally patronized the businesses of her aunt's friends and protégés,
buying such items as lace, ribbon, and shoes from Jane Eustis, Jannette Day, and the Cuming sisters.[36] Shops were comfortable, familiar
spaces for them, places of feminine interaction and conversation,

where the latest fashions might be discussed and gossip exchanged. For women, shops may have been the functional equivalent of taverns and coffeehouses, the typical sites of male community. The social aspect of shopping finds additional support in other contemporary accounts. In Philadelphia, for example, Elizabeth Drinker reported afternoons devoted to shopping in 1759 and 1760; some women may have enjoyed shopping almost as a form of leisure.[37] In an urban area, visiting shops was an acceptable public pursuit for women, one they could engage in without chaperons.[38] Moreover, as managers of household budgets women needed to have some expertise in shopping. While unremunerative, shopping comprised a form of labor that required knowledge and proficiency for its successful execution. Why then did James disapprove? Perhaps the key distinction in James's mind was that Dolly frequented shops as a consumer of fashionable fineries, rather than following Elizabeth's steps as a retailer. Like J. Hector St. John de Crèvecoeur, who described "the multiplicity of shops with English goods" as offering such "irresistible temptations" that "young girls" had to be "philosophers" to resist their allure, James Murray may have seen shopping, feminine consumption habits, and extravagant indulgence as closely related.[39] James denounced his daughter's schedule and her shopping, identifying the latter, along with visiting, as a popular recreational activity for young women and one that occupied much of their day, and he linked both pastimes to idleness and frivolity.

Despite any criticism Elizabeth may have heard regarding Dolly, she became responsible for the education of other nieces. Their training became a central preoccupation of her domestic life. In 1761 Elizabeth's nieces Betsy Murray and Annie Clark came to Massachusetts to pursue their education under her direction. Since Annie was already a teenager and needed a variety of teachers not available in the countryside, Elizabeth decided to board her with her close friend Jannette Day, whose location in the center of Boston provided easy access to a range of schools. Five-year-old Betsy needed more attention and supervision; she therefore stayed with Elizabeth and attended school in the neighborhood of Brush Hill.[40] Although Elizabeth saw to it that all her nieces received training in both the practical and the decorative accomplishments, she discovered that the girls could be indifferent pupils when it came to learning the arts

of housewifery. She particularly tried to impress on them the importance of domestic skills, but neither Annie nor Dolly ever achieved
complete mastery in such areas and acted affronted when she lectured them about the necessity. Elizabeth expected they would one
day "repent not attending a little more to family affairs." In contrast,
Betsy learned such lessons well. Rather than face the ridicule visited
on her cousin Annie, Betsy went into the kitchen for cooking instruction, learning the art of making pastry.[41]

With a new husband, a beautiful estate, and a house full of nieces,
Elizabeth's domestic circle was briefly complete. To Elizabeth's and
Dolly's dismay, however, Betsy's arrival in Boston in 1761 prompted a
separation. Not wanting to burden Elizabeth unduly with these new
charges, James took Dolly back with him to North Carolina when he
dropped off the other two girls. Thus Elizabeth exchanged the company of one niece, to whom she was deeply attached and who would
"not chuse" to leave her, for the responsibility for two others.[42] Perhaps James's view that Dolly was not spending her time industriously
contributed to his decision to bring her back to North Carolina. In
his eyes Elizabeth had seen to it that Dolly had received the necessary
polish for one of her station; now, she had reached an age appropriate to more responsibility and more serious endeavors. Perhaps more
important, he had renewed his commitment to family life in North
Carolina and wanted his daughter to take her place in his new household. James's remarriage and decision to have his older daughter
rejoin him disrupted Dolly's young life; away in New York visiting
friends, Dolly learned of her father's remarriage by mail and burst
into tears at the news.[43] Just as a stepmother could never take Elizabeth's place in Dolly's heart, neither could young Betsy supplant her
older sister in Elizabeth's affections.

While Elizabeth and Dolly were both unhappy about parting,
Dolly's spirits must have sunk even further when the ship carrying
her clothing and other possessions to North Carolina was wrecked.
Traveling by another vessel, she arrived in her new home without any
clothes other than those she had on the journey. A Boston friend
tried to cheer her up about her losing her things, reassuring her that
she did not need fine clothing to look agreeable: "For, my Father
often tells me, that Virtue and Modesty are the most charming Ornaments, a young Lady can possibly be dressed in."[44] It is difficult to

imagine seventeen-year-old Dolly, homesick for Boston and missing Elizabeth, being fully consoled by thinking about wearing virtue and modesty in lieu of the fashionable wares which she had no doubt carefully selected during her many hours of shopping and which were now ruined.

For Elizabeth, the separation was also trying. In letters full of advice and affection, Elizabeth urged her niece to continue to study and improve on the skills she had acquired during her years in Boston. Dolly should beg her father to do his bookkeeping, Elizabeth insisted, because "the learning of it" as she had done at school meant "nothing without the practice." In pushing this course, Elizabeth reminded her niece of the importance of a woman's familiarity with finances. She reminded Dolly how many families were "ruined by the women not understanding accounts," recalling to her niece's memory the many instances she had seen of this tragedy.[45] Like other eighteenth-century proponents of educating women in this skill, such as Benjamin Franklin and J. Hector St. John de Crèvecoeur, Elizabeth saw accounting as an indispensable aid for women in maintaining family finances and fortunes.

Despite Elizabeth's encouragement and counsel, Dolly was miserable in North Carolina. Isolated on the Point Repose plantation several miles outside Wilmington, Dolly spent her time overseeing the dairy, writing, and doing arithmetic that her father assigned her. Although a friend pressed her to spend more time in town, Dolly was not allowed to enjoy Wilmington's diversions. James dismissed the idea because it did not "answer" his intentions "in bringing her here."[46] If Dolly felt less than content, she had good cause. For seven years she had lived in bustling Boston with an aunt who had become like a mother to her. Now a young woman, she found herself bereft of her former companions, diversions, and belongings, far removed from all she had known and enjoyed. The fact that her younger sister had taken her place in Elizabeth's household likely increased her sense of isolation and longing for the North.

Before long, however, Elizabeth regained control of Dolly's whereabouts, asserting the authority that her wealth and emotional role in her niece's life accorded her. She succeeded in persuading James to return Dolly to her household. By the beginning of 1764 Dolly was back with Elizabeth, again pursuing her education. Elizabeth's claims on her niece, combined with Dolly's own desires, had superseded James's wishes. James confessed that he frequently longed for his daughters' presence, if it could have been "consistent with [Elizabeth's] satisfaction."[47] Because of Elizabeth's resources, place of residence, and emotional attachment to Dolly, James sacrificed his own wishes for a filial presence in his life. A decade before, James had repeatedly invited his sister to join his wife and children in North Carolina. Now, she had all that remained of that family with her in Boston. His offspring became the daughters she never had. With her nieces near at hand, Elizabeth was able to raise them as she saw fit and provide them with the advantages and opportunities her situation afforded.

Involved with her nieces' education and busy caring for her aged spouse, Elizabeth nonetheless found time to help other young women prepare for their future, in the process putting to use the experience she had gained as a shopkeeper. With her own commercial career behind her, Elizabeth committed herself to acting as adviser and mentor to the young women around her. She delighted in preparing them to be competent adults, whether in the household or in the shop. Sisters Ame and Elizabeth Cuming directly benefited from her support. After their mother's death Elizabeth stepped in and set them up in a shop devoted to imported millinery and fashion-related items. In the sisters' opinion, Elizabeth did not stop to consider how her own financial interests might suffer "in the hands of two young unexperinced Girls" who were in "no way qualifyed for Business." Ignoring the risks, Elizabeth provided the two with the means to support themselves in the way that would most contribute to their "Mutual Happiness." She was a "kind adviser" who took care of them when they most needed help.[48]

As single women with limited resources, the Cuming sisters faced the same problems Elizabeth had confronted when she first started in business. Neither Ame nor her sister had been bred "to hard labour" and were therefore "unfit" to get their "bread in that way."[49] Knowing nothing of business, they were clearly unprepared to meet the challenge of supporting themselves. Nor did they possess the resources to attract well-to-do suitors. Only Elizabeth's aid made their self-sufficiency possible. Ame asserted that her sponsorship made it possible for them to stay together and made them independent of everyone but her. The Cuming sisters' sense of gratitude and independence built on another's assistance echoes Elizabeth's own relationship with James in her early years of shopkeeping. In both cases, single women pursued shopkeeping with the financial assistance and advice of someone experienced in trade.

Throughout this period, Elizabeth maintained her view of shopkeeping as an occupation that could bring a measure of self-sufficiency to such women as the Cumings. Although she gave up retailing during her second marriage, Elizabeth continued to believe that if women did not marry, they could, with some help, achieve a life of economic independence. In both the 1760s and 1770s, she successfully backed other women in shopkeeping ventures. Occasionally, these women forged close ties. When Elizabeth's protégé and close friend Jannette Day decided to leave Boston, for example, the Cuming sisters stepped in and expanded their range of services. In April 1768 Ame and Elizabeth Cuming advertised to announce that "Mrs Day's School For young Ladies" was being discontinued and that they would open "A School on the same Plan" on the first Monday in May. At their house across from the Old Brick Meeting House, they would teach embroidery, accept young ladies as boarders, and continue to sell a variety of imported wares.[50] Undoubtedly, they embraced this program with Elizabeth's advice. In doing so they followed the path that their benefactor had carved out for herself as a shopkeeper and teacher, finding a niche just as Elizabeth had done the previous decade.

By the mid-1760s, Elizabeth's sphere of benevolence encompassed not only such young women as the Cumings and her nieces but her brother James as well. Her goal of assisting her family and attaching them to her, which had failed with John, eventually succeeded with James. With his daughters firmly ensconced in Elizabeth's household and his second wife desirous of returning to the town life she had been accustomed to in Boston, James began to consider severing his ties to North Carolina. As early as 1762, while Dolly was in North Carolina, Elizabeth had suggested that James, who had never found the degree of economic success or peace he had hoped for in the South, resettle near her. A real possibility in Boston opened with James Smith's retirement. Elizabeth thought her brother would be a good replacement for continuing the sugar-refining house and urged him to relocate. By 1765 James had agreed to the plan and abandoned his plantation, taking over the Smiths' residence in Queen Street and assuming control of the sugar business. The political climate, however, inhibited his ability to pursue that line of work. The Sugar Act of 1764 had hurt the industry so much that sugar refiners found it difficult to make a living; parliamentary legislation, coupled with bad crops in the West Indies, drastically reduced the importation of raw sugar. Thus James had to close the sugarhouse in 1765. Although he reopened the refinery a year later with his nephew John Innes Clark as his partner, James never made a success of the business.[51] Before long, the sugarhouse was devoted to other purposes.

Although Elizabeth's actions in bringing her brother to New England were designed to provide him with the benefit of her resources and complete their family circle in a prosperous and harmonious way, the consequences of her benevolence were dramatically different. Indeed, one can draw a connection, albeit an admittedly circuitous one, between Elizabeth's private decisions—to marry James Smith and to assist her brother James—and the political crisis in Boston that precipitated the Revolution. Arguably, the political situation of the 1760s imbued Elizabeth's private acts of benevolence with ultimately fateful consequences that affected her family, her community of Boston, and colonial-imperial relations in a unique and profound way.

Given the jubilant mood that followed the end of the French and Indian War in 1763, when colonists gloried in the British victory, thrilled to the prospect of expansion to the west, and counted themselves fortunate to be members of the empire, few could have anticipated the deterioration of relations with Great Britain that took place over the course of the 1760s. Proud of their contribution of men and support of the military effort, colonists were outraged when the British government imposed new taxes on them after the war. Adopting legislation designed to raise revenue to offset some of the costs the Crown had incurred in waging the war, Parliament embarked on a course that ultimately divided the colonies and the mother country. The legislation of the 1760s, especially the Sugar Act of 1764, the Stamp Act of 1765, and the Townshend Acts of 1767, incited colonial demonstrations and animosity.

Particularly violent was the reaction of Bostonians to the Stamp Act. After learning of the passage of the act, which would have generated money through the use of a special stamp on newspapers, playing cards, and all sorts of official documents, residents of the port town engaged in a variety of protests. They eschewed the consumption of British goods, signing nonimportation agreements with the hope of persuading merchants in England to pressure Parliament to repeal the act; denounced the political powers that Parliament was attempting to enforce; and pursued more violent actions, such as harassing stamp distributors, marching through the streets, and attacking the property of both the appointed distributor, Andrew Oliver (who resigned his post before selling a single stamp), and the chief justice and Oliver's brother-in-law, Thomas Hutchinson.[52] The unprecedented mob violence and ransacking of private property shocked British officials and many colonists as well.[53] Although colonists elsewhere also protested the act, Bostonians gained for themselves a reputation as rabble-rousers and troublemakers. Their extreme response stemmed in part from their comparatively more difficult economic circumstances. More so than other colonial towns, Boston in the mid-1760s had a struggling economy, with heavy taxes, swelling ranks of the poor, and an increasing concentration of power and wealth in the hands of the elite.[54]

In the aftermath of the Stamp Act riots, the relationship between Bostonians and the Crown grew more fractious, with the royal governor receiving instructions authorizing him to request troops to quell the rebellious citizenry if he saw fit, and customs commissioners, who arrived in November 1767, repeatedly calling for military assistance.[55] The Townshend Acts, a series of duties on a variety of imported goods, further antagonized colonists, who protested once again. Inspired by the retraction of the offensive Stamp Act and outraged by the renewed attempt to deprive them of their wealth and liberty, colonists reacted with nonimportation agreements and harassment of crown officials. It was in such actions as the boycott that women, as both consumers and purveyors of British wares, experienced the beginnings of Revolutionary politicization. If a woman chose to give up tea or wear homespun, she did so to support the colonial cause. Buying and selling merged private decisions and economic activities with larger political concerns.

Among those who supported a 1768 nonimportation agreement was Elizabeth's good friend Jane Eustis, one of seven women who signed "A List of the Subscription of Those Gentlemen . . . immediately concerned in importing Goods from great Britain." By subscribing, Eustis promised not to import any goods for a year.[56] What is especially interesting about this agreement is that Eustis's commercial stature as an importer rendered her politically one of the "gentlemen" whose support for the cause was valuable. (A year later, however, she was again ordering goods from Bridgen and Waller. When a 1769 nonimportation pact was circulated, she did not add her name to the list of ninety-five male and eight female supporters, two of whom had endorsed the earlier action.)[57]

Given the unrest in Boston, the level of colonial antagonism toward parliamentary measures, and the spreading popular support for protest, the royal governor found himself in a delicate and difficult position. Although Governor Bernard hesitated to invite the enmity of the people by calling in troops, he believed the situation had become quite untenable by the summer of 1768. The British government took steps to squelch the rebellious behavior seemingly centered in Boston and sent two regiments to the town.

The decision to send troops to Boston in 1768 created many problems. The idea that troops would be sent in peacetime to control them alarmed colonists deeply; they were citizens of the Crown, with the rights of Englishmen, not enemies whose conduct merited the punishing presence of the military. Thus, when troops began to arrive on 30 September 1768, a hostile reception awaited them (figure 8). How the troops were handled in the following weeks seemed designed precisely to antagonize town residents. Instead of discharging their men at Castle Island, where a fort built with colonial funds stood empty, British officers had the ships drop anchor in the harbor. The colonists felt themselves besieged, "surrounded at a time of profound peace, with about 14 ships of war."[58] The next day, with their muskets charged and bayonets fixed, over seven hundred troops landed and marched through the town to the Common, accompanied by a train of artillery and the martial sounds of fifes and drums. Demands from British commanders that the town provide them with quarters went unanswered. As far as colonists were concerned, the barracks for the troops were those standing empty on Castle Island.

8   *A View of Part of the Town of Boston* . . . [1768 landing of British troops], engraving by Paul Revere, 1770. Courtesy, American Antiquarian Society.

Unable to find quarters, the troops began to cover the Common with tents and also to take refuge in Faneuil Hall, home to the chambers of the colony's representatives. By 3 October, British commander Colonel Dalrymple had been able to procure housing and appeared before the council to demand billeting for the troops.[59]

The British found quarters, in spite of the opposition of local officials and animosity of Boston's populace, because James Murray agreed to house troops in the sugar factory and townhouse belonging to his brother-in-law and sister. In making such an unpopular offer, he immediately made himself many enemies and became a target of public censure. *A Journal of the Times* announced the news of 4 October tersely: "Report, that James Murray, Esq; from Scotland, since 1745, had let his dwelling house and sugar houses, for the quartering of troops, at £15 sterling per month."[60] This item highlighted two facts: James was not a Bostonian by birth, and he stood to profit from a situation that appalled many of his neighbors.

Over the next few weeks the tension grew, as the need for more quarters remained and cold weather approached. Council members flatly refused to consider quartering troops in town as long as the island barracks stood empty. Confronted with this obstinacy, the royal governor, Bernard, searched for other means of shoring up his hand, such as getting his own men into positions of power. On 26 October Bernard nominated and appointed James Murray as a justice of the peace for Suffolk County. When Bernard proposed Murray's name, he was greeted with silence and then expressions of disgust. It was only the governor's impassioned entreaties that persuaded the council, with a majority of only two, to accept James Murray. According to *A Journal of the Times*, "No appointment of this sort could have been more unpopular, or have raised a more general indignation."[61]

The connection between James Murray and James Smith, publicized in the wake of the justice of the peace appointment, exposed Elizabeth and her family to the hostility of former neighbors and friends. On 28 October the *Journal* reported that the troops that had been occupying Faneuil Hall "had been placed, or had quartered themselves in the buildings, which had been hired of James Murray, Esq; but owned by James Smith, Esq; of Brush-Hill." This report intimated that James Smith, even if not complicit in the initial decision to quarter the troops, had supported it and was therefore at least partially responsible for the current situation. According to the *Journal*, the relocation of the troops in the barracks flew in the face of an act of Parliament and might lead some citizens "to think that some gentlemen of the civil or military order have concluded that they have a right for *certain purposes*, of dispensing with those acts at their pleasure." In short, James Murray and James Smith were being accused of taking the law into their own hands with impunity and doing so in the most obnoxious way possible.[62]

As the fall of 1768 progressed, the situation deteriorated. The punishments British soldiers received for what colonists considered minor infractions appalled them. Dolly was disturbed by the report of a man sentenced to a thousand lashes, who fainted after 170, "his back as raw as a piece of Beef."[63] In response to a petition signed by many Bostonians, the officer in charge canceled the remainder of the man's punishment. Adding to the climate of violence and unease were conflicts that erupted between soldiers and angry citizens, who harassed men on guard and occasionally attacked those who were off-duty.[64] Devoted to chronicling the depredations of the troops, *A Journal of the Times* duly noted every attack on a woman, described the nuisances caused by drunken troops, and detailed incidents in which soldiers accosted peaceable Bostonians. When Irish transports with additional troops were allowed to unload, despite reports that they were carrying smallpox, the *Journal* cried foul. As the year drew to a close, James Murray once again became the object of public vitriol. On 2 December a fire broke out in the barracks "called Murray's." If not for its quick discovery, the paper reported, the fire could have been fatal not only to the soldiers, women, and children quartered therein "but might have occasioned the destruction of a considerable part of the town" as well. The sugar buildings stood in the very center of Boston, "within a few feet of the largest pile of wooden buildings in the province." Already condemning him for housing a peacetime standing army in their midst in violation of their will and their rights, the writers for the *Journal* were ready to blame James Murray for whatever destruction befell the town.[65] Showing hospitality to British officers, quartering British soldiers, and serving as a justice of the peace made him one of the most politically unpopular men in Boston.

What Elizabeth thought of her brother's decisions or of the public criticism that attended them is largely a matter of speculation. Deeply attached to Boston, grateful for the success she had met with as a shopkeeper, and fond of her neighbors, she had ample reason to rue the imbroglio in which her brother's public-spirited, patriotic acts had enmeshed her. For over a decade she had made Boston her home and had developed her own reputation as a retailer. James's conduct put that reputation at risk. Like James, she continued to think of Great Britain as home in a sense and of herself as a devoted subject of the Crown. Yet she decried the corruption of the customs service, seeing in its actions ample cause for colonists' anger. Over the course of the next decade, as members of her family took opposite sides in the Revolutionary struggle and friends began to flee, Elizabeth found her loyalties increasingly in conflict.

For Elizabeth, James's political activism can only have added strain to a difficult year marked by household crises and separations. In 1768, in short order, Jannette Day sailed for Great Britain, James Smith fell seriously ill, and Dolly Murray married and moved to Flor-

ida. These occurrences disrupted Elizabeth's life. Domestic difficulties came to the fore as Elizabeth's marital relationship and other
close ties became sources of pressure, stress, and sorrow.

The bonds that Elizabeth cherished were challenged by the marriages of her female intimates. Jannette Day, who left Boston to
marry, found the separation from Elizabeth difficult to bear. For the
eleven years they had known each other, Elizabeth's every word, look,
and action "proved to me the Goodness of her Heart and Esteem for
me."[66] In the weeks before her wedding, Jannette found herself grieving over the loss of Elizabeth's friendly presence, longing for her
feminine companionship, and unable to replace it. She was hesitant
to unburden herself fully to her absent friend: "I am Afraid to say all I
think, but you know I am no Flatterer, and you know I Love you." She
pleaded with Elizabeth to take care of herself, not to trifle with a life
on which many people's happiness depended.[67] From across the Atlantic Jannette could not restrain herself from praising Elizabeth and
calling to mind their last time in each other's company, their days
together, and even their last ride to Brush Hill. Her exuberance had
no bounds; indeed, she would not exchange her memories of Elizabeth's companionship for anything. Even her union with her spouse
could not assuage her sense of loss. "Happy as I am in the Tenderest
of Husbands, there is still a want," Jannette admitted. "I long to sit
with you as formerly and talk without resarve which it is imposible to
do by letter." When her husband tried to ease his wife's loneliness for
female friendship by introducing her to a woman whom he thought
she would like, Jannette was not altogether pleased. Mrs. Selie, she
told her spouse, could never be a Mrs. Smith to her: "My Friendship
for her is of more then a day's Standing." Although "a very Sensible
and an improving Acquaintance," Mrs. Selie's talkativeness made her
less than a wholly satisfactory companion.[68] In short, Jannette could
never find a replacement for her beloved Elizabeth.

The depth of Jannette's attachment—as well as the declarations of
love and friendship made by many other women to Elizabeth — raises
questions as to the nature of their relationships, whether they were
purely platonic or had some romantic or sexual dimensions. In examining women's diaries and letters, historians have found evidence of
intense emotional ties between women in the late eighteenth and
early nineteenth centuries. Female love served an important function

in these women's lives, tying families and friends together across time and distance in networks of mutual support, and was not seen as incompatible with heterosexuality.[69] It is clear that Elizabeth cherished the women in her life, nurturing nieces as daughters, sponsoring young women's work, and maintaining close and caring friendships for decades, even though she did not resort to the kind of emotionally charged language that typified Jannette's and other friends' prose.

Busy with caring for her husband, Elizabeth did not respond to Jannette's outpourings to her friend's satisfaction. Not usually effusive, Elizabeth considered Jannette a "romantic" and "an Enthusiast in Friendship."[70] After Jannette pleaded with her to write and tell her that she held "the same place" in Elizabeth's esteem as always and no letter came, her husband teased her about her behavior. He said that she acted like the heroine in a romance and jokingly suggested that the feelings of friendship were all on his wife's side. The jest pained Jannette. Yet in letters showing her well-developed sensibility, she persevered in her expressions of attachment and in her confidence that Elizabeth returned her sentiments. She told her husband that she would not doubt Elizabeth's affection even if she never heard from her again; Elizabeth's friendship and generosity toward Jannette had been voluntary and sincere. In her eyes, Elizabeth, "far Exalted above her Sex," was an exceptional woman with a steady soul. "As long as I have Breath," she told Elizabeth, "Neither Time or Distance can Shake my Attachment to you."[71] How Elizabeth reacted to these many heartfelt declarations can only be imagined. Over the course of the previous decade, she and Jannette had been neighbors and friends and had taken part in each other's family and affairs. When Jannette left Boston, Elizabeth probably said good-bye with mixed feelings of joy and sorrow at her friend's good fortune. As Jannette rightly predicted, Elizabeth remained a good friend. She continued to take a very active interest in Jannette's life, later tending her as she lay on her deathbed and subsequently assuming responsibility for her orphaned daughter.

More upsetting to Elizabeth than Jannette's migration was Dolly's marriage. After breaking off an early attachment to her cousin John Innes Clark, which her father had discouraged, Dolly met a clergyman from St. Augustine, Florida, while he was visiting Boston. Far too rapidly for her family's liking, she and John Forbes pursued their courtship in the summer and fall of 1768.[72] A few months later, in February 1769, the pair married in a ceremony at Brush Hill.[73] Dolly's marital choice and subsequent move worried and saddened her friends and family. For her aunts in Britain, Anne and Jean Bennet, her move to a warmer, southern climate evoked memories of Dolly's mother, the sister they lost to an early grave. They feared that she would meet a similar fate in Florida.[74] Only letters from Dolly informing them of her well-being would provide any relief or comfort.[75]

For Elizabeth, Dolly's marriage meant another separation, a more permanent and painful one than they had experienced earlier in the decade. Jannette Day Barclay, newly married herself, could not help thinking about how much Dolly's move to Florida would pain Elizabeth: "How Sensibly will she feel your Seperation." While Betsy remained a part of Elizabeth's household and family, she could never take her older sister's place. "You are to her like an only Child," Jannette told Dolly. "Even Betsy will never be to her like you."[76] When she went to Florida, Dolly left behind heartache and a hole in the lives of her loved ones. James Smith spoke of her often. "Sick or well, he talks much of you," Elizabeth told her. "He says he loves you better than he does any one except me." She asked her niece to write a few lines to him: "You know he likes to receive letters." Yet there was little that could reconcile Elizabeth to her niece's absence. She found her grief at Dolly's distance difficult to convey and measure: "Words cannot express nor pen write what I have suffered and am like to suffer by parting with you," she told her niece. She tried to derive some comfort from a promise Dolly's new husband had made to her: "It was that he would make a visit here soon." The thought roused Elizabeth's drooping spirits and made her "wish to live" to see the newlyweds "happy in each other." [77] Given the combination of James's illness and the daily burden of his care, her friend Jannette's departure, the political turmoil surrounding her brother James, and Dolly's move to a distant, dangerous shore, it is not surprising that Elizabeth suffered from depressed spirits.

Indeed, Dolly's relocation prompted one of Elizabeth's few emotional outbursts. Usually reticent in her letters, she confessed her thwarted hopes and disappointed dreams to Dolly. "Whenever I have thought of your settling in the world, it has been the height of my

ambition to have you near me," she admitted. "It is ordered otherwise and I must submit."[78] Just as her brother James had discovered
several years before when he wished to keep Dolly at his side in North
Carolina, Elizabeth now found her own claim weaker than another's.
Where James had submitted to his sister's wish to have Dolly back in
Boston, Elizabeth realized that Dolly's new allegiance overruled all
other ties. Marriage, a central aspect of women's lives, could tear at
the bonds that united women such as Dolly, Elizabeth, and Jannette.

Elizabeth's sense of loss and poor spirits deepened with her husband's increasingly poor health. With the responsibility for nursing
him devolving on her, Elizabeth spent her days caring for him in the
confinement of the sickroom and refusing any assistance. During
1768 and 1769, James remained largely indisposed. As Elizabeth
busied herself with caring for him — finding that he required more
attention when he was up and about than when he was bedridden —
and also worked to oversee the Brush Hill estate, she lost her robust
constitution.[79] Her friends worried that her duties would hurry her
to a premature grave.[80] Finally, at Dolly's insistence, Elizabeth placed
herself under a doctor's care, although apparently to little effect.[81]
The reports Dolly received in Florida were not encouraging. Nursing
James had obviously eaten away at her health and strength, yet Elizabeth claimed she was fine. Repeating such remarks to Dolly, Christian
Barnes added her own doubts: "You know she never complains but if
one may judge by her countenance She is far from being well."[82] The
picture that emerges of Elizabeth's life at this time is not a happy one.
Self-sacrificing, refusing to accept help, and denying her own health
concerns, Elizabeth had few joys and many sorrows. With her darling
niece gone, her aged husband's life slowly ebbing away, her brother
reviled in the press, and her community in uproar, little remained to
comfort her. A bleak widowhood stared her in the face.

As the spring of 1769 wore on, Elizabeth undertook minor steps to
restore her constitution. "With a View to her Health," she and James
traveled to nearby Marlborough to stay with Christian and Henry
Barnes. The strain of the journey, coupled with the difficulty of making James comfortable, robbed the visit of any beneficial effects and
led Elizabeth to cut it short. Christian was disturbed, discerning "a
strange fatality" in Elizabeth's "undertakings." Exhausted by caring for a dying man, Elizabeth seemed to be declining herself. Her

friends hoped for the release that James Smith's death would bring. The Cuming sisters and Christian Barnes, for example, "heartily wish'd the good Man in Heaven, for thither he is bound," but thought he was making "but a Slow progress on his jurney."[83]

In the last weeks of her husband's life, Elizabeth behaved in a way that alarmed her friends. On the June day she and James left Marlborough, Elizabeth "went off in the Morning Mounted upon a Single Horse, with out taking leave of any Body."[84] Failing to say good-bye properly astounded Christian on its own. Remarkable as that action seemed, however, it struck Christian as less troublesome than the way Elizabeth raced away. She appeared to have no sense of herself and to be entirely thoughtless regarding her own well-being. The scene is easily imaginable: forty-three-year-old Elizabeth, graying, as she said, from the strains of her life and middle age, tearing away on horseback, fleeing from caring for her aged spouse, riding wildly, but futilely, away from inescapable responsibilities. After her sudden departure Elizabeth rode twenty miles without stopping to eat or to dismount even once, an exhausting and impressive feat. Christian was aggravated. "I was very impatient to hear of your safe arrival," she told Elizabeth. "What is the reason that in every thing you undertake you will give your Self unnessisary trouble"? Riding away in the fashion she did suggested that Elizabeth went out of her way "on purpose to Seek adventures." Christian would not tolerate such actions: "You must give over these freaks." Exasperated, Christian wondered whether anybody in her right senses would ride twenty miles fasting and then eat only biscuits. "I cannot think of it with Patience," she told Elizabeth, declaring that her whole family had been worrying about Elizabeth and that "even the Strong Beer has freted to such a degree that it is grown sour in the Bottles."[85] Fortunately, despite Christian's worries, the ride did not injure her friend in any way; Elizabeth reported that she was in "very good Health & Spirits."[86] Even in the midst of such difficulties, Elizabeth kept her eye on financial matters, busying herself with selling the year's cherry crop. Acknowledging that "business must be minded," Christian wished her friend good luck with her cherries.[87]

Two months later, on 4 August 1769, Elizabeth's husband died. The *Boston Evening-Post* of 7 August noted the passing of a prominent citizen: "Last Thursday Night died at his Seat at Brush-Hill in Milton,

Mr. *James Smith*, late of this Town, Sugar Boiler, in the 81st Year of his Age." The announcement also described the arrangements: "His Funeral, we hear, is to be attended from the House of James Murray, Esq; in Queen-street, this Afternoon precisely at Five o'Clock."[88] As part of the mourning ritual, Elizabeth gave out two dozen mourning rings, each valued at a pound apiece, mementos of her husband.[89] After the funeral, James was interred in a crypt in the burial ground adjacent to King's Chapel, the church to which he belonged for many years.[90] (He was not buried with his first wife; later, Elizabeth and her nieces Dolly and Betsy were all buried in the same tomb, united as a family in death as they had been for a time in life.)

August 1769 thus found Elizabeth a widow again, this time rich in wealth but poor in health. James had bequeathed her a greater share of his estate than their prenuptial agreement had stipulated. Whether she would live to enjoy it, however, seemed uncertain. In the days after James's death, Elizabeth began to fail rapidly. With James dead and Dolly far away in Florida, the idea of either returning to Brush Hill, the scene of illness, or staying in Boston, the seat of unrest, may have been very unappealing. Trying to improve her friend's "very bad State" and "hoping that Rest and Change of Air might be of service to her," Christian urged Elizabeth to visit. When Elizabeth arrived in Marlborough the week after James was buried, her appearance shocked Christian, who soon concluded that the change was not a temporary one occasioned by the fatigue of James's final illness, death, and funeral. Elizabeth's "disorders were not triffling," and she grew worse quickly. Neither medicine nor exercise "had any good Effect."[91] As the summer and Elizabeth's health faded, the new widow astounded her friends by announcing a sudden decision to go to England, planning to sail as soon as possible. Although "greatly alarmed" at the prospect of Elizabeth undertaking such a journey, no one "dared to object to what Seemed the last cast for her Life."[92]

In August and September 1769, as Elizabeth prepared to unloose her ties to Boston, the situation in the town grew increasingly grim, with politics assuming a violent aspect and James Murray putting himself in the middle of a tense situation. On 5 September at the British coffeehouse in King Street, patriot leader James Otis was assaulted by John Robinson, an attack from which he never fully recovered. The following evening, a man implicated in the beating was brought to Faneuil Hall. Hearing about what was happening and believing the man to be unjustly accused, James Murray hurried to the hall. The "multitude" attempted to eject him from the premises, but a town selectman helped him to a seat. Hissed at by the crowd, he bowed, was hissed at again and bowed in response a second time, and then was finally applauded before taking his seat. When no one offered to put up bail for the accused, James did so, not, he told the other justices, to condone the man's behavior but simply "to stand by him now the torrent was against him." James's willingness to embrace unpopular causes and individuals exposed him to the anger of patriotic Bostonians. Ready for "more sport," those assembled refused to disperse. As James attempted to leave, he found himself suddenly bereft of his wig, his bald pate exposed. The crowd grew more aggressive, and James could barely walk as men attempted to trip him. Friends formed a protective phalanx and escorted James out of the hall and safely home, accompanied by rebel leaders who "admonished" the retinue, "No violence, or you'll hurt the cause."[93] In the wake of this incident, the *Boston Evening-Post* published an attack on James's conduct, accusing him of "airs of insolence" and "foul deeds," of not knowing what he was talking about "and then voluntarily offering himself to be bail for the man that had so greatly violated the laws of honor, humanity and his country."[94] While the political situation was turning ugly and touching Elizabeth's family, another crisis hit the town in the form of a smallpox outbreak.

Surrounded by disease and disorder, Elizabeth hurried to prepare for her trip and say her good-byes to close friends. Although initially hesitant to visit the disease-infested port, Christian forced herself to come in to town, unable to reconcile herself to Elizabeth leaving without a last farewell. Admitting that she was "no enthusiast in friendship as our Friend Mrs Day says she is," Christian declared her "tenderest affection" for Elizabeth: "Believe that I Love you."[95] The bonds among these women inspired them to intimate expressions of their feelings and to acts of bravery. Solicitous of one another's well-being and happiness, they offered their friends tangible assistance as well as constant emotional support. Thus, when Christian overcame her fears of smallpox to join Elizabeth in Boston ten days after they had parted in Marlborough, she rejoiced to find her in a much better state. With Elizabeth's household affairs in an uproar, confu-

9   Mrs. James Smith (Elizabeth Murray), 1769 by John Singleton Copley,
American (1738–1815); oil on canvas, overall 49⅝ × 40 in. (126 ×
101.6 cm). Gift of Joseph W. R. Rogers and Mary C. Rogers, 42.463.
Courtesy, Museum of Fine Arts, Boston. Reproduced with permission.
© 2000 Museum of Fine Arts, Boston. All Rights Reserved.

sion reigned. But the pleasure they enjoyed in each other's company
made all the aggravations disappear.[96] Dreading their separation,
Christian believed that none of Elizabeth's friends would miss her or
suffer so much from her absence as she would. Distinguishing herself
from others, perhaps Jannette Day, the Cuming sisters, or even some
of Elizabeth's relations, Christian opined that her friendship with

Elizabeth was truly disinterested "on both sides" and that she loved and valued Elizabeth "only because she deserves it."[97] Christian's remarks on what was special about their relationship suggest that Elizabeth's wealth and exercise of benevolence made her the target of self-interested offers of friendship.

As she readied herself to leave New England, Elizabeth decided to leave behind something of herself and sat for a portrait by John Singleton Copley (see figure 9). The painting may have originally been intended for Dolly. At least Christian, who accompanied Elizabeth to the artist's studio, thought it was. Although Elizabeth's hair had changed color rather quickly during her illness, she was in excellent health as she sat for the painting.[98] Although depicted in a dark dress, similar in hue to those worn by some of Copley's other mature women subjects, Elizabeth wears a low-cut gown, set off by a vibrant and elaborately draped scarf; sports pearls and an exotic turban as hair ornaments; and holds luscious looking fruit in a fold of fabric.[99] Often symbolic of fecundity, fruit could also signify a woman's interest in gardening. Because Elizabeth had no children of her own and no known fondness for tending her orchards, it is possible that Copley included the overflowing basket simply for decorative purposes: Elizabeth as mythological figure of bounty. The suggestion of a cornucopia certainly captures Elizabeth's generous benevolence, as well as her wealth.[100] For this work, Elizabeth paid a little over forty pounds.[101] Popular among Boston's fashionable elite, who favored portraits above any other kind of painting and provided him with many commissions, Copley is perhaps most widely known today for his portraits of important Revolutionary figures such as Samuel Adams and Paul Revere.[102] Son of a woman retailer who kept a shop on Boston's Long Wharf, Copley captured the images of a few hundred colonists before moving permanently to England. Among them were a number of the Murrays, including Dolly, James, and Elizabeth. Copley also completed a pastel portrait of Ralph Inman, the man who became Elizabeth's third spouse.[103]

In addition to having a portrait done, Elizabeth made arrangements that put her Boston life behind her, disbanding her household and in effect eliminating the trappings of her time as Mrs. James Smith. She parceled out her servants, sending one woman to another household in the neighborhood of Brush Hill, leaving one to stay in the house with the best garret as his apartment, and apprenticing a third.[104] Jack, a slave, joined the Goldthwait household and made an immediate good impression on the family, quickly gaining "the favor of the upper as well as the lower House."[105]

The most important act Elizabeth undertook on the eve of her departure was writing a will.[106] Signed 30 September 1769, days before she sailed, the document reveals her priorities. She ordered first that her funeral expenses be paid as soon as possible after her death; her executors could bury her in whatever manner they thought "proper." The rest of the will was devoted to gifts. To her childhood companion, her brother William, she bequeathed five hundred pounds sterling. Her nephew John Innes Clark would be given half that sum, having already received £250. Elizabeth ordered that Jacobina Day, the daughter of her friend Jannette, receive one hundred pounds and that her friend Ezekiel Goldthwait receive two hundred.

Under the terms of this will, James Murray stood to receive tremendous wealth. Elizabeth promised him a lifetime annuity of one hundred pounds. More substantial than the cash was the property Elizabeth had conveyed to him two days before. Her will simply confirmed that she had given him several tracts of land and buildings in Milton and Dorchester. Betsy, Elizabeth's namesake and traveling companion, would receive thirty pounds yearly until she reached the age of twenty-one. At that point, she would be given a lump sum of one thousand pounds, making her a woman of fortune. The residue of Elizabeth's wealth and property would go to her brother John, with the income from it to be paid to him annually during his life and the property to be divided among his heirs at his death. As executors, Elizabeth named her brothers William and James and her friend Ezekiel Goldthwait. The three would share responsibility for making disbursements, settling the estate, and selling her property, if need arose.

Elizabeth rid herself of Brush Hill, her home for the duration of her second marriage. At some point she had decided to leave the estate to her brother James, assuming that it would go eventually to Dolly and Betsy. James had long preferred a retired country life to that of towns and delighted in his new home, telling his sister how happily he was "settled as a Farmer" again. Leaving the turmoil that surrounded him in Boston must have been a relief. While giving up

Brush Hill seemed to cost Elizabeth little regret, accepting it placed James under a heavy sense of obligation. "You have laid a very difficult task on me and mine," he informed her, "that of behaving not unworthy of so much generosity on your part."[107] The burden James felt only serves to underline how much the lines of patronage, dependence, and authority had shifted direction over the course of the 1750s and 1760s. Once his sister's adviser, mentor, and substitute parent, James had become the recipient of Elizabeth's largesse in the 1760s, joining his daughters as beneficiaries of her wealth and resources. While James welcomed the solitude of Brush Hill almost as a tonic, Elizabeth prepared to seek solace in the diversions of London.

When Elizabeth sailed in early October, a large party of friends gathered to see her off.[108] Bidding farewell to her friends "with Heroick resolution," Elizabeth went immediately from church to board the ship. Christian Barnes, one the well-wishers at the dock, found the scene painful. After taking leave "of the Best Woman in the World," Christian felt like her heart was bursting. Silently supplicating God to grant her friend a safe journey to England and a safe return to America, Christian felt sure that she was joined in her prayer by thousands, "for never was any Person more beloved or more lamented." Among those who regretted Elizabeth's departure were her protégés, such as the Cuming sisters. Although Elizabeth might leave them "with aching Hearts," Christian was convinced that she did not leave them "with Empty Hands."[109] (Christian was probably right, for during Elizabeth's absence, the Cuming sisters received over £120 pounds from her estate.)[110] While Christian comported herself with restraint, afraid to show her "inward anguish" at saying good-bye even though her "Passion struggled for a Vent," others made their grief obvious. Apparently, Margaret Mackay Murray, James's second wife, embraced Elizabeth and screamed violently. Without "the least inclination to follow" such an inappropriate and shocking example, Christian nonetheless had "earnestly wished for a Parting Kiss had the time and place been proper."[111] Elizabeth's good friend Ezekiel Goldthwait found himself similarly silent. Despite his love and esteem for Elizabeth, he could not speak "one word" at parting when he accompanied her down the wharf.[112] Believing that silence could speak volumes, Elizabeth interpreted such behavior as proof of the depths of her friends' attachment to her. "I know by experiance," she admitted, "the heart is often most affected when we shew no Visable signs of emotion." Indeed, Elizabeth considered such self-restraint prudent and perhaps more appropriate than her own forced high spirits. By concealing her true feelings, Elizabeth made it easier for herself to say good-bye. Yet she suspected her conduct may have puzzled her friends. When she thought back on the moment, Elizabeth concluded that her gaiety must have appeared ridiculous.[113]

At the dock was another friend who did not say good-bye, almost certainly the man who became Elizabeth's third husband within weeks of her return to America. Rather coyly, Christian asked if Elizabeth had noted the longing appearance of "another gentleman who look'd as if he would have given his eyes for a tender farewell."[114] Presumably, the man with the wistful, fond expression was Ralph Inman, an intimate of the family and a friend of Elizabeth's since the early 1750s. When Elizabeth traveled to London in 1754, she had carried with her a letter of credit from Ralph, a tangible expression of his respect for her skills and possibly an indication of warmer feelings. At that point, he was married. After his wife died in 1761, he remained a widower for the next decade. During that time, he socialized regularly with Elizabeth and her second husband, attending dinners and parties with them.[115] A member of their regular social circle, Ralph upon occasion even traveled with the couple, as in May 1767, when he "set out with James Smith & wife" and some others for a visit to Marlborough and other towns.[116] Although it is impossible to know the degree of their attachment to the other on the eve of her departure, it seems clear that Elizabeth and Ralph had had opportunity to come to know each other fairly well.

When Elizabeth left, she did not single out Ralph or express visible sorrow at leaving Boston. She gave her hand to her friend John Rowe and her lips to her sister-in-law and said good-bye to the rest cheerfully. Finally released from caring for an invalid, she was wealthy and without crushing responsibilities for the first time in years. Perhaps she anticipated that the trip would "relieve her from some of her vexations in America" and put her mind "more at ease."[117] Elizabeth seemed ready to seek pleasure for herself rather than expend her energies primarily in service to others. The press carried a brief acknowledgment of her departure. On 9 October the *Boston Evening-*

Post noted the sailing of the ship *Boscawen* under Captain Jacobson, "in whom went Passengers *Joseph Harrison*, Esq; Collector of his Majesty's Customs for this Port, Capt. *John Cerrance*, of the 29th Regiment, and Mrs. *Smith*, Widow of *James Smith*, Esq; of this Town, late deceased."[118]

Fifteen years after her last voyage, Elizabeth crossed the Atlantic once again. In 1754 she had been unmarried and full of energy and ambition for her shopkeeping career, so anxious to return to her business that she neglected to see her family. Now, with financial concerns behind her, she was older, grayer, and twice widowed. When she left, some of her friends suspected they would never see her again. Although aware that she planned to return in June 1771, some doubted that she would stick to that date. They knew she was only too ready for a change of scene. Ready to renew old family relationships and visit childhood haunts, Elizabeth set sail, leaving behind her home of twenty years.

4

LEISURE AND INDUSTRY IN BRITAIN

AND AMERICA

When Elizabeth set sail for England in October 1769, numerous troubles lay behind her. Her years of nursing an invalid had ended with her husband's death, her responsibilities for housekeeping had been dissolved with her transferal of the Brush Hill estate to her brother James, and the political turmoil of Boston had receded, at least temporarily. Yet the ease and freedom she may have anticipated as a new widow of means failed to materialize. During the course of her two-year sojourn abroad, part of which she spent renewing her health, enjoying London, and reacquainting herself with old friends, Elizabeth faced crises similar to those which had plagued her in America: she dealt with new familial obligations, debated the role of women in the economy, took on the care of needy, ill friends, and confronted the shocking political debacle of the Boston Massacre. The myriad demands that she felt on her return to New England in 1771 contributed to her decision to relinquish her own independence by marrying again. Before that homecoming, however, she intended to lay in "a stock of health" in Britain. Exercise and change of air appealed to her more than the advice or prescriptions of physicians, and she intended to pursue her plan for a more "Effectual cure" with all her "might" as she revisited the scenes of her youth.[1]

Leaving friends behind her on the Boston shore, Elizabeth faced rough waters, both real and metaphorical. Imagining Elizabeth braving the winds and high seas of the North Atlantic, Christian Barnes accurately envisioned her friend lurching "upon the merciless Ocean, sick" and unable to hold up her head.[2] A week into the trip Elizabeth was covered with "black and blue spots" from "tossing about the cabin." Occupying a stateroom did not protect her from the tempestuous crossing. Now on her sixth such journey, however, Elizabeth proved a better sailor than her niece and namesake. Betsy felt so ill that she did not even dress properly for the first several days of the voyage. After Elizabeth finally insisted that the girl go out on deck to get some air, Betsy complied but soon complained that "she was dying." Once belowdecks again, Betsy "lay some time quite stupid" and revived only when Elizabeth plied her with some orange juice and a little preserved ginger. The medicine seemed to do the trick, for within an hour Betsy managed to eat some roast duck, a dish that seems rather rich and heavy for someone suffering from seasickness.[3] Unfortunately, good food and good spirits did not last long. The following week brought wind that "blew like guns" and rocked the ship, forcing the crew to scurry to prepare the vessel for severe weather. The sailors removed doors and windows, placing in their stead dead lights, metal plates designed to cover and protect the openings. On another occasion, rapidly shifting winds nearly swamped the ship at four in the morning. The *Boscawen* suddenly was laid "so much upon her side that she lay quite still and alarmed all hands on deck." Hurriedly, the crew sprang into action, pulled the sails down, and restored the ship to its proper keel. The excitement was a little too much for Elizabeth, who recommended to a friend that she "must not go to sea until she is more reconciled to death."[4] Given that any ocean voyage posed hazards, writing a will, as Elizabeth had, was a wise precaution for overseas travelers.

Although it is not apparent whether Elizabeth was reconciled to her own demise when she undertook this journey, it is clear that she embarked with the intention of regaining her health, making a break with her recent past, and reestablishing and shoring up old relationships and contacts, both familial and mercantile. The journey to England and Scotland represented a homecoming of sorts, but it was as a colonist of almost thirty years' standing that Elizabeth visited Great Britain. As the ship neared land on 5 November, Elizabeth found herself contemplating the return to her homeland and shores she had not seen since before her first marriage. Within weeks of leaving friends, property, responsibilities, and her husband's new grave behind her, Elizabeth soon arrived safely in London, ready to begin a new phase of her life. Exchanging familiar faces and scenes for the novelty of travel, she set about enjoying all that the capital had to offer, seeking distraction and pursuing pleasure, embracing London's diversions and renewing old friendships. At the same time, her two-year stay abroad clarified how firmly attached Elizabeth was to her chosen home, even with its painful political crisis, and how deeply she believed in its myriad opportunities for young people — especially young women — who were willing to work hard and embrace industry and ambition.

Importantly, both for her aspirations to benevolence and for her young female relations, being in Britain gave Elizabeth the opportunity to promote her own view of femininity. As she had done in America, Elizabeth continued to serve as a mentor to and pursue opportunities to help young women. Traveling throughout the United Kingdom, Elizabeth evaluated the place of leisure and industry in the lives of women. She sampled the first herself with some pleasure and carefully weighed the impact of the latter on young women, especially her nieces. In the process she engaged in debates with friends about the content and purposes of education for women. In this regard she was like scores of contemporaries for whom the instruction of the young was assuming increasing importance. Because gentility required a certain kind of polished behavior and comportment, training in politeness, decorative accomplishments, and practical skills had to be balanced.[5] As those in the middle orders of society struggled to attain for themselves and their children a certain standard and style of life, the education of girls in particular raised many economic, cultural, and moral questions about the effect on their character of genteel training, given the less direct economic value of their education in comparison with that provided boys.[6] What drove this model in part was the marriage market; parents hoped that by educating their daughters according to genteel prescriptions, they would give them a competitive edge in finding a well-to-do partner. An accomplished woman had desirable traits that might attract a mate not fixed solely on his bride's dowry. Yet for Elizabeth an ideal woman was a useful one who possessed a certain amount of polish and refinement but who could support herself if need be through industrious involvement in the world of commerce.

Acting on these beliefs, Elizabeth pushed two of her nieces into retailing and sent them to America to follow in her footsteps, in spite

of the political unrest plaguing Boston. With Boston occupied by
redcoats, some of whom were quartered in the sugar building that
had belonged to her deceased spouse and was now hers, Elizabeth
certainly knew of the town's problems in the late 1760s. Yet before her departure her pressing concerns with her husband's failing
health had occupied her time, while her residence in Milton had
kept her out of the immediate fray. When she decided to send her
brother John's children to Boston to take up trade, Elizabeth did not
anticipate how fully commercial endeavors would force women to
engage in political discussions and actions. In Britain, far removed
from the tumult of Boston's streets, Elizabeth found herself justifying
both her actions regarding her nieces and her political loyalties.

Once she arrived in London, however, before grappling with the
repercussions of women's involvement in trade or evaluating colonial
protests regarding imported goods, Elizabeth was engaged in her
own consumer splurging. Before she could set about enjoying the
capital's delights, Elizabeth sought to acquire some new, stylish clothing. The city contained the most fashionable shops in the British
world. As a woman of position and a former shopkeeper, Elizabeth
probably looked forward to acquiring appropriate metropolitan attire. She did not, however, find the process wholly enjoyable. To her
chagrin she found that clothes do make the woman. After traveling
thousands of miles to enjoy London, she could not go into its streets
right away. Until her new outfits were ready, she was "a prisoner," she
declared ironically. Responsible in Boston for promoting consumption of British finery as a shopkeeper and mentor to other women in
trade, she was now constrained by it.[7] Elizabeth saw humor in the
rituals of fashion. Changing her habits and attire, Elizabeth transformed her appearance. "I have submitted to all the forms of Dress,"
she reported, "except blacking my hair." Instead, Elizabeth paid a
barber to come to her quarters every other day to curl and powder
her tresses. On the days the barber did not make a house call, she had
someone tend to her locks for her.[8] In the mornings, before going
out, Elizabeth covered her head with a queen's nightcap that made
her look "a strange figure." Once it was off and her hair elaborately
styled, Elizabeth wore a "genteely made" outfit with ruffles and a
high crowned cap. "You would be pleased with my appearance," she

told a friend. While Elizabeth made fashioning her new look sound like a bit of a chore, she did not really complain. "I am in very good spirits," she announced.[9]

With her health now fully restored, Elizabeth cut a figure very different from the one she had only a short time before. Feeling well and energetic, with graying locks styled and wearing fancy new frocks, she seemed to have put behind her the exhausted and ill woman who had worried her friends in Boston. For her, London was an invigorating tonic that brought a kind of rebirth. Instead of attending to a dying spouse, she now spent her days socializing and being entertained, living what she described as a droll life. Receiving company at home in the mornings, she often went out to dine and drink tea. Elizabeth immersed herself fully in the social rituals of genteel London.

Part of her pleasure came from seeing old friends. After anxiously awaiting her visit, they kept her busy. Reunited with Jannette Day Barclay, Elizabeth witnessed her friend's marital happiness for herself. The two women spent much of their time together. Elizabeth also deepened her relationship with Edward Bridgen, the merchant who had shepherded her through London's mercantile maze in the early 1750s, and his wife. Shortly after she arrived Elizabeth also renewed her relationship with Anne Elliot, the woman who had assisted her in her shopkeeping venture twenty years before. Their initial encounter reveals a playful spirit on Elizabeth's part. Arriving at Elliot's house, Elizabeth, without revealing her own identity, asked if the Misses Elliot were at home. When a maidservant ushered her into a large, handsome room where Anne Elliot sat alone at a tea table, Elizabeth walked softly up to her, laid her "hands on her shoulders & kiss'd her." Stunned by this greeting, the woman started up. "Madam," she demanded of the stranger, "who are you?" Elizabeth's only response was to tell her to look at her. After examining Elizabeth's face, the woman replied that she looked like Betty Murray; Elizabeth answered that she was. Clasping the newcomer to her, Anne Elliot cried out. Concerned by this outburst, the other woman in the room, Peggy Elliot, moved toward the pair and told her sister not to be so alarmed, that the stranger could not be Betty. Approaching the doubter, Elizabeth demanded to know what sixteen years had done that her friend would not know her. "I am sure I have slept many nights with you," Elizabeth reminded her. Realizing her mistake, Peggy caught Elizabeth around "the neck and almost smothered [her] with kisses." Excluded from the excitement of the emotional scene before them, the gentlemen in the room apparently felt themselves either intruders or extraneous. "We set down & made such a noise the Gentlemen were glad to make their bow & walk off," Elizabeth recalled.[10] Such encounters, replete with memory and affection, were repeated throughout Elizabeth's British sojourn.

As 1769 drew to a close, Elizabeth kept herself busy with London's diversions, visiting gardens, tourist attractions, and the theater. She visited Westminster Abbey and saw an exhibit of wax figures, with eyes and features that were "so lively" that her niece Betsy mistook them for real.[11] For Elizabeth the highlight of various wax statues was that of Queen Anne. The royal mannequin was attired in the manner Elizabeth's husband James, who had attended a royal audience as a young man, had described to her. Among the forms of entertainment that Elizabeth enjoyed was the theater, an important component of genteel and popular culture. Outlawed in Puritan Boston, the theater attracted huge numbers of rich and poor alike in eighteenth-century England.[12] Rather than being considered immoral as it was by many in provincial New England, the theater was viewed as beneficial in England. Lady Pennington, the author of a popular piece of advice literature, declared that the theater had "been brought to very great perfection" and could afford "rational and improving entertainment" to its patrons.[13] Clearly Elizabeth's circle of friends in the colonies viewed the theater in the same light, anticipating that her niece Betsy and Jannette Barclay's daughter Jackie Day would attend plays together. Going to the theater suited their age, sex, and tastes. Christian Barnes even sent the two girls some chestnuts "to Gnaw upon between the Acts at the Play House."[14]

In England the theater was fashionable and received the approval and attendant social cachet of royalty. One evening's excursion to see *The Spanish Lady* rewarded Elizabeth with a view of the king and queen, "a most agreeable . . . & happy looking pair." Some in the audience found the royal couple more interesting than were the actors onstage. Jannette Barclay "was in raptures with them." Indeed, seeing the two rendered her practically speechless; yet Elizabeth thought her friend could say more with her eyes and hands "than

words can express."[15] Not as effusive as Jannette, Elizabeth was nonetheless impressed by the monarchs, including that evening as one of
the early high points in her stay. As she noted to one of her many
colonial correspondents, "I have had the pleasure of seeing thier
Majesties at the play."[16] Fashionable and entertaining, theaters were
places one went to see and be seen. Enthusiasm for the theater even
affected Elizabeth's travel schedule in England; she forestalled her
plans to leave London by a day because Edward Bridgen insisted that
she accept tickets to a play, "to the great joy of Jacky & Betsy."[17] After
attending the theater, Elizabeth, Betsy, and Jackie Day, whom Elizabeth was bringing along as a treat to the young woman, prepared to
set out from London in late December.

Absent from London for fifteen years, Elizabeth did not leave the
metropolis so soon again without regret. She had found the capital
altogether pleasant. In her opinion the city had "never appeared
more to advantage." Money was plentiful, public credit good, and the
"places of Entertainment [were] crowded & more gay than ever."[18]
Reports of her enjoyment of Jannette's company and London's diversions gave pause to old friends in Boston, who began to doubt that
Elizabeth would return to New England, despite her announced
plans to come back in June 1771. "I cannot harber such a thought in
my Brest," Elizabeth Goldthwait maintained. She insisted that Elizabeth must come back, telling her friend that "never was a woman
Better Beloved in New England" and assuring her that she was "one
of the Sincerest of [her] Lovers."[19] Elizabeth seemed to have an
abundance of ardent admirers, but such declarations from distant
friends did nothing to dissuade her from enjoying the delights at
hand. She found the opportunities for "elegant entertainments"
and other activities in the mother country nearly inexhaustible and
somewhat mesmerizing. She reported being enthralled by the public
places of London and walking five miles without noticing the distance or feeling tired. While delighted with gardens "beautiful beyond description" and even the endless variety of sights and sounds
in London's streets, Elizabeth did not hesitate to voice a preference
for the less sophisticated life of the provinces. "However agreeable
England with all its amusements may be," she averred that she would
leave them "without regret to return to my Boston friends where I
hope to enjoy more solid and unmix'd pleasure."[20]

Despite such pleasurable inducements to prolong her London stay, Elizabeth felt the pull of family obligations drawing her away. Her brother John, living in Norwich, wanted to see her again. He had a house full of children whom Elizabeth had never met. Partly moved by John's invitations, Elizabeth was also willing to travel on to Norwich to implement her plan for Betsy, whom she wanted to put into a boarding school there. Acquiring some polish for Betsy had been a major motivation for Elizabeth in bringing her niece along on the journey. Since the teachers had persuaded her that Betsy would gain little benefit if she did not stay in school six months, Elizabeth thought it best to take her niece to Norwich and begin her education there promptly. Less than thrilled at the prospect, Betsy left London reluctantly. Quitting "all the amusements of that gay Place for the confinement of a Boarding School" could only provide Betsy with "a sad contrast for one at her years."[21] After bidding farewell to their friends and London's many charms, Elizabeth and Betsy journeyed on to Norwich, taking Jackie Day with them. Arriving in England's second largest city a day later, Elizabeth was reunited with her family. Meeting for the first time her many nieces and nephews, she also greeted her brothers John and William. When she saw William, her former companion and childhood favorite, Elizabeth excused herself, went to her room alone, and cried. After some initial awkwardness, the two of them sought each other's company constantly, reviving their youthful intimacy.

Not everything that Elizabeth saw in Norwich pleased her. Especially worrisome, in Elizabeth's eyes, was the situation of John's oldest daughter. After meeting her niece, Elizabeth had concluded that the girl lacked an adequately useful upbringing. Then sixteen, Mary Murray, or Polly as everyone called her, had finished her education. Presumably, it was time for the young woman to enter the world. But what could she do? Elizabeth knew that her niece did not possess a fortune adequate "to support the appearance she must make" in public. Nor would she be able to compete well on the marriage market. Unfortunately, Polly's class, income, education, and aspirations were at odds. Yet with no productive employment at hand, Polly had little to occupy her time in a meaningful way; she would have to busy herself in pursuit of "all the gayitys of Norwich."[22] The product of a genteel upbringing that left her unprepared for the economic realities of her family's position, Polly struck her aunt as bright, capable, and altogether at loose ends.

Polly had been educated in line with the ideals current in eighteenth-century England and America, which celebrated the gentlewoman's possession of a number of ornamental skills. Detailed in prescriptive literature, the desirable refinements of the accomplished woman included the ability to dance, do fancy needlework, speak French, sing, and play a musical instrument.[23] Part of the purpose behind acquiring proficiency in these arenas was to provide a genteel woman with activity; industry was its own reward, with busyness preferable to idleness.[24] Integral to such a woman's ability to shine in company were material possessions. While displaying her talents at home or abroad, a lady had to be attired appropriately, that is, in the latest style. Notions of genteel identity fused behavior with appearance. The material component of self-fashioning was an important one in an era of expanding consumer choice and the proliferation of goods.[25] A woman could develop the attributes of polite culture, receiving improvement as she attended the theater and assemblies, visited, and read. Her education, in effect, could be considered that of a cultural consumer. Yet a fine line distinguished polish appropriate to the genteel lady and cultural consumption indicative of dissipation and character corruption.

It was that balance which Elizabeth worried about with regard to her niece. Economic concerns lay behind the strategy of devoting time to both genteel accomplishments and industrious endeavors. Too much of the former could have disastrous economic repercussions, especially if the young woman in question failed to find a prosperous spouse. Undoubtedly reflecting on her own youthful training and activities, as well as those of her American nieces, Elizabeth discerned numerous pitfalls in Polly's path. First, the "gayitys" of Norwich could endanger a young woman's character. Even Jackie Day's brief indulgence in leisure activities in Norwich could be cause for alarm. Her mother worried that it would "Spoile her for the Woman of Business."[26] While inherently harmless, diversions could become a source of corruption. Seen as "improving" in small doses, because they contributed to one's cultural education, such pastimes as attending the theater posed threats when enjoyed immoderately, fostering a passionate, idle, and enervated character. Even if Polly achieved the proper balance and did not overindulge in amusements, she would face difficulties. She simply could not afford the apparel required in the elite sphere of socializing for which she had been prepared. For Elizabeth, the problem was clear: Polly had no fortune to support an expensive lifestyle or attract a spouse, no worthwhile occupation to fill her time, and no preparation for being anything other than a decorative and expensive young gentlewoman. Elizabeth shared with many contemporary commentators a dim view of the utility of female education. Critics argued that girls' education prepared them for a genteel lifestyle replete with decorative accomplishments and high standards of consumption. In one such tract from 1759, the author complained that too many daughters of tradesmen were schooled in ways suited only to the nobility and gentry. The end result was disappointment for parents and a vain, expensive young woman. A shopkeeper might find his daughter ruined: "Though ignorant of everything else, she will be so perfect in the lessons of pride and vanity, that she will despise him and his nasty shop, and quit both, to go off with the first man who promises her a silk gown and a blonde cap."[27] Consumption and corruption were linked.

Not surprisingly for a former shopkeeper who was an advocate for women, Elizabeth was ambivalent about cultural consumption. Her own economic successes and independence had been built on others' willingness and desire to indulge in the acquisition of fashionable imported wares. She had catered to the kind of consumer Polly was trained to be. Yet Elizabeth wanted to remove her niece from the decadent influences of polite culture. As she contemplated her niece's situation, Elizabeth condemned the educational system and its repercussions for the young in general and for her niece in particular. Expressing distaste for its effects, without openly criticizing her brother and sister-in-law for the choices they had made regarding Polly's training, Elizabeth described how "young people [were] being brought up in idleness and entering the world with all its gaietys, triffling away the most active part of their life or marrying imprudently." In Elizabeth's mind, Polly, "brought up in the lap of indulgence," perfectly embodied this practice. At a young age, "she had finished her education and must have appeared the fine lady," declared Elizabeth, "if she had stayed with her acquaintance." To save Polly from that fate, Elizabeth felt it necessary to give her niece some other way to occupy her time and perhaps some other sphere of "acquaintance" as well. Never one to eschew a challenge herself, Elizabeth hoped that going among strangers would rouse Polly's faculties "and make her industrious." Having achieved great success herself as a hardworking, ambitious retailer, Elizabeth hoped to see her niece become equally diligent. Helping Polly become an industrious woman would be "more agreeable" to Elizabeth than seeing her turn into one of "the fine delicate creatures that fly about for amusement."[28] Although Elizabeth was at this time devoted largely to diversions herself, she had earned the right to amuse herself and possessed an income sufficient to do so, neither of which was the case for her niece.

Elizabeth seized the moment and decided to model Polly's future on her own experiences and educational ideals. While she could have done nothing or given Polly some of her riches and transformed her instantly into a young woman with prospects — a small fortune would have afforded her more possibilities on the marriage market — Elizabeth came up with a novel offer. She proposed that Polly move to Boston and become a shopkeeper. Reminding one friend of their frequent discussions "on the education of youth," Elizabeth pronounced the value of her plan. By sending Polly abroad, Elizabeth would put her commitment to benevolence and belief in women's abilities into action. Her ideal was "to give a young Lady an usefull education [and] so soon as she has finished that to put her upon some scheme to improve her mind time & fortune." This philosophy or approach to raising a young woman could help her become what Elizabeth preferred: "an usefull member of society" as opposed "to all the fine delicate creatures of the age."[29] Even if Polly had possessed the fortune to support a genteel life of leisure, Elizabeth would have wanted her to be active and "usefull" rather than a "fine Lady."[30] Becoming a fine lady might spoil Polly so much that business would "ever be irksome to her."[31]

Elizabeth's solution, one with roots in her own adventures in shopkeeping, would provide the cure that Polly needed. Learning how to keep shop would enable Polly to develop "some way of providing for herself."[32] By giving Polly the opportunity to become financially independent, Elizabeth would put into practice her schemes of benevolence for her family, enabling Polly, as the eldest of ten children, to assist her younger siblings if she did well. Given the size of his family and his financial struggles, John probably welcomed his sister's offer to support Polly in such a venture. His wife's response was more hesitant. Elizabeth reported that her sister-in-law had taken the matter "under consideration." Although aware that it would be difficult for her to part with her oldest daughter, Elizabeth thought the move essential. Unable to think of any other way of providing for her brother's children, she declared herself unwilling simply to set them up with money. "As to holding them up as fine Ladys," she insisted, "if it was in my power I would not do it."[33] Society had enough of such delicate creatures. Elizabeth's enthusiasm and resources, her willingness to take an active role in the girl's future, and her earlier successes as a shopkeeper soon won approval for her plan.

Ensconced in her brother's Norwich home and surrounded by the cold, gray gloominess of an English January, Elizabeth began to plot her niece's future in Boston, evaluating the mercantile options for young women and the costs to her own pocket. She wanted Polly to be as prepared as possible to travel the path she had followed two decades earlier. Given her own early difficulties as a "broken shopkeeper" and one who was largely unprepared for commerce, she consulted with Edward Bridgen and James Waller, her merchant friends and associates in London, about what steps she should take. Bridgen suggested that Polly spend some time training "with some prudent Milliner and there learn the Genteel way of Making up things" and in the process "also learn the Nature of Shopkeeping."[34] While the plan had its appeal, the ever frugal Elizabeth questioned its value. Such training in a genteel shop would not come cheap.[35] Bridgen and Waller investigated the cost of an apprenticeship in London and found it prohibitive. Part of the reason was that Elizabeth thought a year's training would suffice. Uninterested in such an arrangement, the London milliners whom the merchants approached would "demand a larger Sum" for taking on an apprentice for a year than if she stayed with them four or five years.[36] After inquiring in local shops, Waller discovered that the biggest ones demanded from eighty to one hundred guineas and refused to negotiate for a smaller sum. Presumably, if they kept Polly for only a year, they would receive little return on the investment of their teaching. By the time she was ready to contribute some skilled labor to their business, she would be leaving for America. Given the expense attached to training in London, the merchants wondered whether Polly's needs could be satisfied in Norwich, where there were "many good Shops" which did "a good deal of Business" and which made "up things very Genteel."[37]

Ultimately, the differences between running a shop in England and America derailed any ideas Elizabeth had for training Polly before she left England. Although a stint in a London shop could help a young woman, lending her career in the colonies the cachet of origins in the fashionable metropolis, Bridgen doubted it was necessary. Indeed, he believed training in England could not fully prepare Polly for colonial retailing: keeping shop was a very different endeavor in America. It would be impossible for Polly to learn "the Generall Method of Shopkeeping used at Boston."[38] Perhaps more important than the accounting issue was the fact that American shopkeepers stocked a variety of items. Bridgen noted that owners of Boston shops carried all sorts of goods in one shop, whereas in London twenty shops existed for one type of merchandise. London shopkeepers specialized; Boston ones did so to a much lesser extent. With such substantial differences between shopkeeping in London and Boston, Polly would benefit little from learning the system in the capital. Upon arriving in New England, she "wou'd have it all to learn over again." Ultimately, all Polly needed, according to Bridgen, was "an exactness in arethmitic [and] an acquaintance with the people & the money." The first requirement Polly had already fulfilled. After six years at a boarding school, Polly was "a very capable girl" who could write and do sums "very well."[39] The latter requirement — familiarity with local currency and consumers — simply could not be met in London.

Based on her own knowledge of trade and background as a shopkeeper, as well as her mercantile friends' counsel, Elizabeth decided to send her niece abroad as soon as possible to gain the experience she needed in America. Bridgen and Waller thought her decision a good one, believing that since Elizabeth did not intend to set Polly up in business in London, any time she spent there would be a waste of money. By spending a year in Boston instead, she would become "Acquainted with the People before she Enters largely into Business."[40] With Polly already skilled with her needle at "making up things," Elizabeth concluded that a London apprenticeship would accomplish nothing. It is difficult to know which factors ultimately held more sway with Elizabeth. Certainly, if the financial return on training in London would not warrant the expense, she would not choose to throw away her money. Yet she had seen such young women as the Cumings, who had no training, embark on a shopkeeping venture with little difficulty. Perhaps she had so much faith in her own ability to put her niece on the path to prosperity by drawing on her own expertise that she felt delay was unnecessary.

The plan Elizabeth developed for Polly drew on Bridgen and Waller's advice and her contacts with women shopkeepers in Boston. Anticipating the assistance of her friends and protégés the Cumings and her brother James, Elizabeth devised a scheme that would ease her niece into the world of commerce. Polly would sail to the colonies with some goods that she could sell to local shopkeepers, board with the Cuming sisters, and closely observe their business practices. With a little help from James, Polly could keep the Cumings' books. By doing so, she could become familiar with trade and the townspeople before she set up on her own, thereby gaining experience without running all the risks associated with having her own business.[41] Elizabeth asked James to control the flow of goods: "You'll please let her have only a few at a time & such sort as is agreeable to Miss Cumings." If neither the Cumings nor Mr. Pearce, a man who had once worked with Jane Eustis, proved willing to trade with Polly, perhaps another woman retailer would. Elizabeth recommended that perhaps James "could make an agreement with Miss Rand to go into business with her."[42] These tentative partnerships point to the fluidity of trading relationships as well as Elizabeth's familiarity with other women's business practices.

After a winter spent in considering and revising these plans for Polly's future, Elizabeth decided to send her niece to Boston in the spring of 1770. Elizabeth expanded her patronage to include Polly's younger brother. Like his sister, Jack would make the move to America to pursue a career in commerce. Rather than going into shopkeeping, the fourteen-year-old would be trained in the mercantile house of some Boston trader or be apprenticed to his older cousin John Innes Clark, whose firm was in Rhode Island. By setting the siblings on these separate paths, Elizabeth preserved the gender distinction that generally dictated men dominate the ranks of merchants and women primarily act as retailers.

As she prepared Polly and Jack to make their first transatlantic voyage, Elizabeth may have thought of her own first journey, when she and William came with James to North Carolina. Polly's and Jack's parting from their parents was wrenching and distressing to observe. To give some comfort to her brother and sister-in-law, "a most affectionate & tender Father & Mother," Elizabeth journeyed to London to see her niece and nephew safely on board the ship that would carry them to Boston.[43] Although not melancholy about what she was witnessing, Elizabeth declared herself "very thoughtfull." The scenes they went through moved her deeply. "If my heart was not allmost as hard as a marble table," she averred, "they wou'd be too much for such a constitution." While she viewed sending Polly and Jack to make their way in the colonies as the best possible plan — and, indeed, it was not uncommon for parents to rely on extended family networks to provide connections and training for their offspring — Elizabeth remained troubled. "Poor things," she mused, "they part early from their fond parents & family." The two were not much older than she and her brother William had been when they had lost their mother, come to America, and said good-bye to each other. Yet where the upheaval in Elizabeth's young life had followed the deaths of her parents, no such losses forced Polly and Jack's separation from loved ones. Elizabeth's decisions about how to use her resources to help them prompted the siblings' fateful journey. "Perhaps I am to blame," she reflected. It was entirely because of her "advice" that they went.[44]

Elizabeth hoped that her niece and nephew would meet with the same kind of friendship and civility that she had experienced in Boston and, ultimately, with the same degree of success, despite the disturbances that continued to eat away at the town's calm. Although colonial protests and turmoil may have initially seemed at a far remove in London, the situation back in Boston had grown more critical in the months since Elizabeth's departure. Returning to a strategy that had seemed successful in bringing about the repeal of the Stamp Act, patriot leaders had promoted a boycott of British goods in response to the Townshend duties. Agreeing not to import taxed items after 1 January 1769, merchants in Boston had gradually gained the backing of others in such major ports as New York and Philadelphia. Even as support for the boycott became more widespread, however, cracks appeared in the united front. Some larger merchants and smaller shopkeepers continued to sell imported goods. Frustrated and zealous, Boston patriots went door-to-door, enlisting support for nonimportation and threatening those who violated the policy.[45]

Shortly after Elizabeth left New England the nonimportation crisis began to touch her friends, as those who failed to support the boycott found their prosperity undermined and their peace imperiled. Elizabeth's neighbor, friend, and fellow shopkeeper Jane Eustis, who had signed a 1768 agreement but not the one adopted in 1769, found that her decision put her at odds with popular opinion. After being named in the press as an importer in October 1769, she announced her decision to quit shopkeeping. In November she took out a large front-page advertisement in the *Boston Gazette*, declaring her intention to go to England. She asked those indebted to her to settle their accounts promptly; "otherwise," she warned, "they may depend upon being sued . . . without Distinction." She wanted to clear out her wares, which consisted of cloth and "a variety of other goods," including three cases of blue and white china dishes, coffee cups, and saucers, which she planned to sell "at a very low Advance for Cash."[46] By May 1770 her business had dwindled. Forced to return the goods she had imported, "Poor Mrs. Eustis" suffered greatly.[47] Her income and credit were tied up in goods that she could not sell.[48] Yet Jane Eustis was far from alone in encountering hostility.

Ame and Elizabeth Cuming quickly discovered that commercial endeavors exposed them to public pressure and censure. After Elizabeth arrived in London, she learned that the Cumings had come under attack for dealing in British wares. On 5 October 1769 the *Boston Chronicle*, the paper published by John Mein and partially subsidized by James Murray, printed the names of local traders who ordered and imported goods. "A. & E. Cumins" were noted for receiving two trunks of cloth and haberdashery; Elizabeth's friends Gilbert Deblois and Jane Eustis were also listed for their importation of a variety of wares.[49] Over the course of the next several months, the Cumings were repeatedly chastised in the pages of the *Boston Gazette* for violating the nonimportation pact. The first item on the front page of the 22 January 1770 issue attacked them and Christian Barnes's husband, Henry, for audaciously counteracting "the UNITED SENTIMENTS" of merchants throughout North America by "importing British Goods contrary to the Agreement."[50] Both the Cumings and Henry Barnes were reviled in this manner. The whole incident made Christian long for "one political Laugh" with Elizabeth, whom she thought might be diverted "to see Squire Barnes and the Two little Miss Cuminges Posted together in a News Paper as Enimys to their Country."[51]

When the Cuming sisters reported their experiences to Elizabeth, they expressed surprise that their economic actions had inspired so much resentment. Aware that the sisters were selling imported goods, a committee of merchants had come to their shop to investigate their activities and politics. When questioned, Elizabeth Cuming told the men that she and her sister had never entered into any agreement not to import. The reason she gave for their failure to do so was that their business was both very small and very necessary to their survival. They had to keep shop to support themselves, she told them. Not satisfied with the sisters' response, the merchants asked the women to relinquish the goods they had imported. The Cumings, however, could not and would not comply. By the time the committee visited their shop, the sisters had already unpacked their wares and sold some of them. Clearly, it was difficult for the merchants committee to control access to imported merchandise. Just as the Cuming sisters retailed goods in defiance of nonimportation agreements, so, too, did others throughout the colonies. Violations abounded in Boston, New York, and Philadelphia. Without concerted efforts to constrain such traders, the boycott would collapse and, with it, the vigor of colonial opposition to the Townshend Acts.

The reaction that the Cumings encountered demonstrates in no uncertain terms that women's participation in commerce had a larger significance in the decade preceding the Revolution. Their economic activities forced them to engage in political debates. While the sisters never expected that anyone would take notice of them or try to injure two industrious "girls," as they described themselves, who were "Striving in an honest way to Git there Bread," they learned that their shop was visible in the larger mercantile community. Unmoved by the Cumings' pleas, the merchants warned them that they would have to face the consequences of their noncompliance.[52] Knowing that reports of this confrontation were likely to alarm their mentor abroad, Ame Cuming did her best to reassure Elizabeth that she and her sister were fine. Rather than being "uneasy" on their account if she had seen them described as importers in recent Boston newspapers, Elizabeth should be cheered. The attack in the press had had the effect of improving business. Repeatedly the *Boston Gazette* printed resolutions from various nearby towns which named the Cumings as violators of the nonimportation agreement and in which the townspeople promised not to purchase goods from them or allow others to do so.[53] Clearly, what transpired in Boston also mattered in the countryside, as expressions of support for Boston's commercial policies galvanized and unified the populace. In the wake of such declarations, after being held up to public scorn, Ame and Elizabeth found themselves profiting from the highly charged political connotations of consumption. With friends inspired to buy goods from them, they had "more custom then before" and wished they had imported six times the quantity of goods they had.[54] By purchasing imported English wares from the Cumings rather than boycotting them, those "friends" who frequented the sisters' shop expressed both their personal loyalties and political leanings.

Just as women who sold British goods felt compelled to address the political context surrounding their business decisions, so, too, did women consumers. Boycotts of British goods involved women and girls who previously considered politics as outside their realm, demanding their commitment. A woman retailer might sign a nonimportation agreement, whereas a woman buying goods for her family's consumption faced important choices about whether to give up tea or imported fabrics. Throughout the colonies women accepted the challenge, putting their names to nonconsumption agreements, as did a group in Edenton, North Carolina, whose action become the subject of political satire. Spinning bees proliferated as women gathered to meet the demand for cloth with homespun material. While many expressed their opposition to Britain's taxation through such gestures, many others made it possible for shopkeepers such as the Cumings to sell their wares.

The news Elizabeth received from her friend Christian Barnes was less encouraging than was that from the Cumings. Even after Henry

Barnes was named as an enemy in the press, he still intended to advertise his goods, an action that Christian thought would actively antagonize the rabble. She determined to use her "influence with him not to be the first" to publicize his wares.[55] When goods arrived for him, a committee from "those dareing Sons of Libberty" waited on Henry to demand the wares be stored. Disturbed and concerned, Christian hoped for the imminent fall of the men, whom she saw as oppressors solely in pursuit of private gain. Once the people—"the deluded multitude," in her view—recognized them for what they were, they would refuse to follow their lead. She hoped peace would return soon, confessing to Elizabeth that she expressed only her "Private opinion."[56]

Almost apologizing to Elizabeth, Christian declared that her offering an opinion at all was a mystery, because she "never chose to dabble in" politics. She excused her exercise of political voice as the result of the intimacy of her relationship with Elizabeth. Writing to her friend and giving "vent to every sentiment" in her heart gave Christian "a peculiar pleasure."[57] The private emotions that bound these women made it possible for Christian to articulate opinions about public matters that she would have otherwise kept to herself. Soon, Christian began to provide Elizabeth with reports on the political views of servants and slaves, a striking sign of her broadening view of who could exercise political judgment. She believed one of the family's slaves, Prince, whom she thought a more talented artist than Copley, was "of tory principles" but could not be certain as he had "not yet declared himself."[58] In this tense and highly charged climate, Christian moved in a relatively short time—the course of a few weeks—from rationalizing and excusing her commentary about current affairs to asking Elizabeth for the latest news. Christian neatly connected politics and commerce in a simple request. "Send us a Little Dash of Politics from t'other side the Water," she urged Elizabeth. "Our well disposed import such a vast quantity of lies with their other articles that they begin to find a Difficulty in vending them."[59] Whether one bought imported British goods or a political bill of goods, the implications were both moral and economic. By describing the merchants committee as filled with the "well disposed," Christian echoed the popular critical view that many of those who enforced nonimportation violated the agreement on the side for their own gain.

When both the Cuming sisters and Henry Barnes refused to mend their ways, they were publicly reviled. In March 1770 a town meeting voted to condemn their actions. Unanimously, the council approved a motion to enter their names, along with those of ten other traders, into the records of the town "that POSTERITY may know who those Persons were that preferred their little private Advantage to the common Interest of all the Colonies." Corrupt and greedy, they stood out when all other traders suspended importations in order "to obtain a redress of the Grievances so loudly and Justly complained of." By continuing to import and sell goods "with a design to enrich themselves," Elizabeth's protégés and friends and their fellow reprobates excited the "Astonishment and Indignation" of the town, whose representatives expressed their surprise and disgust "that any of its Citizens should be so lost to the feelings of Patriotism and the common Interest, and so thoroughly and infamously selfish."[60] Without going into detail, James Murray reported to Elizabeth that there were "Mobbish doings upon those they call importers, among whom they were so mean as to include your poor Miss Cumings."[61] Interestingly, the same issue of the *Boston Gazette* that printed the names of the Cumings also carried the advertisements of several women shopkeepers who continued to retail newly imported British goods.[62] These six women, however, specialized in seeds, which were not taxed under the Townshend duties; three of them had signed a 1769 nonimportation agreement.[63] In her notice for seeds and "all sorts of English goods," shopkeeper Susanna Renken alerted potential customers that she had imported this other merchandise "before the Non-importation Agreement took Place."[64]

Despite accounts of political upheaval and attacks on her friends involved in shopkeeping, Elizabeth persevered in her plans for Polly and Jack and even argued in favor of the colonial protesters' actions. She believed that those who opposed British policy saw it as their "duty to stand up for so valuable a country & not be tax'd to feed the worst set of men that ever lived." In fact, she declared, "if I was in Boston I wou'd drink no tea and advise all my friends to sign" agreements foreswearing British goods. Although she did not go as far as did Abigail Adams did in calling tea "this weed of Slavery," Elizabeth was willing to give it up.[65] With limited success, colonists urged their compatriots to switch to various local brews, such as Labradore tea, which was made from the leaves of a bush that grew abundantly along the banks of New England's rivers but had a less than optimal taste.[66] Whether Elizabeth ever consumed this alternative is unknown. Clearly, she came to embrace opposition to the current tax system as a result of her travels. In England she saw firsthand "what a vile set of Placemen and pentioners lives upon our industery." Their "wickedness & bad management" were responsible, in her mind, for the suffering of "many poor creatures."[67] Aligning herself with those who protested parliamentary legislation, Elizabeth voiced a kind of patriotism and political opinion that colonial women were just beginning to express. Notably, Elizabeth was also rejecting the allegiances of her youth and upbringing, identifying with the American rather than the British perspective. Indeed, she thought herself entitled to express "a partiality for a Country & people where & from whom I have receved unmarited friendship & civilitys that I shall ever Glory to Boast off." In 1770 her "partiality" for America was quite pronounced, despite the problems her brother and friends had encountered, news of which she had gradually received.[68] By decade's end, however, her political loyalties would be sorely tested and undergo substantial shifts.

Although Elizabeth made some of these defensive pronouncements after her niece and nephew had sailed for America at the beginning of April, it is difficult to know if she would have kept to her decision to send them abroad if she had known how much the political climate had changed that March with the Boston Massacre. Tensions and minor altercations between Boston's residents and the British troops who occupied the town, a regular feature of town life since the redcoats' arrival in the fall of 1768, erupted into bloodshed on 5 March. That evening, a group of Bostonians walking down Cornhill were insulted and assaulted by several soldiers walking through the streets with their weapons drawn. A fracas ensued, with reports flying throughout the town that soldiers, moving toward their barracks — James's former sugarhouse in Brattle Square — were fighting townsfolk. Quickly, a crowd gathered and, with snowballs and clubs, pressed the soldiers toward the sugarhouse. Two officers locked their men in and tried to calm the crowd outside. Meanwhile, a couple of blocks away, a soldier on duty alone in front of the Customs House yelled at some boys who were insulting a passing officer and found himself pelted by snowballs. One boy ran into a church and began ringing its bells, the signal for fire and one that immediately drew the crowd from the barracks, as well as other townspeople, into King Street. There, Private White, still at odds with the group of boys, called for help. When reinforcements arrived, they found chaos and a crowd of two hundred. As people yelled "Fire," some believing there was a blaze, others daring White to shoot, the crowd closed in on the soldiers. In the confusion the soldiers fired their weapons, one at a time, killing or mortally wounding five men and injuring six more. Within moments Governor Hutchinson appeared on the scene, demanding to know why the officer in charge, Captain Thomas Preston, had given such an order (which he denied doing) and taking him away to be interrogated.[69]

Word of the bloodshed — quickly dubbed the Boston Massacre — and the public outcry that galvanized the populace in its aftermath reached Elizabeth six weeks later, leaving her shocked, worried, and "very sick." The news "of the riot in Boston" kept her awake all night. "Murder comitted in Boston, no letters for me, horrible indeed," she wrote.[70] She hoped that friends would escape the disturbances, declaring that one friend's involvement "would certainly banish me from a place and people I esteem and have the greatest reason to admire"[71] (figure 10). James was glad Elizabeth was not there, certain that it would have pained her greatly "to have continued in or near the Turbulent Town of Boston."[72]

In the weeks after the massacre, the situation continued to deteriorate. In response to the public anger, in short order, Captain Preston and the soldiers involved in the shooting were imprisoned, the other troops were confined to their barracks, and plans were made to move all the regiments out of the town. By 14 March the soldiers had decamped, vacating Elizabeth's building and Boston. James Murray was concerned enough about the safety of Preston that he wrote to the local commander, Colonial Dalrymple, to recommend that he bring some troops back into Boston, to "Smith's Barrack," to serve as a guard during Preston's trial. Otherwise, he feared, the man might fall victim to a violent crowd. Although his suggestion was not fol-

10   Elizabeth [Murray] Smith to [Mrs. Rowe], 24 April 1770.
Courtesy, Margaret Howe Ewing Papers, Private Collection.

lowed, the fact that James was willing to make it underlines both the depths of his loyalty and his indifference to popular opinion.[73]

Throughout the spring, attacks on those accused of importing goods increased. Elizabeth's good friend, merchant Gilbert Deblois, was chased through the streets, called "Importer," and pelted with old shoes. A mob fouled both his house and shop. Friends insisted that his life was in danger, that the mob planned to tar and feather him, and that he should allow goods that had recently arrived to be shipped back to England rather than insist on their being stored. He held wealthy merchant and patriot leader John Hancock partly responsible for his predicament. If not for that "Villain" offering to send the goods back to England free of freight charges, the townspeople would have allowed the wares to be stored. As it was, he and Jane Eustis were both forced to return their orders. In short, the town was "in a most shocking situation, ten times worse than when [Elizabeth] left," yet it was impossible for her to recall Polly and Jack, then in the mid-Atlantic.[74]

En route to New England before word of this uproar reached England, the pair landed on 4 June, the point of their journey having been rendered even more risky by the current political climate. Anxiously awaiting news of their ship's docking, Ezekiel Goldthwait found the two within half an hour and took them home. The following day, James Murray came into town to take his niece and nephew back to Brush Hill, where they remained. James had been staying in Milton for some time. Many of his friends in Boston took "great pleasure" in his absence, for they believed he would not be safe in the town, given his political loyalties and propensity to express them openly.[75] From England, Elizabeth worriedly urged James not to involve himself in politics and to devote himself instead to caring for Polly and Jack. He should try to befriend those from whom they had received so much friendship rather "than try to reform them."[76] The refuge of Brush Hill did not, however, protect the newcomers from soon learning how dangerous their commercial plans might be. The week after Polly and Jack's arrival, a group of disgruntled townspeople made an effigy of Christian Barnes's husband, Henry, labeled it an "infamous importer," hung the stuffed figure all day, and then burned it at night.[77] Shortly thereafter, while Polly was visiting Christian, a letter attacking Barnes was discovered, written presumably by members of the same mob that had made the effigy and attacked a wagon full of goods belonging to him. Before Polly left Christian's house, news from the Cuming sisters arrived, reporting angry crowds carting the targets of their hostility out of town "in a most ignominious manner."[78] The violence was coming frighteningly close.

While Polly and Jack had arrived safely, it was not clear that the cargo they carried with them would escape unscathed. The goods

Elizabeth had ordered for her niece were in danger of being seized by the merchants committee. Gilbert Deblois thought it extremely unlucky that the goods had come when they did. Trying to help the young woman and Elizabeth, he and other friends endeavored to have the goods stored in a Boston warehouse privately rather than shipped back to England. If they could keep the merchandise out of the committee's hands, it might be possible for Polly to sell it privately in the fall. Deblois's own cargo on Jacobson's ship, totaling one thousand pounds sterling, was seized by the committee for shipping back to England. Fortunately, Polly's goods had come in her cousin John Innes Clark's name. "Had they been in Miss Murray's," Deblois declared, it would not have been in the power of any friend to have prevented their seizure; the Murray name would have attracted attention. As it was, they escaped unnoticed and were safely stored.[79] When she learned of this good news, Elizabeth expressed hope that Boston was "returning to its former good order." While acknowledging that she had been "much condemn'd" by some friends for advising her brother to send his children "to such a riotous place," Elizabeth insisted that her counsel was sound. She anticipated that the kindness the pair encountered would convince them and their friends that the opinion she had formed of New England and its inhabitants "was not mistaken."[80] Elizabeth had already begun to consider bringing Polly's younger sister Anne back to Boston when she returned the following spring.

Given the chaos reigning in Boston and the attacks on those involved in trade, it was clear that Polly had "no prospect of doing any business."[81] The political climate in the summer of 1770 precluded it. Although Elizabeth had intended for Polly to "set up Shop in Mrs. Eustis or Miss Cumings way" with some imported merchandise, "the fury of the People at Boston [put] it out of her power."[82] Three months later, the situation remained unchanged. Polly told her aunt, "It has been impossible for me to do anything in the way you proposed since I came." A shipment of fashionable goods had arrived just the previous week, but, said Polly, "Tis uncertain when we shall get them out." She had nonetheless attempted to get involved with retailing, asking shopkeeper Jane Eustis to sell six caps that she had brought with her. Although they sold four caps soon, Polly could not report wholly positive transactions. Because the items were not on the invoice, they "were obliged to guess at the price." She admitted, "I am afraid we sold them to a disadvantage."[83]

While Elizabeth's niece made only tentative forays in 1770 into the world of commerce, her friend Christian Barnes found herself increasingly thrust into trading activities. In the midst of the "great disturbances" of that year, she was hard at work in her husband's shop, so busy "ploding behind a counter from Sun to Sun" that she had no time to write Elizabeth. Christian did not relish the shopkeeping life as much as Elizabeth had, asserting that it could "Stagnate the Blood and Stupifie the Senses."[84] Deeply ambivalent about her work, Christian complained about her own ignorance, lack of ability, and mistakes. At the same time, she took some satisfaction in her labor. "It would divert you," she told Elizabeth, "to see what a parade I make with my business. To one Gentleman I write for insurence, to another to secure freight, to a third to purchase Bills." In summing up her accomplishments and activities, Christian declared, "All this is done in such a Mercantile Strain that I believe many of them think me a Woman of great capacity."[85] Christian's hesitant assertion of feminine "capacity" in matters of business highlights the intersections between familial enterprises and female entrepreneurship, women's economic activities and their sense of their own abilities. Clearly, she undertook commercial endeavor in a family context. Like many other women who kept shop, Christian did so as an adjunct to a trading spouse, filling the role of "deputy husband" in his absence.[86] Yet her shopkeeping transcended family duty. She saw her work as a challenge and opportunity on the grounds of gender. Moreover, Christian's sense of the relative ease with which she took up trade to assist her husband added to her view of shopkeeping as accessible to women. The world of men and business lost some of its mystery once she entered it.

While Christian polished her mercantile skills, Polly had little employment. Without Elizabeth's presence and advice, her shopkeeping venture did not get off the ground. Her brother James declared himself "so fond of" Polly, that he did not choose to set her up in business until Elizabeth arrived. While she agreed that it would "do better to defer it" given the unsettled times, Elizabeth's dream — that Polly become a shopkeeper and, by going among strangers, rouse her faculties to become useful and industrious — appeared unlikely to be realized.[87] Instead of laboring in a shop, Polly pursued pleasure. A few months after she had arrived in New England, Polly sent home an account of her activities that troubled her father. She reported days passed entirely in idleness. John feared that such a "length of leisure" would turn Polly's "head too much from Business."[88] When another, similar letter arrived, John could not contain his anxiety. He alerted Elizabeth that Polly's correspondence "contained nothing but an account of the Parties of Pleasure" she was pursuing with her aunt Margaret, James Murray's second wife.[89] Much more fond of town life than James was, Margaret sought out company and diversions enthusiastically. Some contemporaries thought such indulgence clearly a feminine flaw; Dr. Gregory, author of a popular piece of advice literature, saw women as needing the restraint of religion to check their "rage for pleasure."[90] When John Murray heard of Polly's activities, his reaction was prompt and specific. He advised his daughter to be industrious, "not to forget her needlework nor her Arithmetic."[91] News of Polly's idleness troubled Elizabeth. It seemed that the future she had attempted to alter was unfolding nonetheless, the only difference being that her niece was becoming a fine lady in Boston rather than in Norwich. "I fear [Polly's] young Brain will be turned with frolicking about," she worried. Like her brother, Elizabeth feared that instead of developing into an economically independent and self-supporting, useful woman, Polly would be corrupted by too much "frolicking" and excessive attendance at public places.

Just as Elizabeth had sent Polly to America for its opportunities and to balance her youthful genteel education, she had brought Betsy with her to England with similar ends in mind. She expected that her niece would be able to complement her colonial education with the abundant polish offered by boarding schools and improving diversions in such cities as London. Elizabeth's underlying ambition for her nieces was not wholly at odds with contemporary standards of gentility. The methods she employed for achieving that end, however, as well as her specific definition of industry, grew out of her understanding of the economic options offered by the expansion of Atlantic commerce. Born in the colonies, Betsy went to England for polish, whereas her English cousin Polly traveled to Boston to keep shop. In both instances Elizabeth's objective was to cultivate the proper balance between social refinement and industry.

The summer of 1770, one of pleasure for Polly in America, was one of idleness for Betsy and nostalgia for Elizabeth. Niece and aunt spent a few months traveling around Scotland revisiting the scenes of Elizabeth's youth, an excursion that deepened their feelings of attachment to the place. As they neared Unthank, Elizabeth was overcome by emotion, so much so that a cousin traveling with them observed it and tried to divert her. "He quitted his English and talked Scots in a very droll manner," she reported. When they arrived at the farm, Elizabeth questioned the current tenant at length about her former neighbors. Gazing at a stream she used to wade to see her "first friend," Elizabeth remembered the girl's death at age seven. Everywhere she went, Elizabeth was confronted by bittersweet memories. One morning she and Betsy spent some time in the kirkyard where her mother was buried. Shortly after leaving that "melancholy place," she was approached by an old woman who told Elizabeth that she had lived with the Murray family and that Elizabeth had lain in her arms many nights. The woman gave Elizabeth news about her former schoolmates. Before the visit to Scotland was through, Elizabeth found the "place and family" so natural to her that she felt as if she had not been gone a year.[92]

During these months of traveling around Scotland, Elizabeth worried that the leisure of Betsy's days would undermine her progress and that she stood "a great chance of being ruined."[93] Endless numbers of cousins doted on the girl, taking up so much of her time that she neither wrote nor sewed.[94] Betsy was growing spoiled before Elizabeth's eyes. Something had to be done. A relative urged another stint in a boarding school, believing that a few months' study in Edinburgh "wou'd be a great advantage" to Betsy.[95] Not too surprisingly, the idea did not appeal to Betsy. After six months of studying in Norwich and a summer spent in travel, Betsy did not want to return to school. In Elizabeth's opinion, that would be the best option; otherwise, Betsy "wou'd be ruined with visiting & the indulgence she meets with."[96]

Elizabeth arranged for Betsy to stay at a boarding school in Edinburgh, where the girl would also visit friends of the Murray family and "attend the p[u]blick diversions."[97] Quickly, these new activities and acquaintances filled all Betsy's time. Back in Florida, Dolly felt neglected when her younger sister failed to write. While Elizabeth agreed that Betsy should be a better correspondent, she allowed her more leeway: "I have often been angry at her for not doing it, but now I excuse her." Betsy "must take some time to recolect the many very agreeable scenes she goes through before she can find words to express her sentiments." Hopeful that these activities would provide Betsy with polish, Elizabeth was equally hopeful that "the indulgence [would] not hurt her."[98]

Before long, Elizabeth had changed her mind about her niece's shortcomings as a correspondent, linking them to overindulgence in leisure, diversions, and entertainments as well as to possible character flaws. When two weeks elapsed between Betsy's letters to her, Elizabeth reprimanded the girl for her thoughtlessness. She asked rather sarcastically whether Mrs. Hamilton, the woman who ran Betsy's boarding school, had deprived her of pen and ink. "Or," Elizabeth inquired, "has the amusements of Edin[burgh] taken up your time & attention in such a manner that you cannot spare one hour in a week to indulge your friends"?[99] From her boarding school, Betsy promptly answered Elizabeth's charges, saying she wrote as usual, sent the letter the regular way, and was very sorry her aunt had not received it. Sounding slightly hurt, Betsy added, "I am sorry you had not rather imputed it to the neglect of [the Carrier] than me." She assured her aunt that not a week would go by without her writing. "I own I am fond of public places," she admitted, "but that or anything else should not take up my attention so much as to neglect those who by nature and gratitude I owe so much to."[100]

Elizabeth did not really begrudge her niece the pleasures of town life. Indeed, she considered attending plays and other public entertainments an expected and desired component of Betsy's education. Of course, the risk remained that Betsy might indulge too much. Elizabeth Goldthwait, one of Elizabeth's Boston correspondents, asked her friend to send Betsy her love and "tell her she must not be to much taken up with the Vannityes of this world for thay are not Durabel."[101] Betsy's Edinburgh activities highlight the links between town life, participation in cultural activities, and consumption of goods. Before Betsy could attend races and genteel assemblies, she needed to procure the right attire. With her aunt, Betsy made caps and flouncing gowns "to Cutt a figure" at upcoming balls.[102] In some cases, however, it was the public activities that Betsy pursued which raised concerns. After one play she attended, an actor performed an epilogue that contained shocking material. The following day, a minister delivered a sermon about the incident. In addition, "a long paper went about the Town informing the people the great sin which was comited at the play house." This news of scandal and immorality could not have given much comfort to Elizabeth, concerned as she was about her niece's potential ruin. Betsy became a little more cautious. Invited to another play the following Saturday night with some women who had taken a box, Betsy initially said yes. Before the appointed evening arrived, however, they "heard it was a bad play" and did not go. Betsy assured Elizabeth that this turn of events pleased her: "I am very glad of [it,] as evry body who was at the last Saturday night play was ashamed of it."[103] This one experience did not signal the end of Betsy's theater-going, however. Shortly thereafter she attended *The Conscious Lovers*, with two women, a play that she declared "an exceeding good one and very well acted."[104] Richard Steele's work was the epitome of the proper play when first produced a half century before.[105] Yet Betsy anticipated her relations' criticism: "I dare say you all think that going to the play once a week is too much; so do I and it is a practice I do not intend to follow for time to come."[106]

While Betsy had plenty of time to attend the theater during her stay in Edinburgh, she did not fail to participate in other sorts of improving employments, including regular lessons in singing and playing the guitar. Betsy's boarding school instruction mixed acquisition of decorative skills with academic ones. Absent from her curriculum was French, a common element of female education. She chose not to study it given the brevity of her stay, deciding that it would be impossible "to do any good at it" and that it would distract her from perfecting her command of other subjects.[107] In early December she began studying dancing and geography. The latter was perhaps included at her father's insistence. "I desire she may learn Geography to enable her to read History," James requested, "which is better reading than those Novels so much in Vogue."[108] He thus closely echoed Lady Pennington's 1761 recommendations to her daughters: "Learn so much of *Geography* as to form a just idea of the situation of places . . . and this will make history more entertaining to you."[109] Novel reading could endanger a young woman. As Maria Edgeworth argued in *Practical Education* at the end of the century, women "have been much addicted to common novel-reading" to no good effect. "Sentimental stories, and books of mere entertainment . . . should be sparingly used," she contended, "especially in the education of girls. This species of reading . . . induces indifferences for those common pleasures and occupations" that make up daily life.[110]

Ultimately, Elizabeth approved of Betsy's progress, viewing her education as a sound investment. She thought the visit was "of great service" to Betsy and would "be of more use than three thousand pound wou'd ha[ve] been."[111] Elizabeth's comment neatly captures her view of education as a means to a social and economic end, in this case marriage; she defined Betsy's cultural improvement in terms of the size of a dowry. Gentility could be purchased, as one historian has argued, "but only if the code of genteel conduct was sufficiently flexible to fit the diverse social and educational circumstances of the purchasers."[112] In Betsy's case the experiment had worked, and the expense was clearly justified. The largest cost Betsy had incurred during her stay at Mrs. Hamilton's school was for board. Clothing bills, for millinery items and shoes, exceeded the total educational costs for instructors and materials. With Elizabeth spending more for proper clothing than for training for her niece, it seems clear she valued external markings of gentility as well as internal accomplishments.[113] Betsy's behavior did not finally receive censure. Instead, her friends and family praised her polish. Jackie Day thought her friend had improved "prodigiously in her writing" and seemed "to be very Happy in her Sc[ho]ol."[114] James concurred with this positive assessment of his younger daughter's accomplishments. Betsy "has been much improved at home," he informed Dolly, having attended "one of the best boarding Schools" in Edinburgh.[115]

While she worried about Polly and the political situation in the colonies and oversaw Betsy's education in Britain, Elizabeth encountered new troubles. As 1771 began, the health of close friends in London became a cause for alarm. Having fled Boston after burying her spouse, Elizabeth now found herself anticipating the loss of other friends and loved ones. Jane Eustis had returned to England in the fall of 1770, arriving just before Christmas. During the trip she apparently contracted some illness, which her friends characterized as a nervous disorder. Quickly, her condition went from bad to worse as the new year opened. Insomniac and despondent, she talked as though guilt-ridden about her life. Her "distemper" alarmed her friends, who tried "to keep her Case as secret as possible" and allow no visitors "but necessary attendants."[116] For a time, "more outrageous than ever," the ill woman had to be restrained in a straitjacket. In that condition she received doses of some medicine that acted as a laxative and a sedative. When she awoke she spoke "Calmly" and rationally, declaring that she "had been used cruelly, but that there had been a necessity for it."[117] Persuaded that Eustis had regained her senses, the nurse removed the straitjacket; her doctor predicted a speedy recovery. His optimism proved unfounded. When James Murray, who had recently arrived in London to try to gain some sort of political preferment, went to visit her, he found her gravely ill and decided to stay with her for the day.[118] Before it was over, she was dead. The sudden, unexpected event stunned everyone.[119] Informing Elizabeth of her friend's death, Edward Bridgen acknowledged that she would need to grieve, to pay "the natural tribute of a tender, sincere and affectionate Friend" at the loss of a "dear Good woman." He tried to encourage her to see the woman's passing as a blessing of sorts. If she considered the severity of her friend's "Violent attack," Elizabeth would have to contemplate the misery that even a prospect of its return would cast on the rest of her life.[120] Sharing his partner's perspective, James Waller admitted that he at times could not believe she had died, so "sudden and Unexpected" her passing had been. Yet he took solace in her release from the "Melancholy Situation that Dreadfull disorder had fix'd on her."[121]

Reeling from the loss of one friend, Elizabeth was preoccupied by the condition of another. In October 1770 Jannette had informed Elizabeth, still in Scotland, about her own poor health. Ill with what sounds like breast cancer, Jannette believed that her doctors thought she would not survive. "I know their privat Opinion is the same as my own," she averred, "that it will be a Miracle if this lump as hard as a Stone can never be disolved but with the whole Frame."[122] Describing her pain and bidding her friend farewell, Jannette declared her confidence that Elizabeth would assume responsibility for her daughter, Jackie; the death of Jannette's husband that year meant that her own passing would leave Jackie parentless. He had failed to make adequate provision for Jannette and Jackie's maintenance before he died, and his relatives were urging Jannette to put her daughter into business.[123] With Betsy in boarding school, Elizabeth had not planned to leave Scotland for London for some time. If need be, however, she would change her plans and return sooner, unwilling to miss seeing her friend alive. Preparing to leave Scotland in early February, Elizabeth departed with regret, returning to London with a heavy heart. She had renewed ties with her extended family and felt unhappy about leaving them. Her relations shared her sorrow. After saying good-bye, a Scottish cousin was tormented by remembering their farewell. "If I dream it over again," she told Elizabeth, "I shall be quite vext."[124] News from the capital was not wholly unencouraging. Jannette was feeling somewhat better, hopeful that she would survive the disease, for her lump had become smaller and softer. If she lived, she would be happy to return to Boston with Elizabeth.[125] When Elizabeth arrived in London, however, she found Jannette in a great deal of pain and very ill. With her health very precarious, Jannette could do little to take care of herself. Rescuing her friend once again, Elizabeth made the arrangements to take Jannette back to New England with her.[126]

As the end of April 1771 neared, Elizabeth prepared to sail back to Boston. She booked passage on the *Osterly-Lizard*, "a fine large Mast ship" engaged in the West Indian trade, which would carry her party to Casco Bay in Maine; there she would board a trading schooner for the final stretch of the journey. Elizabeth preferred taking the larger vessel and indirect route to making the crossing on a smaller ship going straight to Boston.[127] In accord with the promises she had made her friends in New England, Elizabeth was scheduled to arrive just as planned. Neither the pleasures of her wandering life abroad nor the new responsibilities she had acquired had either delayed or hastened her homecoming. When she sailed on the first of May, Elizabeth brought with her a larger group than she had taken. The *Boston Gazette*, which reported the ship's arrival in Maine, noted the names of the passengers, information of interest given their status and associations in Boston. Among those listed, Elizabeth and her party comprised the bulk: "Mrs. Smith, Widow of the late Mr. James Smith, Mrs. Berkely, formerly Mrs. Jane Day of this Town, with her Daughter, and a Daughter and Niece of James Murray, Esq."[128] Crossing the Atlantic to return to a town where her homecoming prompted an item in the press, Elizabeth readied herself to meet a variety of obligations. And after a year and a half of visiting and traveling, she may have been tired of her journeys and felt ready to return to her former life.

Elizabeth's two-year interlude abroad came to an abrupt close with her assumption of new responsibilities. In England she had formed an "extensive & benevolent plan of usefulness" that she intended to follow in Boston.[129] The chief beneficiaries of that program, her nieces Polly and Anne, had to be cared for, trained, and supported. Acting as a mother to these two greatly enlarged Elizabeth's familial duties. Because political unrest had forestalled Polly's pursuit of a commercial career, Elizabeth would have to set the business in motion herself. Yet the planning for these nieces and their futures was a task that Elizabeth welcomed. Taking care of Jannette Barclay and Jackie Day was a responsibility Elizabeth had not anticipated.

After a difficult ten-week crossing, Elizabeth arrived in Boston in low spirits. As they sailed, Jannette's health had deteriorated markedly, and she was in great pain. Witnessing such misery was agonizing. "Your Tryals must have been great on the Passage," a friend sympathized with Elizabeth, "owing to the Tender feelings you have for the Dear Woman."[130] By the time Elizabeth and her charges arrived in Boston, it was clear that Jannette would not live much longer. James Waller tried to cheer her, to tell her that she had reason to rejoice, that God had blessed her and would reward her for her "Tender love and care of the Afflicted."[131] Whether Elizabeth derived any comfort from his words, we cannot know. It is possible, however, that the circumstances surrounding Elizabeth's trip recalled memories of the days before she left for England nearly two years before, a time of grief and exhaustion after James Smith's final illness. The sources of satisfaction in Boston must have looked somewhat bleak, and the political situation at hand, less than perfectly calm. The city remained a powder keg, with the regular arrival of British warships, the seizure of colonists' goods, annual commemorations of the massacre, and restive crowds in the streets. Shortly after she returned, a mob targeted a house of prostitution and ejected the women working there. In late July the trial of John Robinson, the man who had attacked James Otis just before Elizabeth left Boston in September 1769, concluded, its proceedings a source of public unrest.[132] Over the subsequent two years, however, the situation calmed down, so much so that such rebel leaders as Samuel Adams were hard pressed to find receptive audiences when they complained of colonists' grievances.

Regardless of what the political situation may have been upon her return, Elizabeth's immediate responsibility was to attend at her friend's deathbed and assume responsibility for Jackie Day. Watching at her friend's side, Elizabeth found what Jannette went through extremely painful.[133] By 5 August Jannette was "so low" that the doctor thought she could not last much longer,[134] and on 11 August she died.[135] One friend tried to take comfort in the fact that the "poor woman" was "happy after many Sufferings & Cares."[136] For Elizabeth, the last moments of Jannette's life cemented their bonds. Jannette's dying wish had been that Jackie not be left friendless. As long as Elizabeth survived, that would not happen. Elizabeth's promise to care for Jackie as her own daughter and to place her on an equal footing with her nieces Polly and Anne fulfilled Jannette's wishes.[137] Elizabeth had reassured Jannette that her love for Jackie was "as near that of a mother" as she could wish and that she hoped Jackie would look on her "as her Dear Mother friend & intamate."[138] Deprived of a doting mother, Jackie found her life substantially altered within the span of a few months, and not for the better. In England she had known a fond stepfather, enjoyed a circle of relations, taken pleasure in many fashionable diversions, and fallen in love. Without the approval of his guardians for a match or an adequate income to support a household, the pair parted tenderly, Jackie sailing away and her lover staying behind to plot their reunion. Robbed by death of both her stepfather and her mother and separated by an ocean from her betrothed, Jackie faced an uncertain future with no income and no way to support herself. Without Elizabeth's aid, she would have been wholly without resources. But Elizabeth decided that Jackie would join Polly and Anne in their shopkeeping enterprise.

As she watched her friend's life ebbing away and contemplated the new burdens she had shouldered, Elizabeth began to consider sharing her responsibilities with a new partner, Ralph Inman, a man she had known since her earliest years in Boston. Christian Barnes teased Elizabeth about the prospect of her marrying again and changing her living arrangements. Apparently Elizabeth had shared with Christian Barnes her thoughts about where she might settle. Until she knew whether Elizabeth was "in Jest or Earnest," Christian refused to offer her own opinion of Elizabeth's plans. Urging her friend to follow her own desires, Christian wished she were able to partake in the excitement in a more direct manner. "If you like the Situation . . . why I say Amen," she told Elizabeth, "but I think it is a little hard that I cannot be Present when all these affairs are in agitation."[139]

Christian thought her friend needed to act with her health in mind—and marriage could be a cure. The main requirement for mending Elizabeth's constitution, perhaps weakened again by nursing Jannette Barclay or the Atlantic crossing, was "retirement and ease." Christian insisted, "In order to procure that you must fix upon some worthy Person who will relieve you from the fatigues and cares of life or at least share them with you." Her advice amounted to an endorsement of matrimony. "Perhaps you will say the remedy may be as bad as the disease," joked Christian.[140] Unfortunately, Christian proved as prescient in this case as she had in her imaginings of Elizabeth's rolling, nausea-inducing journey to England two years before; Elizabeth's third marriage was marked by periods of acrimony and her declaration of unhappiness.

Regardless of Christian's advice, Elizabeth was back in Boston less than three months before changing her situation dramatically by marrying a man she had known for two decades (figure 11). Her courtship with Ralph Inman coincided with the period of Jannette's final illness; she accepted his proposal six days after her friend's death. The speed with which Elizabeth and Ralph decided to marry raises questions about how well the two knew each other before Elizabeth went abroad and when they first considered marrying. Although we do not know the extent of their correspondence during Elizabeth's sojourn in Britain, it is clear that they communicated both indirectly and directly. A few months after she had arrived in England, she told a friend that she had received a card from Mr. Inman, but "being a novice in politeness," she could not answer his missive properly and so would not even attempt to do so.[141] Perhaps that note contained intimations of a marriage offer. Mutual friends in Boston occasionally acted as conduits of information, sending Ralph's regards to Elizabeth in their own letters.[142] Along with Ralph's "best compliments," Polly wrote that she hoped her aunt would "not engage [herself] in England." Polly wanted to "have a chance for the pleasure of calling [Mr. Inman] Uncle."[143] Another friend let Elizabeth know that Ralph had extended an invitation to her to be his houseguest. Elizabeth declined the offer, asking her correspondent to give her compliments to Mr. Inman and tell him she was much obliged to him.[144] Ralph also sent offers of credit to Elizabeth in England. Wishing to assist her in promoting her business plan for Polly, Ralph contacted the mercantile house of Lane, Son, and Fraser, promising credit of four hundred pounds for Elizabeth, and wrote to her about his action as well.[145] In addition to inviting Elizabeth to be his guest and offering her financial backing, Ralph proposed visiting her in Scotland. His willingness to travel such a distance to see her invites speculation. How much did Ralph miss her? How strong had their attachment been before Elizabeth left Boston? It seems likely that the issue of marriage came up before Elizabeth returned to Boston. Yet Elizabeth dissuaded Ralph from visiting, much to the disappointment of her Scottish relations. One of her family declared it "both a Sin and a shame" for her to deprive them of "so much Pleasure as his visit" would have provided. This cousin deduced that Elizabeth had forbidden Ralph to come because she had already decided to marry him and wanted to do so in Boston, a course of action that a Scottish visit would have derailed or delayed. "You wanted to have your weding in your own way," she suggested, guessing about Elizabeth's plans.[146]

Regardless of how much the two may have danced around the issue of marriage during Elizabeth's absence from Boston, within two weeks of her return, Ralph had proposed. Thanks to John Rowe's diary and his intimate connection with Ralph Inman, we have detail, albeit from the outside, of the progress of the match. Rowe archly described an encounter between the two on 22 July, only eleven days after Elizabeth landed in Boston: "After Dinner Mr Inman Introduced his Design to Mrs Smith."[147] Although his "design" may not have surprised Elizabeth, she delayed giving her suitor an answer.

Finally, almost a month after Ralph had proposed, Elizabeth accepted him. On 16 August Ralph went to the Goldthwaits to visit Elizabeth and returned home "well pleasd & agreed on his Plan of Matrimony." That evening Ralph dined at the Rowe home, with Jackie Day and his soon-to-be nieces Polly and Anne Murray.[148] Two

11   Ralph Inman, portrait by John Singleton Copley, ca. 1770.
Courtesy, Boston Athenæum.

weeks later, their betrothal was announced in church.[149] Although
marriage was a civil contract in New England, banns were published,
or announced, in public meetinghouses, and ministers often performed the ceremony. On Thursday, 26 September 1771, a day of
"still pleasant weather," Elizabeth Murray Campbell Smith and Ralph

Inman wed.[150] The *Boston Gazette*, which carried few marriage announcements, reported the couple's nuptials.[151] Before twenty-five witnesses gathered at Goldthwait Hall, the Reverend Mr. Caner performed the ceremony. Among the guests were several of Elizabeth's nieces and nephews: John Innes Clark from Providence; Polly, Jack, and Anne Murray; and Betsy Murray. Jackie Day and Ralph's three children attended as well. Afterward, the entire party — except for the officiating clergyman — went to dine at Ralph's house in Cambridge, where they were joined by more friends, a "very Chearfull" company. Several friends and relatives, including the Rowes, spent the evening with the newlyweds and stayed at their home overnight.[152]

While the wedding celebration may have been "Chearfull," it is clear that not everyone was thrilled by Elizabeth's decision to remarry. Family opinion was divided. The Murrays' reaction was markedly less enthusiastic than it had been to her previous matches. Given her great wealth and advanced age — she was all of forty-five at the time — some members of her transatlantic family worried about what would happen to her estate and, by extension, to their financial circumstances. With her new attachments, would Elizabeth be moved to cut off her assistance to her family or reduce their portions in her will?

Ever aware of financial considerations, Elizabeth anticipated her family's concerns. When she informed her brother John of the marriage, Elizabeth suggested rather bluntly that he would think she had "acted imprudently" and guessed that he would see her new situation as "a disadvantage to [her] friends."[153] Those "friends" included John's many children, who stood to lose much if an interloper robbed them of their aunt's affection and promises of future munificence. Although John was perhaps at fault to doubt his sister's sense of commitment, he had cause for concern, given the financial promises she had made and the coverture laws that deprived married women of their property. While visiting John's family in Norwich, Elizabeth had pledged to contribute to the support of his two oldest children, Polly and Jack. Signing a bond of financial obligation, she promised jointly with her brother John to discharge debts that his daughter and son accrued while setting up business in the colonies with the assistance of her London merchant friends Bridgen and Waller.[154] In addition, Elizabeth arranged to have Bridgen and Waller disburse a quarterly sum to her brother to supplement his physician's income.

John was troubled by the news, he said, on behalf of his children, and hoped that her marriage would not affect them. Their interest, he assumed, would "suffer nothing" from Elizabeth's action, as long as "their behavior and conduct" continued to merit her "notice and encouragement." Yet he could not help worrying. In a sense, John saw his children as orphaned, both by their distance from their parental household and by Elizabeth's decision to remarry. Despite his statements to the contrary, John was apprehensive that his offspring would suffer from the change in her domestic situation. "Oh my Children! Orphans in a Strange Land!" he wrote, "what will become of you, if Providence should remove your Aunt or any Cause alienate her Affection?"[155] The most likely "Cause" would be Ralph Inman.

After considering Elizabeth's move, John offered tempered approbation while reminding her of her financial promises to him. Because she had been a person of consequence in America before her recent trip to Britain, according to her brother, she ought to have a home and family of her own, rather than "be degraded to a kind of nothingness" without them; she deserved to be mistress of a household. John explained that he had assumed that Elizabeth would remain single, that her "attachment to the interest" of his children might preclude remarrying. Yet he insisted that the chief obstacle to remarriage he had anticipated for Elizabeth was difficulty in finding a worthy spouse. From what he had heard of Ralph Inman, both from Elizabeth and others, John did not doubt that she would be "as happy in this" as in her former marriages. "Having already got so much" from her, John knew that he and his family had "no right to expect, far less to claim, more." Her previous generosity precluded any demands or complaints on his part. Any favor she showed him in the future would be the generous expression of Ralph's and her "affection and benevolence." Such protestations aside, John made it clear that he depended on Elizabeth's support. Telling his sister about his financial difficulties, John informed her that he continued to draw on Bridgen and Waller "for the usual sum, but [had] been obliged to anticipate a quarter" and draw money in advance on account of extra expenses related to moving into a new house.[156] Thus John felt free to take advantage of the arrangement, to anticipate her goodwill, and to exploit her mercantile contacts' willingness to help her kin.

Feeling somewhat compelled to explain her reasons for remarrying, Elizabeth tried to deflect John's criticism and justify her actions. She did not list affection among the factors that led her to wed again, although she and Ralph had been on friendly terms by 1753 and had socialized regularly in the 1760s. Interestingly, she argued that Ralph Inman would prove an economic help. Despite what her friends and relations might have thought, Elizabeth's financial affairs were neither comfortable nor well ordered. She assured John that the circumstances were in fact "very different." During her absence, the estate she had inherited from James Smith had been "reduced one thousand pounds Sterling." Upon her return to the colonies she discovered disarray: "I found things in a Situation that was very disagreeable to me." Apparently, accounts had been handled poorly, with no receipts made or securities taken. She needed some assistance and found the solution in Ralph, "an honest generous Man" who would "render a faithful Account."[157] The task of administering her property was a sizable one. A list of her real estate compiled that September details her substantial holdings in Boston, including twelve houses, the sugarhouse, and land, which generated an annual income of over three hundred pounds from tenants. She was also a creditor to several dozen individuals in and around Boston.[158]

Even more important than Ralph's ability to act as Elizabeth's steward was his willingness to sign a prenuptial contract that acknowledged the significance of Elizabeth's wealth and her right to keep it for herself. Two days before the marriage, Ralph signed the six-page document.[159] The "Indenture" recognized that Elizabeth was possessed "in her own absolute right of a very considerable Estate, both real and personal, the greatest part" of which she had received as the bequest of her late husband. Before marrying again, Elizabeth wanted to insure that she could "reserve for herself the whole" of this estate, except the income from it during the period of her forthcoming marriage. The prenuptial agreement would keep her estate intact and preserve her control of it unimpaired. Ralph would gain financially from marrying Elizabeth and handling her affairs, however. The "income, interest and profits" on her property would go to

Ralph for "his own use." Out of this sum Ralph would pay Elizabeth's trustees two hundred pounds sterling per year for her "separate use and benefit" and keep the excess for himself. To insure that Ralph was handling the estate correctly, Elizabeth and her trustees demanded that he keep "an exact account" of bonds, mortgages, other securities, and rents due his wife. Upon request, he had to turn over these accounts. This arrangement was designed to allow Ralph to profit while ensuring that he did not do so at his wife's expense. Elizabeth may have trusted Ralph, but she nonetheless took legal steps to guarantee his good behavior and the preservation of her property. He promised one thousand pounds security as his bond for fulfilling his pledge.[160] Most important, Ralph renounced a husband's claims to the privileges of coverture. "By contract [he] has put it in my power to Will away every thing as if I was not married," Elizabeth explained, trying to reassure her brother John that the provision would preserve her ability to take care of his family.[161] The prenuptial agreement canceled Ralph's rights to her property and legally authorized her to make a will. Ralph promised that if she predeceased him, after making a will, that he would permit it to "operate in the same manner as tho' she was not under Covert at the time of making such will." If she failed to make a will, her property would go to her next of kin "as tho' she had died sole and unmarried."[162]

Both Ralph and Elizabeth would benefit from the terms of the agreement. Just as Ralph would gain income from Elizabeth's estate, so would she profit from his. Although she renounced her dower rights to a third of his real estate, Elizabeth would have "full power & Right to possess Enjoy and improve the whole farm and lands" that Ralph had in Cambridge, "together with the dwelling house stables outhouses and buildings." If she survived him, she would hold these substantial properties rent free for the remainder of her natural life and keep the income and profits from them. She would also enjoy "forever" the contents of the house, "all such plate household Goods furniture of every sort and kind beds bedding and linnen" in the house at the time of his death. Similar personal household property that Elizabeth brought into the marriage would be Ralph's if he survived. These provisions made it plausible for Elizabeth to argue that her family stood to gain from this man's assistance in administering her extensive properties rather than lose from his legal and emotional attachment to her.

While some of Elizabeth's family may have had concerns about her marriage, other friends were delighted by the news. Even before her return to Boston, it was "a settled Point" among her friends there that she not "set down again in a Single State."[163] Elizabeth Hamilton, the director of the Edinburgh boarding school where Betsy had studied for several months, believed that the marriage had to be gratifying to all of Elizabeth's friends "and particularly so" to Betsy, whom Elizabeth loved "as a mother does a favorite Child."[164] Another Scottish correspondent congratulated Elizabeth, convinced that she had "done well & wisely."[165] Free of the financial self-interest that plagued John Murray, these women saw the marriage purely in terms of its personal benefits for Elizabeth. Edward Bridgen berated her for not sharing news of the match with him before she left England. Like other friends abroad, he seemed to believe that Elizabeth knew before she returned to Boston that she would marry Ralph. Bridgen needled her about her reticence: "There is not a woman in the world can keep a Secret better than I can," he insisted, "but you, My Dear Madam, would not trust me." Nonetheless, he graciously conceded to forgive her, congratulating her on her marriage "with a Gentleman of so much merit as Mr. Inman."[166]

Along with his good wishes, Edward Bridgen sent Elizabeth tongue-in-cheek advice on how to have a good marriage. Outlining appropriate behavior for a married couple, he doubted that Elizabeth would be able to practice it. He suspected that the couple's good dispositions would preclude "those pretty bickerings & contradictions" that enabled outsiders to recognize married folk. Nonetheless, he urged Elizabeth to consider the benefits of "some polite Altercations." Indeed, he proclaimed, from the vantage point of his London residence, "I don't believe you know enough of the Beau-monde to be thoroughly acquainted with the polite matrimonial life; therefore, as you are a new-married woman I shall take the liberty to give you some advice." In his minutely detailed prescriptions, he offered an amusing and illuminating characterization of polite matrimony. "If Mr. Inman says, my dear shall we take a ride out?" he told her, "be sure say, no, I am not well. When he is not well, be sure to leave him, but if you can't help going with him, as sometimes you can't, never fail to look out at the opposite window of the Chariot, least strangers should judge you were not married." Clearly, looking within would suggest that the passengers interested each other more than the passing scenery, proof that they were not wed. Crossing a spouse at every turn was the essence of Bridgen's advice. "If Mr. I. is fond of a particular dish be sure to be tired of it yourself, and so in every thing else, if he approves be sure, never to be of the same opinion." By disagreeing with her husband whenever possible, Elizabeth would attain "the pleasure of living in as polite a Style" as any other married pair of genteel Londoners.[167] If the new Mrs. Inman chose to ignore her friend's dictates and pursue an impolite connubial state, he could not tell her otherwise. "If you don't approve of this my advice," he declared, "follow your own inclinations, and be as ungenteel as the most happy couple of your Acquaintance." That, of course, was his wish. Bridgen anticipated the couple's enjoyment of "a long series of happy years."[168]

For a time it appeared as though Elizabeth would enjoy the happy union that Bridgen predicted, one distinguished by harmonious family relationships. Settled in Cambridge, Elizabeth tried to ingratiate herself with her new family. Her opportunity to prove herself came in the summer of 1772, when Ralph's son, George, graduated from Harvard. To celebrate the occasion, Elizabeth threw an impressive party at their home. The three-story house, a mansion that stood just off what is today Massachusetts Avenue, behind the Cambridge City Hall, possessed an impressive veranda, grounds full of pine and locust trees, and a pond. Although Elizabeth, as mistress of the household, had some responsibility for planning the hospitality, everyone had an opinion as to how the affair should be. Giving her a "proof" of the freedom she had to conduct herself as she wished, Ralph desired she would act as she chose in every detail, regardless of the opinions of other relatives and friends. "This roused my invention," she said.[169] The celebration Elizabeth planned for her stepson's commencement awed the guests. John Rowe thought it the "Genteelest Entertainment" he had ever seen. "Such an entertainment has not been made in New England before on any occasion," he declared. Three hundred forty-seven gentlemen and ladies attended the party, 210 of them dining at one table.[170] With some pride, Elizabeth noted that everyone wondered "at the Elegence & variety of meats hot & well dress'd & cool liqures in such hot weather

for such numbers." Among those in attendance were the Massachusetts governor and lieutenant governor, as well as their families.
Given such a crowd and the political climate of the day, it would not
have been surprising if some factional behavior or verbal sparring
had occurred. Yet Elizabeth reported no such outbreaks, asserting
that the celebration successfully abolished party lines for a time.
There was neither Whig nor Tory in attendance; rather, "every one
joind to make the day & evening compleatly agreeable."[171] Others
agreed. The *Boston Gazette* reported that "the *polite, cordial* Reception
given to the Guests and their *bene-volent* Festivity were mutually a
Credit to each other."[172] In short, the party delighted everyone.

The extravagance of the affair attracted attention outside Cambridge. Luxurious entertainments — with the conspicuous consumption and display that distinguished some of the colonial elite — not
surprisingly could become the targets of public scrutiny and criticism.[173] In the *Boston Gazette* published just after the graduation gala,
the editors reported minute details of the celebration, making fun of
its lavishness. The issue that contained a list of the names of the men
receiving their bachelor's or master's degrees also carried a special
item of local news: "Among the young Gentlemen who received their
first Degree at this Commencement, was the only Son of Ralph Inman, Esq; of Cambridge." The paper offered a vivid account, announcing that Inman "gave a very extensive Invitation, in the Name
of Himself, Lady and Son, to the Circle of their Acquaintance, to
dine at his Seat." Insiders gave the paper the scoop. "We are informed by some of the Company present, that they found a Table of
about 150 Feet, under a Canopy on the Green before the House."
There, "spread with an Elegance as if directed by the Fancy of a Fairy
Queen," the guests found an amazing repast. The "Fairy Queen" —
Elizabeth — had provided a meal that was both elegant and delicious;
it was "capable of giving the most solid Satisfaction to the whole
School of Epicurus." The editors lampooned the whole affair, declaring that "the Sideboard Range would have put a new Smile upon the
Cheeks of Bacchus and his jovial Train." All the gods would have
been moved: "Poor Venus indeed and her Nymphs must have burst
with Envy, had they been present to examine, at one single Prospect,
a brilliant Group of more than eight Score Ladies." After ten o'clock,
the company adjourned "to the Pleasures of a Ball at the Court-

House."[174] To a readership well attuned to the political connotations of consumption and excess, such extravagance may have appeared inappropriate and unseemly.

After the party, Elizabeth acknowledged that she was highly pleased with her efforts on behalf of her new family. All her friends were very proud of her performance. Equally important, the Inman family recognized her success. Father, son, sisters, uncles, and aunt all "said they felt so happy, words cou'd not express." They promised that their future behavior would convince her of their gratitude.[175] She had proven herself a worthy mistress and stepmother, and they would accord her the respect and appreciation she deserved. Word of the affair reached Scotland, where a friend heard of the "Noble intertainment" Elizabeth had given. "I take it you dazzled the new world," she wrote. "I hope you continue to be a good Step Mother & a happy Wife."[176] Another celebration of a family milestone followed in September when Ralph's eighteen-year-old daughter, Susannah (or Sucky), married Captain Linzee, a British officer. Twenty-six friends and family gathered at the Cambridge estate to witness and celebrate the nuptials.[177]

The joys of 1772 gave way to the next year's discontents as illness hit Elizabeth's new family. In the two years since she and Ralph had married, Elizabeth had worked especially hard to take care of the youngest of her husband's three children, Sally, motherless since infancy. Moving into Sally Inman's life and home when the girl was twelve, Elizabeth succeeded in befriending her. She enjoyed Sally's company, and the girl confided in her. Equally gratifying, the relationships between Elizabeth's nieces and Sally were affectionate, like those of sisters. With an engaging personality, Sally "delighted" all around her and "was her fathers darling." Suddenly falling ill with a throat distemper, the "most mortal" of any that had ever struck the area, Sally died within ten days of falling sick.[178] With grief, Elizabeth recalled how Sally "left us to Mourn the Loss of her we loved." Yet submission to "the will of Heaven" was difficult. Elizabeth found herself plagued by headaches and was ordered to go riding daily for her health.[179]

By the fall of 1773 Elizabeth had grown dissatisfied with her marriage. Even so, she did not explicitly blame her husband: "If I am not a happy wife it is my own fault. No one has more of their own Will &

few so much as I have."[180] She recognized that she had much more freedom to do as she pleased than other wives. Despite such autonomy, Elizabeth's spirits were not especially good. She wondered that her husband had ever thought of seeking "so grave a wife" as she was.[181] Her "drooping spirits" lingered.[182] What caused her unhappiness cannot be determined with any certainty, although Sally's recent death no doubt contributed. Perhaps she found this marriage and its responsibilities especially constraining. Even with a detailed prenuptial agreement, she may have found herself inhibited from using her wealth as she desired. Cambridge may not have suited her. Or maybe she and Ralph simply did not get along well.

As the contentment of Elizabeth's domestic situation deteriorated, the world around her was growing increasingly unsettled. In the early 1770s, relative calm had prevailed. Despite annual orations on the anniversary of the massacre, for example, Boston's political problems seemed to have little resonance outside the town. And regardless of the continued tax on tea, consumers throughout the colonies sated their thirst with large quantities of the beverage. In this climate, radical Samuel Adams's denunciations of British plots and parliamentary conspiracies designed to deprive Americans of their rights fell largely on deaf ears. Only the continued presence of British troops inspired much propagandistic ink.[183] In late 1772 and early 1773, however, the situation began to change, and the Revolutionary crisis heated up once again. In November Samuel Adams rallied fellow Bostonians who opposed British authority to support a series of resolutions listing the colonists' grievances, from the payment of royal officials' salaries by the Crown — a policy that removed whatever leverage local legislatures may have had over administrators — to the abuses of the customs commissioners. The most important element of the protest was the creation of the Committee of Correspondence, which communicated these grievances to colonists outside of Boston. Viewing the report the town meeting ultimately issued as a "declaration of Independency," Governor Thomas Hutchinson felt it necessary to squelch such rebelliousness. In January 1773 he lectured the General Court, the colony's legislative body, about parliamentary authority. The response was far from accommodating. Hutchinson lost further support that summer. In June, letters he and Lieutenant

Governor Andrew Oliver had written years earlier, in which they were critical of Boston patriots, were made public, owing to the machinations of Benjamin Franklin and Samuel Adams. Their disclosure led to an overtly hostile climate, with the General Court petitioning the Privy Council in England to remove the two men from their offices.[184]

While Bostonians were involved in their own struggles to rid themselves of an unpopular governor, members of Parliament were contemplating a piece of legislation that ultimately rid the empire of its colonies. In May 1773, Parliament passed the Tea Act, a bill designed to bail out the struggling East India Company. Under its terms, tea that the company would have had to sell at a loss in England would be shipped directly to particular merchants in the colonies for sale, thereby eliminating the commissions and additional costs imposed by its handling by middlemen. Even with a tax of three pence per pound, to be paid by colonial consumers rather than the East India Company, the streamlined distribution would allow the merchants consigned the tea to sell it at prices low enough to compete with smuggled Dutch tea. When colonists learned of the act that summer, many perceived it as the latest attempt to enslave them, to use their desire for cheap tea to seduce them into acknowledging Parliament's authority to tax them. In New York and Philadelphia, colonists quickly protested the act. In those ports the men consigned to act as agents of the East India Company resigned their posts. In Boston, however, the merchants refused to do so. As October and November progressed, protests and unrest escalated, with mob action and the vandalizing of property reminiscent of the Stamp Act riots. When the first shipment of tea arrived in Boston in November — before anywhere else in the colonies — the situation was yet unresolved. The law required that the ship be unloaded in twenty days, or by 17 December. On the night of the sixteenth, after the first tea ship's captain refused once more to sail back to England with his cargo intact, Bostonians, many disguised as Native Americans, met at the shore, boarded the tea ships, and dumped their leafy contents overboard.[185] Overnight, the Boston Tea Party altered the political landscape. In retaliation for the destruction of property and lawlessness, Parliament responded promptly and harshly, passing legislation known in America as the Intolerable or Coercive Acts, which closed the port of Boston. Problems of poverty and poor relief escalated in the wake of the act.[186] Boston became a symbolic martyr, its problems the focus of protests and support throughout the colonies.

As angry colonists grappled with the meaning of Britain's rule, Elizabeth and her family found their lives disrupted and their loyalties tested. Elizabeth's shopkeeping dreams for her nieces Polly and Anne threatened to fall apart. When the fighting broke out, the discontentment Elizabeth felt with regard to her marriage flared into open discord, with hostilities equally apparent on the domestic as well as political fronts.

5

Conflicting Loyalties and

Fighting the Revolution

In the midst of the turmoil following the Tea Party, Elizabeth decided it was time for Polly to return to England for a while. In her estimation her niece had fully lived up to her expectations. Indeed, she concluded that Polly's "capacity" for business was "so great," that she should be indulged with a visit to friends in England. Equally important, a trip could be "a great advantage" to Polly in a commercial sense, just as Elizabeth's own journey two decades before had been. Back in England, Polly would select more goods for the shop and visit her family before returning the following fall. As Polly prepared to return home in the spring of 1774, the town was in a state of unrest not dissimilar to that of her first summer in town four years earlier. That May, Elizabeth still defended her chosen homeland. "Notwithstanding the many bad things they say of us," she noted, "vast numbers of people" from England, Ireland, and Scotland continued to settle in the colonies. A "glorious" country, it deserved "the protection of good people."[1] Within a few short years, Elizabeth's vigorous defense of her neighbors and attachment to the home of her adulthood would be severely undermined, challenged by the pain and tumult of a war that brought upheaval into every aspect of her life.

In May 1774 word of the Boston Port Act arrived, signaling the escalation of tensions between the colonies and the mother country. Soon thereafter, the new military governor, General Thomas Gage, landed. Elizabeth managed to be both optimistic and humorous about his arrival and what it portended. "Giving us a milletry Governor will make us more gay & social," she opined, in comparison with the "dull times" they had had for the previous three years. "I do not despair of seeing every body as happy as their temper & setuation will admit of in a few months, in the best of times thier is allways Grumbletoneys."[2] By the end of the month only nine ships remained in port. When Polly sailed for England on 31 May aboard the *Minerva*, her fellow passengers included former Governor Hutchinson and his son and daughter.[3] They left just before the port closure act went into effect. On 14 June, the last date that ships were allowed to leave the harbor, a regiment of troops came ashore and pitched their tents on the Common. Throughout June, big town meetings were held as more and more troops arrived and joined the camp.[4]

With Polly gone to England and her immediate domestic circle a source of pain, Elizabeth's great experiments of the early 1770s were falling apart as the political situation grew increasingly unstable. Marriage once again had not brought the ease or satisfaction for which she had hoped. Legal autonomy did not ensure domestic bliss. Moreover, personal losses and disruptions continued to figure in Elizabeth's life, as she attempted to run a household, endear herself to a new family, take care of her nieces, help oversee their business venture, and keep an eye on Jackie Day. A few years into her third marriage, Elizabeth was not content. The seeds of dissatisfaction had been sown, and when nourished by the tensions and difficulties of the Revolution, they grew into blatant discord. As 1774 dragged on, the political situation around Elizabeth worsened. Boston was an occupied town, and General Gage was a military man more than a civil commander. In September, when he decided to seize Charlestown's gunpowder supplies and two cannons at Cambridge, he encountered resistance. The roads around Elizabeth filled with thousands of colonists in arms marching on Cambridge. Although his troops and the colonists did not meet, Gage was alarmed and responded by ordering a fort to be constructed on the Boston Neck, a narrow strip of land that connected the peninsula on which the town stood to the countryside.[5] The conflagration was imminent and came the following spring.

In April 1775 colonists in Boston and the surrounding countryside found themselves in the midst of a war. The nineteenth witnessed the real beginning of the Revolutionary conflict, when British soldiers, on a mission to seize weapons reportedly being stockpiled in Concord, fired on and killed colonial militiamen gathered on the Lexington green. As the day wore on, battle erupted, with armed minutemen hurrying to join the fight against the retreating British troops. The ensuing clash between the king's soldiers and colonial volunteers transformed the route between Lexington and Concord and Boston into a "bloody chute." Colonists harassed the exhausted redcoats, wounding and killing many as they completed their long day's march back to Boston. Once the beleaguered troops had made it back to the city, the thousands of colonial forces that had poured into the fields and roads that day set up camp, beginning a siege of Boston that would last eleven months. Across the Charles River in Cambridge, where Elizabeth was then living, the "shot that rang "round the world" sounded close at hand. A "midnight cry" preceded the encounter, rousing people from their sleep and alarming them, as one of Elizabeth's female neighbors wrote, "that a thousand of the Troops of George the third were gone forth to murder the peacefull inhabitants of the surrounding Villages."[6] Elizabeth's proximity to troop movements was perilous; armed men marched within a mile of her home. In the days that followed, colonial volunteers hastened to the town. Chaos, confusion, and uncertainty reigned. War had undeniably begun. Elizabeth persevered in attempts to fulfill her prewar responsibilities, while others fled theirs. Her priorities, in the early weeks of the conflict, revolved around maintaining the family farm, preserving crops, and protecting property. These economic goals would implicate her and involve her in public affairs more than anything she had ever done as a shopkeeper or promoter of women in commerce.

Over the course of the Revolutionary War, Elizabeth found that her sex rendered her actions problematic, on both a personal and a political level. Contemporaries were not wholly comfortable with women who expressed political sentiments or exercised independent judgment.[7] Torn by conflicted loyalties to family, country, and finances, Elizabeth strove to move within gender constraints of the day even while she challenged them. When others criticized her conduct, she typically tried to couch it in terms of her sense of her responsibilities as a woman. In other words, she attempted to manipulate others' expectations about the extent to which married women could be considered to exercise independent will and political action to pursue her own agenda. Her history, clearly remarkable in some respects, serves to highlight the wide range of negotiations and inno-

12   The Inman House, Cambridge. Courtesy, Cambridge
Historical Commission.

vations women encountered and practiced as they experienced the
Revolution in immediate and personally transforming ways.

Elizabeth's description of her actions in the aftermath of Lexington and Concord, penned at the Cambridge estate to which she had
moved four years earlier (figure 12), captures both the adrenal anxiety of the moment and her distinctive response. Instead of leaving
her home when the fighting broke out, she assumed a military pos-
ture, with a guard near her garden and a number of men patrolling
the marsh and the farm. Because she remained to defend her family's economic interests, rather than flee to a safe refuge, Elizabeth
was in the middle of troop movements. This circumstance did not
daunt her or deplete her store of fortitude. As she reminded one
friend, she was never one who had "seen troubles at the distance
many others have."[8]

In contrast, much of the local female populace abandoned Cambridge in the face of the possibility of the town being overrun by
troops.[9] One woman described a cacophony of ringing bells, beating
drums, and firing that convinced her that "the rising Sun must witness the Bloody Carnage." Anxious to leave before the troops ar-

rived, she hurried to a safe place a mile away, where she found a house "filled with women whose husbands were gone forth to meet the Assailants." Seventy or eighty of these women had gathered, with many infants and small children at their sides. When the next day found the enemy advancing, these terrified refugees were compelled to move again. "Thus we began our pilgrimage," she wrote, "alternately walking and riding, the roads filled with frighted women and children, some in carts with their tattered furniture, others on foot fleeing into the woods." This desperate parade of women and crying infants passed through fields strewn with "mangled Bodies."[10]

Aware that other women responded to the crisis by evacuating the town, Elizabeth knew that her decision to remain behind was unusual. As she explained, "The women & Children have all left Cambridge so we are thought wonders."[11] Even Polly, who admired her aunt's spirit, thought her actions "very extraordinary."[12] Elizabeth recognized that her gender rendered her choice, which held political and personal ramifications, noteworthy and distinctive: her sex made her behavior "marvelous."[13] Elizabeth acted in a manner that was at the very least surprising, as well as potentially unseemly and dangerous. This moment of crisis and drama — a woman overseeing the security of family and farm while surrounded by armies–lends itself to a variety of interpretations about women's involvement in the Revolution and its impact on their lives. Chaotic circumstances could demand new actions and types of behavior from individuals who could be forced to assume modes of conduct altogether unfamiliar to them.

In acting to protect her family's interests, a goal not at all incongruous with acceptable feminine roles, Elizabeth found herself in an unanticipated and, for her, previously unimaginable position of command and political engagement. Although politics and their personal repercussions were not news to her, she had been abroad when her family and friends were having most of their difficulties, receiving reports of the turmoil at a distance. She read the disturbing news about loyalist persecutions and the Boston Massacre in England, rather than witnessing these incidents herself. With the fighting at Lexington and Concord, everything changed: her relationships, responsibilities, and activities. As she put it in the immediate wake of the battle, "I have acted many parts in life but never imagen'd I shou'd arrive at the Muckle [i.e., great] honor of being a Generall."[14] For her, the beginning of the war demanded that she adopt an extraordinary new role, one that underlines the necessity of incorporating individual histories into a Revolutionary narrative that encompasses more than political decisions and troop movements.

Elizabeth's reversals in family fortunes and fluctuations in roles reveal the radical impact of the Revolution, the shock of which "reached into the deepest and most private human relations."[15] For her, the most intimate bond disrupted by the war was that with her husband. Once the Revolution began, Elizabeth found her personal relationships undermined by the stresses imposed by living in the midst of war. In such difficult circumstances, she turned to her own resources, rejecting the authority of men and following her own counsel repeatedly. During the crises of 1775 and later, Elizabeth acted on her own judgment, neither deferring to the advice of the men in her life nor backing down from choices she made that they considered less than perfect. What governed her was a careful calculation of the attendant financial repercussions and personal costs of any decision, as well as a confidence in her own wisdom. On friendly terms with colonial commanders as well as royal prisoners of war, Elizabeth thwarted male authority and ignored the popular will. Thus from time to time Elizabeth's challenges to contemporary mores earned her private and public censure.

As the war began, Elizabeth characterized her decision to stay in Cambridge primarily as one appropriate to a parent and housekeeper, despite her description of herself as a general. Contemplating a retreat from Cambridge, she weighed her "parental" responsibilities for the members of her family, including a number of servants and slaves. None of them would stay on the farm if she left. Aware that the "poor creatures" depended on her "for protection," she did "not chuse to disapoint them." So she determined to "protect them" as far as it was in her "power," feeling so confident of her ability to keep her household and its inhabitants safe that she asked her niece Dolly, with her two young children, to come to the farm and take her chances there.[16]

What makes Elizabeth's insistence on staying in Cambridge during the spring and summer of 1775 remarkable is that her husband Ralph and brother James, who were considered to be loyal to the

Crown, were both behind British lines in Boston. Elizabeth's brother, whose sympathies with the Crown were well known, had encountered patriot hostility earlier. For his efforts in the case of Captain Preston, the British officer tried in the wake of the Boston Massacre, James had been burnt in effigy.[17] Ralph initially had less compelling grounds for remaining in the occupied town. Throughout the war he struggled to preserve an uncommitted political stance, although his son, George, did volunteer for and serve with British forces during the conflict.[18] Ralph's other child, Susannah, was by association a loyalist. Her husband, John Linzee, was captain of the British man-of-war *Falcon*, which arrived in Boston on 16 April 1775, just in time for the beginning of the war.[19] Presumably it was the arrival of Susannah Linzee aboard this vessel that accounts for Ralph's presence in town when the fighting broke out. Ralph stayed in Boston afterward, apparently not even trying to come back to Cambridge.

The onset of war led to other marital separations among Elizabeth's circle. Unwillingly, Christian Barnes's husband, Henry, found himself confined within the occupied town. Anxious for his presence, Christian petitioned the committee of selectmen to advise her on how to procure Henry's return, trying to convince them that he never intended to stay in town. Although they promised her that she would be safe, Christian felt vulnerable to potential insults and wished for some sort of a written protection from colonial general Israel Putnam.[20] Christian thought Elizabeth, who was on friendly terms with the commander, might persuade him to send one. An encounter about two months earlier had given Christian and Henry good reason to worry about their countrymen's view of them. In February, two of General Gage's men, sent out as advance scouts on a reconnaissance mission, stopped at the Barnes's home in Marlborough for food and hospitality. Their presence incited local fury. Before the men had eaten a meal, they had to flee. The Committee of Safety appeared, searched the house, and informed the Barneses that they would destroy the house if the family harbored the enemy again.[21] After that incident, Elizabeth thought her friend should "fly" to Cambridge to join her before anything else happened. The treatment Christian might encounter if a regiment of British soldiers passed through the town made Elizabeth "very uneasy"; her known sympathies for the British might lead her to offer them aid that would inspire the townspeople's wrath. Although Elizabeth was "no coward," Elizabeth assured Christian that she would not put herself "in the power of a desperate people."[22]

Elizabeth's fears for her friend's safety proved true. Before April was over, Christian was terrified by a stranger at her door. Loading his musket, he demanded that Christian serve him dinner. Obeying his commands, Christian set the table with her best food and attempted to pacify him. Yet he insulted and abused her. After he finished eating, the man demanded a horse. "If I did not let him have one," Christian told Elizabeth, "he would blow my brains out."[23] Claiming to have orders from the military to procure one but not producing any such papers, the man frightened Christian so much that she ran into the store and locked the door behind her. Fortunately, passersby heard the man threatening to break the door open. They stopped him and then stayed with Christian until the intruder was gone. During these traumatic days, Henry could not leave Boston.

Like Christian, Elizabeth was without the protection of her husband and therefore more vulnerable than she would have been either in Boston or with him at her side in Cambridge. Initially, Elizabeth tried to reassure her friends that her situation was bearable. Indeed, the tone of hearty aplomb and goodwill that Elizabeth expressed in her writing was equally apparent in the flesh and buoyed the spirits of her companions. An officer from colonial headquarters, dispatched with written orders to check on her safety, visited the farm and told Elizabeth that she and her associates "were the happiest folks he had seen." They acted in some respects as though life were unchanged by recent events. Mild weather that spring had accelerated the agricultural calendar. At Elizabeth's direction, the family and servants were occupying their time with household chores, working in the garden, planting potatoes, and making plans for the corn crop. Despite her air of bravado, the toll of the April days evinced itself in the noticeably bigger and messier scrawl with which she closed one letter; her fading penmanship prompted her to add, "We are sleepy dont think Us drunk."[24] They drank only water and spruce beer.

The period of separation between Elizabeth and Ralph, which began in April and lasted over five months, served as a catalyst to increasing discord in their relationship. The main source of contention was whether Elizabeth should stay outside the occupied town or join her husband in Boston. Although Ralph told her he thought she was as safe in Cambridge as she could be in Boston, he was willing to defer to her opinion: "I know you are more capable of Judging for your Self than any Directions I can give."[25] Not only did Elizabeth follow her own judgment, she also tried to order her husband's movements. In late April, after she learned from General Putnam that Boston would be opened and all those who wished to leave would be allowed to do so, she urged Ralph to visit, telling him that his advice was "much wanted."[26] Even if the rumor proved false about the town's opening, she expressed confidence that he could get special leave to come to her. Despite this rather insistent letter, Ralph did not join her, claiming later that her note to him had been misdirected. Ralph's conduct angered Elizabeth. While she took pleasure, she assured him, in studying ways to increase his happiness, she doubted that he appreciated her efforts. Reminding Ralph that she was not one to complain, she proceeded to do so, listing her exertions on his behalf and her attempts to see him and consult with him about the farm, which, because of his repeated failure to respond, had been "all in vain."[27] Disturbed by her husband's seeming indifference to her fate, Elizabeth reviewed all his notes to her and concluded that she could discern Ralph's wishes, which were neither very reassuring nor affectionate. Clearly, he preferred that she stay in Cambridge rather than move to town. By early May, miscommunication fueled acrimony. Elizabeth thought that her letters to him had been "misrepresented," wishing that Ralph's friends had consented to his meeting her as she "earnestly desired." A face-to-face encounter would have helped immensely, preventing many, if not all their difficulties.[28] The fault was Ralph's, for he had taken other friends' recommendations rather than accede to her requests.

While waiting for advice from her husband, Elizabeth found that her residence in Cambridge made her vulnerable, as rebel troops briefly held her prisoner. Elizabeth learned that Job, a slave belonging to her husband, had told the troops a story that made her out to be some sort of foe to their cause. As a result they made her their prisoner, thereby preventing her from coming to the lines for a potential meeting with Ralph.[29] If she "had not been roused beyond reason to have acted an uncommon part" that day, Elizabeth believed that the encounter might "have proved fatal," as she confronted men who were doing "nothing" but their duty, "considering the story Job told them."[30] Trying to assuage and forestall the Continentals' anger, Elizabeth negotiated with them and made promises to persuade them that she was no enemy. She gave the troops use of her kitchen, the rooms above it, and several others, also pledging not to bolt with the farm's stock. After that terrifying incident she was more calm and acted as though she intended to stay in Cambridge for years, despite forming plans to move to Brush Hill or elsewhere. When her nephew offered to send wagons from Providence to help her move all the stock and property possible, she declined: "I had given my word, by that I must abide."[31]

The fact that Elizabeth gave her "word" to the rebels and cooperated with them indicates either that she was able to present herself in a political sense as her own person or that her reputation and rapport with colonial officials were sufficient to enable her to remain above the fray for a time. The promise not to leave Cambridge was hers, not her husband's, and may account for her name popping up in diaries of Continental soldiers stationed there. They referred to being on duty at "Madam Inman's" or "on guard at Mrs. Inman's with twenty-four men," not serving at Ralph Inman's house.[32] With large numbers of troops around her estate, Elizabeth was uncomfortable and sought reassurance from General Putnam. Clearly holding her in high esteem, he responded by posting guards nearby, providing her with written protections authorizing her to move in safety, and sending his son to stay with her. From the middle of May on, Daniel Putnam lodged in her house every night.[33] In addition, a Colonel Sargent was assigned to protect her. Yet her former equanimity had been shattered and she doubted she could secure a safe retreat if the need arose. Despite the presence of Colonel Sargent, "one of the best men" imaginable, Elizabeth worried that his military duties might suddenly call him away. "Then what will become of us God only knowes," she worried.[34]

As May wore on, Elizabeth's position in Cambridge began to look more precarious, as rumors flew that British reinforcements would arrive soon. From his vantage point in Boston, James emphasized the dangers of Elizabeth's situation, insisting that she could not, for her own safety or his peace of mind, stay outside Boston much longer. If a decisive battle took place, Cambridge would be affected. Regardless of who won, Cambridge would be "the first object," as colonists, whether they won or lost, would attack the houses of Tories. Either "elated pride or dispairing Rage" would lead to the destruction of the property of those who took "Sanctuary" in Boston, as did James and Ralph.[35] In short, their presence behind British lines jeopardized Elizabeth's safety as well as the security of family property in rebel territory, regardless of what leaders of the colonial army may have thought of Elizabeth personally. Contemporaries largely assumed that women did not exercise political judgment, much less hold views that differed from those of their husbands; thus, the Inman property was vulnerable. When women did act on political convictions that differed from those of the men in their families, the committees that confiscated Tory property became enmeshed in legal wrangling.[36]

In the face of mounting pressure and anxiety, Elizabeth decided to leave Cambridge, contemplating both Brush Hill and more distant locations as alternatives. Ralph urged her to "follow [her] own Inclinations." As far as the care of the Cambridge estate went, he felt unable to give her "any advice," arguing that if she could not derive any benefits from the farm, she should not expend any more effort on it. "Let it take its chance with the rest," he told her.[37] Whether Ralph felt unable to advise Elizabeth, given the chaos of the times, or anticipated that she would be unlikely to heed his recommendations cannot be determined. What is clear, however, is that his seeming unconcern continued to fuel Elizabeth's dissatisfaction with him. Repeatedly, Elizabeth tried to persuade her husband of the difficulties she faced while expressing her desire "to be settled in a family way again." Believing residence in Cambridge to be untenable in the long run, Elizabeth proposed a more drastic step than simply relocating in the Boston area. She suggested that she and Ralph could simply leave New England altogether. If he could buy or rent some land elsewhere, she could "move bag & bagage & meet [him] at any Port." Moving into Boston did not make sense, given the expense of providing for everyone. In the midst of considering where and when to move, Elizabeth also tried to plan for the care of the farm's crops and stock. These various issues required Ralph's input. "I earnestly intreat you to consider what is to be done as their is not time to lose," she insisted. His response would determine her actions.[38]

Elizabeth's plans and pleas for advice met with differing responses from her husband and brother. Ralph suggested a move to Point Shirley and thought she could save the farm animals by driving them to Chelsea, whereas James adamantly opposed the plan, insisting that as soon as she made an attempt to save the stock by putting it out of reach of the army or its friends, "so soon will it be driven off or destroyed — things are now come to such Extremity the Stock . . . is scarcely an object of attention." James expected that the war would end quickly. Inexperienced colonists, with equally untrained generals, would soon be routed. Given his expectations, James not surprisingly continued to advise Elizabeth to stay outside the town. At Brush Hill she would be "most comfortable" and as safe "as any where, even as safe as in town."[39] James doubted the security of residing in Boston. Like many other town dwellers, he believed that Boston might be shelled or set on fire from within by Whig elements. In such unsettled times no location could be entirely satisfactory. Following her brother's counsel, Elizabeth began the "most disagreeable task" of moving her possessions "from a once delightfull home" to Brush Hill.[40] Equally reluctant to leave Cambridge, Dolly, who had been with her aunt for some time, was nonetheless hopeful that relocating would make her uncle Inman and the rest of their friends "Easy."[41] Their move would be a gradual one.

In the meantime, in her husband's absence Elizabeth acted in his stead, overseeing crops, financial matters, and business decisions, all the while frustrated by his unhelpful behavior. If he had not denied her the privilege of coming into Boston, she would have done so the night of "Job's affair," regardless of having given her word to rebel troops. When Ralph advised her "by all means to stay" in Cambridge, Elizabeth told him she thought him cruel in urging this course.[42] Instead of doing as she wished, she stayed on her own and without adequate male protection. Although she had some security from Putnam and Sargeant's presence, Elizabeth continued to be ill at ease, partly because Ralph failed to help her or even be sympathetic to her plight. By mid-June, she no longer refrained from telling him of her frustration and disappointment. Throughout April and May, weeks of uncertainty and fear, while Elizabeth worked to fulfill what she saw as her responsibilities to her spouse and his estate — acting the "good wife" — Ralph, in her view, failed to uphold his part of the bargain.[43] Although she had suffered through one instance of rebel wrath, she seemed to think she might not survive the next few months. Elizabeth closed a cutting letter by telling Ralph that she was glad he was in town, safe with other refugees.[44]

This bitter volley provoked an effusive apology from Ralph. "It never was my Inclination to be separated for a moment," he declared, "unless it was your own choice." As to the advice that he had given or failed to give, he told her he was trying "to Comply with what [he] thought would be agreeable to [her]." Nor did he wish her to believe that his life in Boston was one of ease in comparison with hers. Worn down, he could not continue much longer in the distressed condition he had endured in her absence.[45] By early summer, life in Boston had become difficult. The siege had compelled growing numbers of loyalists to take refuge in the city, and shortages had compounded their hardships.[46] In this military crisis, the scarcity of fresh meat was such that it was given only to the wounded. As large numbers of injured men lay dying, disease ran rampant through the town. Living in the midst of such disorder, Ralph found his situation distressing. He needed Elizabeth and argued that her arrival was extremely desirable. "I have wrote you & now do from my soul Request that you will come to Town," he pleaded. As to the farm, he relinquished his interest in any profits the year's crops might generate. He did not care what happened to the hay or the stock. Those servants she could not dispose of satisfactorily she should bring to town. "I will bear any hardship to have you with me," he wrote. "If we cannot remain Quiet here I will goe wherever you please, I know we shall meet with friends in any part of the Globe." For his part, he declared, he could say that he had "injured no man, nor given cause to make . . . an Enemy." Ralph tried to recapture his position in Elizabeth's good graces. "I assure you I can content myself in any little Hovell that will afford me a Bare Sustinence, to have you with me," he professed, "dont think of removing any where but to Town." She should forget every other plan she had considered. Closing this letter full of sentiment, he added, "I cannot think of your removing any where else to be kept longer Absent from me — I am forever yours." The postscript reiterated once more his wish to have her in town: "It was always mine had I not mistook your meaning."[47]

Upon receiving Ralph's moving and "very affectionate" missive,

Elizabeth acknowledged her gratitude and former deep distress but did not finally follow his advice. Telling him that she was obliged to him for clearing up the misunderstanding, she confided her earlier pain and suggested that if she had erred, it was "in Judgement." Believing that he valued his farm more than her presence made her inattentive to her own safety when others told her she "was in a place of great danger." To such warnings she had responded stoically, announcing with a cheerful countenance that everyone could "die but once" and that she was a predestinarian. Coupled with a lack of concern for herself, this belief made it possible for Elizabeth to operate with "no personal fear," even when she stood "before a Company" that made her a prisoner "in a formal manner."[48]

With her doubts over Ralph's feelings for her assuaged, Elizabeth was once again inspired to ignore his advice and to evaluate monetary considerations in determining her moves. She decided it was not financially feasible to bring the servants into town and thought she could take care of the farm adequately. If she did not think it likely she could save the crop, she told Ralph, "I would immediately go to town & convince you how ready I was to obey." But "obey" she did not. Her "opinion," which she proceeded to offer, was that she should sleep at Brush Hill but come to Cambridge during the day until the crops were harvested. If she came to Boston, all her effort would be pointless, and the whole year's produce would be lost. Given the difficulties she had already gone through to preserve it, she was confident that "a little while longer" would accomplish her design. Her "design," rather than Ralph's wishes or advice, ultimately determined her decisions. After explaining why she was not ready to follow her husband's counsel, Elizabeth apologized for giving Ralph "so much uneasyness." She was sorry that her words had unsettled and disturbed him, but she felt she had no choice: "I thought as times were it was necesery to speak my mind." Being frank relieved some of her own stress: "When I have done that my heart is as ease."[49] Elizabeth thus intimated that she might normally have held her tongue and kept her views to herself. In the novel situation in which she found herself, however, she deemed it necessary to claim authority and voice for herself to challenge Ralph and his behavior.

Events beyond Elizabeth's control soon prompted her hurried retreat from the Cambridge farm. After two months of relative peace in the wake of the battle of Lexington and Concord, British and colonial forces clashed at the Battle of Bunker Hill on 17 June. The evening before, General Putnam had given his son special orders. In charge of Elizabeth's nighttime safety for the previous several weeks, Daniel was told to go "to Mrs. Inman's as usual" but not to return to the camp in the morning. Instead, he should stay all day with Mrs. Inman, in case the family wanted his aid. "If they find it necessary to leave the house," Putnam told his son, "you must go with them where they go." This order worried Daniel, who suggested that his father might need his assistance "much more than Mrs. Inman." Unmoved by his son's pleadings, the general insisted Daniel go to the Cambridge farm. Staying with Elizabeth and her family, Daniel was restless, unable to take any "interest in the conversation of her nieces or the maternal kindness" of Elizabeth herself. Retiring early to his bedchamber, he spent a sleepless night seated before a window facing Charlestown.[50] It is unlikely his hostess slept any better. With troops parading on the Cambridge Common and then marching that night, Elizabeth would have had good cause for concern.

The following day Elizabeth spent trying to ascertain troop movements and readying her family for flight. According to Daniel Putnam, she had been expecting that the British would send their men from the bottom of the Boston Common and land them near where the troops had begun their march to Lexington (figure 13). "Her attention had been chiefly directly to that quarter," he recalled. A "furious discharge of musketry," however, made it clear that the troops had left the town by another route and "were engaged in a battle, the issue or consequences of which could not be foreseen." With the percussive, explosive sounds of artillery filling the air as the day drew to a close, Elizabeth debated whether she could stay in Cambridge through the night. Not knowing how the battle would end and "dreading the horrors that might overwhelm her family in the night," Elizabeth began to pack. Only when she learned after sunset that the British "had gained possession of Charlestown Heights, with a loss on both sides that none pretended to calculate," did Elizabeth make her decision. With that territory under control, the British might move on to attack the headquarters of the American army in Cambridge. Well aware that her family would be directly in the line of fire, Elizabeth "hastily and but imperfectly" prepared to leave. As soon as

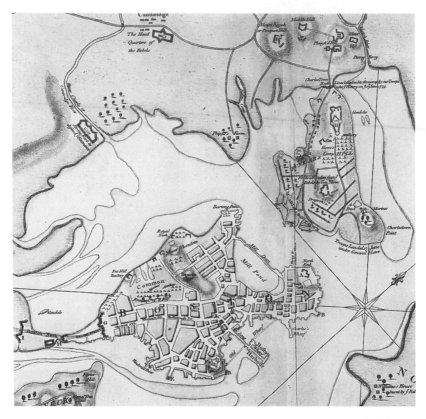

13   *A plan of Boston, and its environs, shewing the true situation of his majesty's army. And also those of the rebels . . . ,* 1775. Courtesy, Massachusetts Historical Society, Boston.

they were ready, Elizabeth, her family, and Daniel Putnam "passed through the scene of confusion."[51] Others on the road, some of them survivors of the battle, told the party of refugees that General Putnam had survived. Relieved by this news, Daniel stayed with his charges until they reached Brush Hill after midnight. From this distance, safely removed from the theater of war, Elizabeth gave Daniel permission to return immediately to his father in Cambridge.

A few days after Elizabeth vacated the farm, the rebels turned the once gracious Inman estate into General Putnam's headquarters. Both the general's regiment and troops from Connecticut occupied the property.[52] The Inman farm was ideally located for the Continentals' purposes. On the outskirts of Cambridge, with a clear view of Boston, the property had extensive grounds and expansive buildings. The construction of barracks began promptly. Indeed, soldiers built so many temporary wood structures for themselves that the countryside was quickly denuded of its trees. The house became known as "Barrack number one"; the property itself became the temporary home of 3,460 soldiers.[53] This turn of events underlines the remarkable and unique position of Elizabeth Murray Campbell Smith Inman in the history of this era. Within a decade, the armies that opposed each other during the Revolution both used her property as their base, the British soldiers being housed in "Smith's barracks," the sugar-manufacturing building of her second husband, at the time of the Boston Massacre and the colonial forces occupying the estate of her third husband at the beginning of the war.

Removed from this scene, Elizabeth thought that by residing in Milton she would keep her family safe and more comfortable and still be able to go to the Cambridge farm during the day to keep an eye on the crops, thus fulfilling her plans and presumably supporting her husband's financial interests as well. She was mistaken in thinking that she and Ralph were fully in agreement. Their reconciliation disintegrated completely at the end of July when Elizabeth learned that Ralph was planning on sailing with John Rowe and his wife for England, with or without her.[54] Other friends were preparing to go to England as well, ultimately becoming part of a large loyalist exile community. Apparently Ralph had tired of waiting for Elizabeth to join him and no longer wished to endure the hardships of life in Boston. "Words" could not describe Elizabeth's "astonishment" when she received his message that he intended to go to London. Shocked by his willingness to be separated from her by an ocean, Elizabeth upbraided him: "If this is a return for the many anxious & fatiguing days I have had[,] I leave it to your better Judgement & will endeavour to submit." Sarcasm sharpened her expression when she related hearing of Ralph's complaint that he had received "but little money since he came to town." The implication was that she had deprived him of necessary income. Sending him an order for one hundred pounds, Elizabeth scornfully urged her husband to cast off his cares, telling him that "anxiety is very bad for the health." He would need plenty of health, as well as money and good spirits, for "seeing & being seen in England."⁵⁵ In short, Ralph needed to be in good shape, physically and financially, to enjoy the leisure and public entertainments that had figured largely in her 1769–71 visit to Great Britain. Her bitterness as she imagined his life abroad was palpable.

Elizabeth's distress about Ralph's imminent departure clearly had many sources. Ralph seemed willing to make their separation permanent. In addition, he treated her in ways that she found thoughtless and unacceptable. As he prepared to leave New England, Ralph compiled a list of debts owed to him and sent it to her with a request that she collect interest on them during his absence. This action Elizabeth found insulting. He had asked her to take care of his affairs yet had failed to enclose a power of attorney for her. Without one, she would be able to do nothing. "No doubt you'll leave one with some friend before you sail," she remarked somewhat snidely. Eventually, Ralph gave one to his brother-in-law James, who then forwarded it to Elizabeth some weeks later. Disgusted by Ralph's selfishness and disinterest in her fate, Elizabeth told her recalcitrant spouse that he need not worry at all about her. He should be aware that she was "not anxious" about a maintenance; experience had taught her that water, gruel, and salt, along with a bit of meat or a few greens or roots were "enough" for her to survive.⁵⁶

Elizabeth was further outraged by the interpretation of her actions that she thought Ralph was spreading among their friends in Boston. She was sure he had misrepresented her conduct—her refusal to come to town—to justify his own behavior and planned desertion. "I think they ought to hear my reasons before they condemn me," she averred. Presumably his friends thought she was failing in her duty to him. But she saw only the inconsistency of his advice to her. He first had told her to stay in the country rather than come to town. Then he informed her that provisions were scarce in town and he could command only seventy pounds a year. After telling her of the shortages—of goods and currency—he invited her to bring their family into town, a family that had required over three hundred pounds per year, as well as the produce of the farm, to support. Clearly, he had not thought through the situation fully. Her decision not to follow his advice should not reflect poorly on her, she believed.⁵⁷ Rumors circulating in Boston apparently intimated that Elizabeth failed to move into town not only because she was a disobedient wife but also because she was guilty of more serious political crimes, specifically of acting as a conduit of rebel correspondence. In response to that charge, she simply explained that she could not deny those who asked her to handle their letters, arguing implicitly that such a purely personal action as forwarding letters should not be construed as a political act. (By the same token that she passed letters to those of differing political bents, Elizabeth benefited from rebels' willingness to convey personal correspondence. That summer, Samuel Adams asked fellow patriot James Warren to serve as a courier and deliver letters to "Mrs. Inman" from William Hooper, her niece Annie's husband, who was then serving as a North Carolina delegate to the Continental Congress meeting in Philadelphia.)[58] These insinuations led Elizabeth to beg her husband to let her "know what else" she was accused of doing and prompted her to declare her willingness to explain herself fully. In the course of detailing her reasons for refusing to move to Boston, she announced that she would "with pleasure account for every action" that she remembered "since the year seventeen hundred & twenty six," the year of her birth.[59]

Trying to smooth over the discord that threatened to flare into open hostility, James tried to placate and advise his sister. Describing Ralph as so upset by the tone of Elizabeth's highly critical letter that he could not answer it, James took it on himself to respond to some of its attacks. Addressing his remarks to Dolly, then residing with Elizabeth at Brush Hill, James suggested that "1726 was at distance enough to learn to make allowance for the vexation the times give." They should all be especially hesitant to criticize the behavior and decisions of anyone — in other words, Ralph — who was "quite out of his usual mode of life & hamper'd in business." James hoped that all the family would judge the conduct of their nearest and dearest generously and interpret their actions as favorably as possible.[60] While advising Elizabeth indirectly about how to deal with her spouse by giving him the benefit of the doubt, James also urged her to be careful about perceptions of her behavior. After James received permission from the commander in chief of British forces to go to the lines to meet his daughter and sister, he sent them a detailed account of his plan and instructions about their own conduct. A

British officer would escort James and his daughter Betsy to the lines, while other officers would accompany them "to be Eye & Ear Witness of all that passes." In urging his sister Elizabeth and daughter Dolly to make the appointment, James suggested that they "use the same precaution, on their side: the Times require it."[61] Exercising such caution might preclude further aspersions about their loyalties.

The political dimensions of Elizabeth's personal choices continued to cloud her family life as the summer of 1775 progressed. With Ralph readying himself to leave America and Elizabeth fully prepared to stay behind, she took steps to complete her family circle in other ways, encouraging James to send Betsy out of Boston to join her in the countryside. Aware that his daughter was anxious to be with Elizabeth, James worried about the political ramifications of such an act and hesitated to accede to his sister's and daughter's wishes. "It is thought very odd," he pointed out, "that while other Tories are loudly complaining of the restraints & hardships their families suffer in the Country, I should voluntarily throw my Daughter into the same Snare." Indeed, such a decision could harm him. "If she fare better than others, the Inference will not be to my advantage." Suspicion from both sides would overshadow his movements and complicate his life in Boston even more.[62] Briefly, James considered sending Betsy to England, a plan that Elizabeth quickly vetoed. Urging James to think about his daughter Dolly, who, along with her two young sons, had moved from Cambridge to Brush Hill with her, Elizabeth argued that if Betsy were not employing her time well in Boston, "she wou'd be usefull to her Sister & Children" in Milton.[63] Even in the context of the Revolutionary crisis, Elizabeth evaluated feminine activities on the spectrum of idleness and industry. And it was on the grounds of sisterly affection and familial duty that Elizabeth swayed her brother. Finally, although Betsy had her father's consent, she left Boston against James's "inclination." Once again, Elizabeth's judgment with regard to her nieces took precedence over her brother's parental will.

After Betsy left Boston, James's fears came true. His neighbors held him in "a State of Diffidence & Suspicion" because his family was able "to make their Quarters good in the Country."[64] The rebel distrust that had earlier fallen on Elizabeth and her household in Cambridge because of James's and Ralph's presence in Boston was now mirrored by that of Tory denizens of the occupied town who suspected Elizabeth and the rest of the family of rebel leanings. Indeed, James found himself on the receiving end of political insults when he attempted to apply for a pass to come to the lines to meet his children. Only after repeated efforts did he obtain one, which carried the "mortifying restraint" that he could not pass the lines or communicate with any friend who met him.[65] At the same time, James was not sure how much longer he or anyone else could remain within the town. Rumors were afoot that the British planned "to lay this town in Ashes and to decamp with the Tories toward New York, where there will be more elbow Room and more of the Country people to Countenance & assist the Kings Army."[66] The British continually hoped that colonists in another region would rise up in wholehearted support of the Crown, one miscalculation among many that contributed to their eventual defeat.

Ironically, at around the same time that Betsy Murray left Boston, Elizabeth went into the besieged town, not finally to "obey" her husband's directives but to assist her niece Anne Murray. Since her sister Polly's departure for England in May 1774, Anne had been running the shop, a task she did not welcome. Elizabeth had established her nieces in a corner shop where they had been very successful.[67] While Polly was clearly in charge of running the shop and Anne and Jackie initially devoted their time to making up hats and other finery, eventually all three waited on customers. Like Elizabeth, the Cumings, Jane Eustis, and many other women retailers, Polly, Anne, and Jackie sold fashionable imports.[68] Business had poured in apace. As beneficiaries of Elizabeth's assistance and largesse, Polly, Anne, and Jackie appeared poised to earn their livelihoods as shopkeepers, doing so well that their performance inspired acclaim. Polly was expected to make "good all the Prophesies . . . viz.: That She would turn out the Notable dilligent & Cleaver Shopkeeper."[69] Confiding her delight, Christian Barnes expressed great satisfaction with the young women's progress and had high hopes for their future achievements. She told Elizabeth that she sincerely hoped that the young women's undertakings would "be crowned with success for their own sakes, as well as for the Honour of the Sex." As she declared with remarkable gender consciousness, "Who shall say we have not equal abilitys with the Men when Girls of 18 years of age discover such great capacitys?"[70] Barnes's assertion that their youth, rapid acquisition of shop-keeping skills, and early promise of financial acumen attested to feminine ability prefigured the claims and demands of reformers who began to reconsider the content and purpose of women's education in the last quarter of the century and urge its redesign for more practical and civic ends.[71] Unfortunately, Polly proved to be much more adept than her sister at shopkeeping. After she left, it was with great difficulty that Elizabeth had convinced Anne that she could tend the business on her own. "Many tears" were shed, reported Elizabeth; some might think her a "cruel monster to plague the poor Child so." Although she doubted her own abilities, Anne apparently overcame her fears enough for Elizabeth to declare her niece very industrious and busy with her needle and altogether "highly pleased with her faculty."[72] Polly, who worried about Anne's shop skills and stamina in her absence, was delighted in early 1775 when Anne made better remittance than she had expected, making Polly "less anxious" than she had been "about her success."[73]

As 1775 wore on, however, Anne grew desperately unhappy, despite Elizabeth's encouragement and Polly's praise. Missing her sister terribly, Anne felt lost, incapable of handling the business herself, and exposed to all sorts of humiliation. Depressed and ill at ease, Anne could list her grievances easily, although she suspected that few would immediately sympathize. She asked her cousin Betsy to try to imagine being in her place, separated from "the best of Parents" and from other connections whom she missed. "You will say, & Justly, that I left them by my own desire," Anne admitted. "My motives were such as I cannot but think good." But she could not help her feelings, especially when she encountered any unpleasantness. When her sister was present, she "felt it less." Polly had consoled her. Since her absence, however, Anne "met with more disagreeable sensations" than she would have otherwise. "I have at times been so chagrin'd," she confessed, "that I have thought my resolution would not hold me up." Nearly distraught, Anne nonetheless felt conscious of the debt and obligation she had to Elizabeth and felt the "warmest gratitude" to her. "Amid every mortification I look with wonder upon her goodness," she avowed, "let me be unhappy, but let me never be ungrateful."[74] Part of Anne's problem was that she felt the business was poorly run in Polly's absence. She had only one assistant, "a Black

Man lame in hands and feet who could make figures on a slate in the way of accounts," and noted that "but for the weekly resource of a visit to Brush Hill or Cambridge I know not what might have been the consequence."[75]

In direct contrast to the views championed by Elizabeth, Anne thought shopkeeping humiliating—inappropriate for someone with her background, class, and education—and attributed her difficulties to this fact. In later years, she portrayed herself at the time she emigrated as "a childish girl of sixteen taken from a boarding school."[76] While Polly had quickly become a capable businesswoman, Anne never embraced shopkeeping. "Painful scenes" stood out in her memory. "The great part of *my* residence in Boston was one of most severe mortification," she recalled, "a plan of life for which from Nature and education I was totally unfit, was marked out for me by those whose will had ever governed my conduct." With no will of her own and little experience of the world, Anne had come to America. "Never was a Girl of 16 so much a Child as myself in person and mind," she remembered, "yet with this childishness I was not insensible to the consequences of loss of Caste."[77]

Although resentful about her lot and unwilling initially to disobey her aunt or parents, Anne ultimately waged her own revolt, questioning her elders' authority and decisions. A couple of years before, Polly and Anne's commercial successes had led the Murrays to consider shopkeeping for their younger sister as well. In 1773 John had "pushed Charlotte forward in her Arithmetic," according to Elizabeth's wishes, and intended as soon as she was "fit for book-keeping" to have her instructed in it as well.[78] As a result of her older sisters' commercial efforts, Charlotte Murray was being trained differently from how they had been, with shopkeeping directly in view. This willingness to modify Charlotte's education and embrace migration for her future points to the Murrays' readiness to adapt their child-rearing techniques and to their ongoing view of geographic mobility as a viable means of achieving self-sufficiency and economic mobility, a strategy that applied to both sexes. When she came to America, Charlotte would not be as unprepared as Anne felt herself behind the counter. Upon learning of this plan, Anne felt compelled to challenge it: "I then begged that no more of the family might be placed in the state of degradation I experienced." Rather than have her sister participate in her "irreparable humiliation," Anne offered to give some of her earnings to Charlotte, even suggesting an annuity.[79] Whether it was Anne's pleading or the disruption of the war that held more sway in preventing her family from sending Charlotte to Boston is unknown.

The business, a questionable success in the months after Polly went home, declined in the summer of 1775. Bereft of maternal supervision, sisterly support, and her Aunt Elizabeth's guidance at the beginning of the siege, Anne complained of overwhelming depression and abandoned the shop. Early that summer, Ralph told Elizabeth she would not have been surprised "at the Ladys Quitting her Business had [she] seen her so determined." Anne told her uncle that she hated her business and could not submit to doing it any longer. With Elizabeth outside the town, Ralph tried to persuade Anne to keep to her work. His words, however, "had but little weight in the Scale."[80] James confirmed Anne's distaste for her trade, describing her as "town Sick" and therefore "quite unfit to attend Business." Dreading getting worse, Anne pleaded with her uncle for permission to make a restoring visit to Newport. Although James thought it would have been better for his niece to cross the lines and join Elizabeth instead, he gave Anne his consent; he dared not withhold it "lest she should have suffer'd." In his mind it was fairly clear that Anne would be incapable of attending to the shop for some time.[81] How Elizabeth received such news can only be imagined. After putting her efforts and resources into making a life of self-sufficiency possible for her nieces, she learned from a distance how bankrupt her dreams had become. Her husband was preparing to abandon her, she had been forced to flee Cambridge, Polly was separated from her by an ocean, and Anne was desperate to leave.

By August it had become clear that the business was falling apart and that other plans had to be made both for Anne and for disposal of the stock. Elizabeth's first thought was that they should simply sell the goods wholesale. James quickly disabused her of that notion, telling her that they would not "fetch ten Shillings for the pound." He suggested that if Anne, the "merchant of them," could "be less engaged & more attentive to the business," then it might be worthwhile to wait until winter to sell them.[82] By then, "goods of her sort" would be "scarcer & of course more saleable." Within the besieged town, supplies were dwindling. Regardless of what plan was followed, Anne had to be involved. James needed her assistance to make up the accounts; moreover, his niece needed to busy herself "to check some improper dangling."[83] How attentive she might be was uncertain, however. Compounding Anne's rebelliousness was her romantic situation. Anne had fallen in love but was trying to be discreet enough not to attract too much notice. Informing Elizabeth of the liaison, Ralph insisted that Anne's matters of the heart required his wife's involvement.[84] After receiving these reports from her husband and her brother about Anne's preference for keeping company rather than her shop, Elizabeth concluded that Anne's situation demanded her presence.

In a clear indication of where her primary loyalties lay, Elizabeth decided in September to come to Boston to take care of Anne, when neither her brother's advice nor her husband's pleading to join them had moved her to do so before. Later events revealed she had gotten permission to come in under the pretense of taking care of an ill spouse, using the excuse of fulfilling her wifely duties to mask her true intentions. Surprising her brother and husband when she appeared at the end of the month, Elizabeth quickly resolved to assist Anne and her lover, William Powell, in their plans to marry and leave America. Apologizing to James for deciding "upon Ann's going Home without first consulting" him, Elizabeth intimated that she had compelling reasons for taking this step and promised to explain them eventually.[85] As a result of Elizabeth's renewed involvement in her affairs, both personal and financial, Anne soon found herself hard at work as October began, writing accounts for the shop from morning to night. Complaining of her long hours, Anne despaired of a prompt release, imagining that a month's labor would not be enough to finish her task.[86] Within a week, however, she had sailed for England.

For the young lovers, Elizabeth paved the way to marriage. Although Anne's betrothed did not ask Elizabeth "to become an agent in the matter," he pleaded with her not to oppose the match. Anne would "be satisfied" if she gave her consent and "the world" would "remain ignorant" of Elizabeth's knowledge of their actions.[87] They needed to marry before they journeyed to England, home to both their families—who would normally be involved in granting permission for the match—because the crossing itself might require William to assist Anne in ways he would otherwise be unable to do with propriety. Elizabeth agreed that they should marry. Profusely, William thanked Elizabeth for her goodness, feeling overwhelmed by her assistance. Once the marriage was solemnized, the two prepared to embark. To hide the news from those on shore, Anne boarded a ship bound for England under her maiden name, and William pretended that he was only escorting the vessel a short distance. Shortly after they sailed, however, the "world" discovered Elizabeth's role. William felt terrible about the news: "I feel with pain how much you must have sufferd from the idle Tongues of a misjudging People when it was known that you was privy to my Elopement, as I find it is stiled in Boston."[88] Braving public and private censure, Elizabeth assumed the role of the head of the family in this instance, as she had in many others.

In the aftermath of Anne and William's departure, Elizabeth moved about with some freedom in the fall of 1775. She was in Cambridge in early November and then back in Boston a few days later. Betsy and Dolly briefly had some ability to cross the lines as well. Betsy attended a ball in Boston, which Elizabeth also invited Dolly to come to if she wished.[89] But before long, Elizabeth was confined to Boston. She could not leave, nor would General Howe, the commander who had replaced Gage after his removal, even permit her to go to the lines to see Dolly and Betsy, both living at the Brush Hill farm.

With Elizabeth staying in the occupied town against her will, the members of a Milton committee decided to seize family property there. Dolly, who had been taking care of the Brush Hill farm on her own, objected strongly and petitioned the Massachusetts Council and House of Representatives for a redress of her grievances. According to her, the men thought themselves "obliged by the Resolve of Congress of June 21st last to take [Elizabeth's] effects." Dolly protested their plans, presenting Elizabeth's actions as the result of colonial leaders' advice. "During the Troubles of last Summer . . . Elizabeth remained in Cambridge till such time as the Danger became so eminent that she was advised by General Putnam and Others to remove to some more distant place for Safety." Taking this advice, she had moved property from Cambridge to Brush Hill. Her "unfortunate" trip into Boston should not render her an absentee, a loyalist whose property was subject to confiscation.[90] Massachusetts laws regarding confiscation protected married women's interests in the war only if they dissociated themselves from loyalist husbands. By going to Boston, Elizabeth was once again associated with her Tory spouse. Massachusetts laws were unusually radical in comparison with those of other colonies, where it was assumed that the wives of loyalist husbands had no political opinions.[91]

Dolly argued that she herself had every right to retain possession of Brush Hill, first, because her aunt had been denied permission to return to Milton and, second, because the resolves prohibited seizure of occupied estates. As the occupant, Dolly believed herself on solid ground in claiming her rights and asked the government for clarification of the policy, to remove any confusion on the part of the committee. She had remained at Brush Hill to protect her family property—just as Elizabeth had stayed at Cambridge—and was thereby "demonstrating, at real personal risk, a conviction that the rebel government would live up to its promises" and a confidence that the government would succeed.[92] Ultimately, the committee did not take action against her or the property. Dolly had successfully petitioned the government, assuming a public, political profile and distinguishing herself as a property holder and responsible woman.[93]

As 1776 began, problems with communication and movement across the lines continued as the Murrays found themselves split between territory controlled by rebels and a town occupied by the British army. Although Betsy and Dolly were able to go to the lines, they were prohibited from speaking to their father and could only pass letters to him. While frustrated by these constraints, James urged his daughters to come again as soon and as often as possible. Their "healthy and chearful Countenances" would console him. "Your very looks will be a feast to your old Father, tho' not a Word pass," he told them.[94] Despite being unable to communicate directly with his daughters, James hoped to assist them by sending them anything they might need from within the town. "I know, from your experience," he wrote, "that there is politeness & humanity enough, *on your Side*, to secure the safe delivery" of whatever he might send.[95] His difficulties with royal authorities in Boston made him critical of their humanity.

Within a few months, as the first winter of the war faded, the situation changed dramatically once again when colonial forces prepared to drive the British from Boston or, if need be, to lay waste to the town. In early March, with frigid weather still prevailing, Continental troops made baskets that they filled with snow and sprayed with water. Overnight, using these icy bulwarks, two thousand troops constructed fortifications on Dorchester Heights, hills just to the south of the town, and put in place cannon hauled overland at tremendous effort from Fort Ticonderoga, in New York.[96] As the sixth anniversary of the Boston Massacre dawned, British commander General Howe was confronted with a new menace and quickly recognized the superior tactical position of the rebels. With heavy artillery, the Americans could easily shell Boston, the fortifications on Castle Island, as well as much of the fleet lying at anchor. Although Howe ordered an attack on Washington's position, a storm dispersed his ships, and he began preparations to decamp.

As the British army readied itself to abandon Boston, the town was in a state of chaos created by the bad behavior of the troops and the panic of the loyalist inhabitants. Although under strict orders to conduct themselves well, the evacuating British soldiers plundered houses and shops, adding further damage to a town that had grown increasingly unkempt during the siege. Troops had used the Old South Meeting House to exercise their horses indoors, and they had chopped down the Liberty Tree, the symbol of early patriot protests. Over the previous year, as they struggled to keep warm, those within the town — soldier and civilian alike — had torn down fences for firewood. With many inhabitants gone, gardens were wild, streets dirty, and buildings in disrepair. As the troops wreaked havoc in the days before their departure, loyalists who were apprehensive of retaliation from Continental troops hurried to pack their possessions and abandon Boston with the king's forces. With Boston in shambles, the British troops finally left on 17 March 1776 (thus giving the city the unique American holiday of Evacuation Day).

Among the thousand colonists who left Boston with the British were some of Elizabeth's family and friends. Her brother James and his wife decided to flee with the army to Halifax, Nova Scotia, where the British had determined that the loyalists would be safe. In his family party were Elizabeth's shopkeeping protégés Ame and Elizabeth Cuming.[97] (Moving to Halifax, however, did not signal the end of their commercial ventures; they were extremely successful in business in their new home. Some of the family's friends also took Polly and Anne Murray's goods with them to Halifax. Over the course of the next few years, reports of their sale trickled down to Elizabeth.)[98] In the wake of the evacuation, Washington and his troops entered Boston, encountering those colonists who had stayed behind — some of them with loyalist leanings — and the scourge of smallpox.

While her brother and friends had fled with British forces, Elizabeth chose to remain behind, negotiating the delicate position of one with both loyalist and rebel associations. Despite the fact that her son-in-law, Captain Linzee, served the British and her brother was a notable Tory, her nephews in Rhode Island joined the American army and her niece Anne Hooper's husband was in the Continental Congress. With such bonds, Elizabeth managed to remain on good terms with colonial military leaders. Indeed, a few days after the evacuation, she and Ralph dined with General Putnam at John Rowe's home. (Like many others torn by the conflict, Rowe ultimately chose the colonial side.)[99] This intimate encounter with a representative of the highest ranks of the colonial army suggests a kind of friendliness that in some ways transcended politics or perhaps the murkiness of loyalties in the midst of a civil war. While her husband Ralph, for example, was Rowe's brother-in-law, he had served as a former member of the king's council and an addresser of Hutchinson — that is, one who had signed an address expressing appreciation for Hutchinson's service. For that act, Ralph was arrested in 1776, an event that placed his property in Cambridge in limbo.[100]

As the American forces celebrated their victory over the British, they left Cambridge, vacating the Inman estate for a time. Anxious to reclaim the property, Betsy Murray and a niece of Christian Barnes, presumably at Elizabeth's direction, returned to the property. They stayed in the house, "just as it was left by the soldiery," without any of the things they needed to be comfortable, except for one bed and a servant. After serving as a military installation, the estate looked awful. The locust trees that shaded the roads leading to the farm, as well as the willows that surrounded its pond, had been cut down to meet the troops' lumber needs. Stripped of all of the beauty and elegance that it possessed before, the place resembled "an unfrequented desert." More worrisome than the appearance of the farm was the vulnerability of its inhabitants. Residing in Cambridge once again, Betsy and her companion lived "in constant fear" that some outrage would be committed against them if their connection to Ralph Inman became known. His politics cast a shadow on the entire family. To try to avoid discovery while occupying the house, they kept Betsy's name out of their business dealings.[101]

As often as she could, Elizabeth managed to come to Cambridge to see her niece and friend. The two young women found Elizabeth's conduct a source of inspiration and enjoyed playing hostess to her when she visited her former home. Christian's niece thought their actions had an air of absurdity during these encounters. "You would really be diverted, could you give a peep when Mrs. Inman visits us," she told her aunt, "to see Betsey & I resigning our broken chairs & teacups, and dipping the water out of an iron skillet into the pot as cheerfully as if we were using a silver urn." Their good humor was almost perplexing. "I cannot tell what it is owing to, unless it is seeing Mrs. Inman in such charming spirits, that prevents our being truly miserable." Nor should anyone pity their patroness for her difficulties: "Tell her friends in England not to lament her being in America at this period, for she in now in her proper element, having an opportunity of exerting her benevolence for those who have neither Spirits or ability to do for themselves." In her view, Elizabeth was like no one else: "No (other) woman could do as she does with impunity, for she is above the little fears and weaknesses which are the inseparable companions of most of our sex." Indeed, from Elizabeth's conduct "one would imagine . . . that all was peace and harmony."[102]

Within a month's time it had become impossible to pretend that tranquillity prevailed. The Cambridge Committee of Correspondence insisted on taking charge of the Inman property. The estate passed on to the Provincial Congress, which rented it out for forty pounds per annum as the property of an absentee.[103] Once again, the inhabitants decamped for Brush Hill. Despite having done all in her power to prevent the confiscation, Elizabeth had failed. The problems continued in Milton, where "the same tribe of Demons" appeared in May to try to take the Brush Hill farm into possession during James Murray's lifetime. Christian's niece doubted that Elizabeth would countenance this new threat well: "I am sure Mrs. Inman's spirits will forsake her when she finds this family in so much trouble."[104] Fortunately for Elizabeth, her nieces, and the family friends who took refuge with them, the committee did not triumph. By June it had become clear that the "*infernal crew*" would not succeed "in taking the farm from this amiable family."[105]

At the same time as Elizabeth endeavored to preserve property and maintain good relations with colonial leaders, her niece Betsy, exposed repeatedly to danger at the hands of rebel forces, expressed fervent loyalist feelings. While in Boston in June 1776, Betsy learned of the capture of some Scottish troops. Although born in the colonies, Betsy cherished her Scottish connections and had been more attached to the country since her visit there. After learning where the prisoners of war were being held, Betsy, along with Prudence Middleton, went into the garden of a house next to the jailyard, hoping to see them. As they walked toward the Common a short time later, she passed more of the troops being moved under guard, hesitated for a moment to speak to them, and then chased them as fast as her feet "in high heeled shoes would carry" her. Too slow to catch them, Betsy seized the next encounter to approach the men and, trembling, conversed with them briefly. Acquainted with the family of one of the young officers, Betsy talked with him about his mother and sisters before they parted company. The meeting threw her into a great "agitation of Spirits." With her father a refugee in Halifax, her own fondness for Britain deepened by her sojourn there a few years before, and her recent experiences ones of turmoil caused by the war, Betsy had ample cause for loyalist sentiments. "While this unhappy War continues," she declared, "I feel that kind of restless anxiety which will never allow me one hours peace." Betsy felt "cruelly tortured" by the suspense of not knowing the war's outcome and doubted that the "Blessings of Peace" would ever be able to compensate for their current sufferings.[106]

When the Declaration of Independence was issued the following month, Betsy made no effort to hide her dislike for the rebels. The document was first read on 18 July from the Towne House in the center of the city, just across from Elizabeth's former shop and residence. That night, a crowd of jubilant and impassioned colonists celebrated the historic act by tearing down the royal standards, a carved lion and unicorn, from the roof. Independence, destruction, and chaos seemed to go hand in hand. In the weeks that followed,

Bostonians heard the Declaration again throughout the town, as ministers relinquished their pulpits to repetitions of the solemn, stirring words. When Betsy attended church one day, she was disturbed to see someone get up to read the document. "Happily it was not till the service was over," she reported. The timing allowed those who wished to avoid subjecting themselves to a hearing to leave; Betsy was one who "came out of the Church."[107]

Betsy's loyalist leanings inspired her to react negatively to the Declaration of Independence and express sympathy for captured British soldiers, but Elizabeth went further some months later, assisting prisoners of war and thus opening herself to censure. On one of the ships of Scottish Highlanders taken that June was Colonel Archibald Campbell.[108] Although the source of their connection is not clear, it seems plausible that the Scotsman was related to Elizabeth's first husband or that she had known him or his family in Scotland; regardless, she chose to help him while he was imprisoned in 1776 and 1777. Held in what he described as a "dungeon," twelve or thirteen feet square, with walls blackened with the grease "of successive Criminals" and a floor covered with their litter, Campbell bemoaned his appalling surroundings.[109] After thirty-four days in this condition, he was released to an apartment in the jailer's house, which happened to be the local tavern. There, he complained, proximity to the public road "exposed [him] to tumultuous noise, and the unmerited insults of the lower class of Passangers."[110]

In an effort to improve his situation, Campbell solicited the aid of Mrs. Inman. He requested that she try to help expedite a prisoner exchange of him for Ethan Allen. He also asked her to send him various needed supplies, including books, cheese, coffee, sugar, butter, candles, linen, and hair powder. Elizabeth assisted him to the best of her abilities, sending him many gallons of rum, for example. On numerous occasions, he expressed his deep gratitude for her continued good offices, thanking her once for her notes, which he received "in the powder," a suggestion that perhaps her letter had been concealed. She may have even effected his relocation or sought to have him released to her custody. "The Intelligence is great and pleasing," he told her. "I shall be happy indeed to see the hour I am Garrisoned in your place and shall gladly partake of a Saturdays vages; near Fort Edward.

As a Practice prevails (fays a Correfpondent) of idle Women reforting to the Prifons where the Britifh and Heffian Prifoners are confined, and as dangerous Diforders generally accompany fuch Proftitutes, it is therefore recommended to thofe whofe Bufinefs it is, to prevent fuch Practices.

Some of the Prifoners above-mentioned, have been conducted from Cambridge to Concord, to fee their Friends, *not to carry Intelligence to, or from, Col. Campbell*; but, perhaps, to acquaint the Colonel of their plerfant Situation, and how they are vifited by Mrs. I m-n, from Bofton, who drank Coffee with them a few Evenings fince.

O America! America! I lament for your Simplicity! May your Children exert themfelves with more Vigour, and look out with greater Circumfpection, or they will be undone!

14   "As a Practice prevails," *The Independent Chronicle,
and the Universal Advertiser*, 31 July 1777.
Courtesy, American Antiquarian Society.

dinner even of Salt fish fruit tea."[111] In assisting Campbell and other prisoners of war, Elizabeth exposed herself to rebel surveillance and invited public criticism.

Elizabeth's benevolent activities with regard to Campbell led directly to the public questioning of her sexual prudence and political loyalties in the press. The 31 July 1777 issue of the *Independent Chronicle, and the Universal Advertiser*, a Boston newspaper with a masthead sporting a patriot with a drawn sword in one hand and a paper bearing the word "Independence" in the other, castigated Elizabeth by name and tied her activities to disorderly women and political intrigue (figure 14). The report decried the presence of "idle Women" around local prisons where British and Hessian troops were confined. "As dangerous Disorders generally accompany such Prostitutes," those in authority should put an end to the practice. Equally appalling, some of the prisoners had been taken to Concord, "*not to carry Intelligence to, or from, Col. Campbell*; but, perhaps, to acquaint the Colonel of their pleasant Situation, and how they are visited by Mrs.

I——n, from Boston, who drank Coffee with them a few Evenings since."[112] Regardless of whether these prisoners of war were carrying valuable information to a British officer, they were engaged in other suspicious, offensive acts: entertaining and showing hospitality to Mrs. Inman. She apparently visited Campbell himself as well. The author of this piece thus connected Elizabeth's visit with the presence of prostitutes, both of which raised the specter of consorting with the enemy in ways that demonstrated a lack of virtue in its sexual and political senses. This tendency to fuse personal, female virtue with political, male virtue during the Revolutionary era supports views of a "historical and symbolic connection between the two definitions."[113]

Contemporaries felt bound to comment on the political activities of a prominent individual, despite her sex or perhaps precisely be-cause of it. Elizabeth's behavior symbolized the many challenges faced by the authorities. No matter how blameless her life had been heretofore, what her reputation as a shopkeeper had been, or how friendly she was with rebel commanders, Elizabeth was suddenly and thoroughly suspect. By including "Mrs. Inman" in a diatribe against prostitutes, the press characterized her as a disorderly woman, a po-tential problem for the patriot cause. The piece closed with a plea for vigilance: "Oh! America! America! I lament for your Simplicity! May your Children exert themselves with more Vigour, and look out with greater Circumspection, or they will be undone!" The moral and sexual connotations of "undone" in this exhortation seem clear: just as a naïve young woman could be "undone" by the depredations of a lecherous rake, so too could the simplicity and innocence of the childlike Americans be ruined and destroyed by those of ill repute and malicious intent. Following the newspaper attack on "Mrs. In-man," Campbell excoriated those who misrepresented her chari-table act. Full of remorse that the kindness Elizabeth had shown him had exposed her to libel, he sincerely regretted "the late audacious liberty of the *Columbian press* with the good Ladies humane Visit to her Captive friend." In his view, benevolence and compassion alone had motivated her. Campbell angrily declared that "such Calumny [was] heartily to be despised" and that she should hold "all such malevolence in Just contempt." In short, he was "very uneasie" that she had encountered "any trouble on this account."[114] Whether he

Queries, by a LADY.

Query. Would it not be as proper for Lieutenant *Campbell,* who refides in Cambridge Prifon, to be fet free, and go wherever he pleafes, as to be at the Trouble of entertaining Mrs. *Inman* and Mrs. *Sargeant* in his Confinement.? Is not this correfponding with our Enemies ?

Query. Did not the former of thefe Women efcape into Bofton, when the Town was fhut up, under Pretence of feeing her fick Hufband ; though her Hufband was perfectly well, and walking the Streets ? Did fhe not clandeftinely convey herfelf and live Stock to Newport, to be tranfported by Capt. *Lindfey* to Bofton, during the Siege ?

Query. Was it never heard that any mafculine Female has had a hand in a Plot ?

15   "Queries, by a LADY," *The Independent Chronicle,*
      and the Universal Advertiser, 7 August 1777.
      Courtesy, American Antiquarian Society.

had seen the latest salvo in the edition of the paper the day before he sent her this note is unknown.

A week after the first attack on Elizabeth's reputation, the *Independent Chronicle* printed a series of pointed questions regarding her political activities and personal attributes, under the heading of "Queries, by a LADY" (see figure 15).[115] The author wondered whether it would not be as proper to let Campbell out of the Cambridge prison as to put him to the trouble of entertaining Mrs. Inman in his confinement. The "Lady" wondered, "Is not this corresponding with our Enemies?" In other words, the visit potentially provided the British prisoner of war with as much access to information as he would have had if free. The subsequent queries attacked Elizabeth even more bluntly. The second asked whether she did not "escape into Boston, when the Town was shut up, under Pretence of seeing her sick Husband; though her Husband was perfectly well, and walking the Streets?" Presumably, then, the "Lady" maintained, Elizabeth had cloaked her request to cross enemy lines in the guise of familial duty, of a wife fulfilling her responsibilities to her husband. Seeking permission to cross lines for this reason was common and accepted by Revolutionary committees, who thereby acknowledged that in some circumstances married women did not have the same kind or level of political commitment as did men.[116] That attempt to mask her behavior needed to be exposed. (Undoubtedly, Elizabeth thought pleading the need to see an ill spouse a better reason to give the authorities for coming into Boston than helping a wayward niece elope.) In addition to traveling into the town, Elizabeth had "clandestinely convey[ed] herself and live Stock to Newport, to be transported by Capt. *Lindsey* to Boston" during the siege, thus violating her earlier promise. Although no other evidence suggests that Elizabeth took advantage of her son-in-law's position to preserve family property, it seems unlikely that the charge was wholly unfounded. Although not always well supplied, Bostonians did receive foodstuffs from the surrounding countryside during the siege. Elizabeth was thus accused of personal profiteering and a willingness to violate acceptable limits on feminine political behavior. In her conduct, then, her critics saw yet another example of the fundamental conflict of the Revolution; self-interest, the antithesis of self-sacrificing virtue, governed this corrupt woman.

The purportedly feminine author of the piece posed one final query that lay bare the gender connotations of women's political consciousness and activism. Highlighting the challenge that politically involved women presented to contemporary notions of distinctive male and female spheres of activity, the author wondered, "Was it never heard that any masculine Female has had a hand in a Plot?" This suggestion of espionage and conspiracy on Elizabeth's part links gender and political life in intriguing ways. Where one week's press lumped Elizabeth together with disorderly women, particularly prostitutes, the next week's column charged her with treacherous, potentially treasonous actions and unfeminine behavior.[117] Significantly, women who prostituted themselves or who engaged in treacherous spying were by definition not good or proper women. They willfully violated society's sexual and political mores, taking license to transgress the bounds of what was considered appropriate when it suited them or benefited their politics or purse. Because contemporaries grouped women with infants and "the insane" as dependent individuals incapable of exercising political judgment on their own, a woman who behaved in such a manner expressed an independence that could be construed as unwomanly and unnatural. In the writer's eyes, then, Elizabeth's challenge to and subversion of gender dictates merited applying the adjective "masculine" to her. Although the sex of the anonymous author is unknown, the assumption of a female identity is intentional. This "lady" claimed special insight into feminine behavior and attempted to disabuse contemporaries of the notion that women were beings without political inclinations.

Ironically, the same page of the *Independent Chronicle* that contained the indictment of Elizabeth's actions — ones that rendered her gender ambiguous or suspect — also carried news from Williamsburg that praised women with political commitments. A correspondent reported that on 4 July, Amelia County women with the best interests of the United States at heart had entered into a resolution to accept the romantic overtures of patriotic men only. They pledged "not to permit the addresses of any person (be his circumstances or situation in life what they will) unless he has served in the American armies long enough to prove, by his valour that he is deserving of their love."[118] Resources and status, the typical currency of the marriage market, mattered not at all. Matrimony, in this context, was a politically charged act. One of the most private and personal decisions a woman could make thus assumed a public, patriotic cast. A woman who eschewed tea before the war and wore homespun cloth could support the Revolutionary cause even more fully and intimately by wedding well.

When was it proper or desirable for a woman to espouse political views? Ambivalence over women's political status and sentiments characterized contemporaries' attitudes. Even James Murray, who clearly esteemed his sister as a woman of great talent and thought her a committed loyalist, was uncertain how to characterize her views of the conflict. In a request for preferment from Sir Henry Clinton, James mentioned his "Sister Mrs Inman, much Respected in Boston, though no Disguiser of her Sentiments."[119] Then he crossed out this last phrase, possibly considering that including a woman's political beliefs was inappropriate or immaterial. Equally interesting is James's assertion that Elizabeth had managed to preserve some of her neighbors' respect, an accomplishment he failed to match.

Published as an enemy to the infant nation in the local press, Elizabeth found the Revolution a test of both family and political loyalties. The commitment of some of her family to the American side was a source of great distress. Especially upsetting was the rebellion of her nephew Jack Murray, who had immigrated in 1770 at her instigation and decided in 1778 to embrace the cause of freedom. When she learned of his intention to join the Continental army, Elizabeth sprang into action, anxious to persuade him that duty to his family had greater weight than did his political inclinations. In Jack's case, the two loyalties were at odds. After spending several years of his young adulthood in the colonies, separated from his parents in England by time and distance, Jack had shifted his allegiance to the infant nation. Trying to preempt this potential disaster, Elizabeth solicited the assistance of her nephew John Innes Clark, under whose tutelage Jack had been learning the mercantile trade in Rhode Island. Telling John that "words [were] wanting to express [her] surprize & concern" at learning of Jack's plans, she confessed her disappointment: "I hope I never have nor never will give so much pain to an enemy as this does to me[,] who has gloried in thinking I was his Aunt & friend." She urged her older nephew to exercise his authority over his cousin, to "Check this youth" and, if his efforts proved unsuccessful, to "make an errand for him to Boston," where she could work on him. When she "took him from his Fathers House," she had looked upon herself "as accountable to Him for the boy till he arrived at the age of 21."[120] He had not quite reached his maturity yet.

If Elizabeth's nephew Jack became a patriot, his action would signal more than her failure at guardianship. Should he decide to take up arms against Great Britain, he would sever his ties to his family and destroy forever "his Father & Mothers happiness." They would bid "adieu to their eldest darling Son & end their days in Sorrow." As an additional impetus to aid her, Elizabeth reminded John Clark that he had his own young children and would not welcome their disobedience. She wondered how a similar situation would affect him.[121] Complicating the situation was the loyalty of at least some members of the Clark family to the American cause. Annie Clark Hooper's husband became a delegate to the Continental Congress, while her brothers joined the colonial army, actions that one relative thought "must be hard upon her" and undoubtedly on Elizabeth as well.[122] Exposed to such conduct, Jack may have been choosing to follow his cousin's example.[123]

The whole messy affair simultaneously raised the specters of parental disobedience, disloyalty, and poor judgment on Elizabeth's part for her earlier actions in persisting in bringing Jack to the colonies despite the unsettled political climate. No doubt the concerns Elizabeth had felt in 1770, when she sent Polly and Jack to America, separating them at an early age from their parents, returned to haunt her. Unwilling to leave the matter entirely to John's discretion, Elizabeth wrote directly to her nephew. Interestingly, she did not broach the subject of politics. Rather, she simply told him she thought he was preparing to "take leave" from them in an "easy manner" and hoped that he would pay her a visit. Cloaking her intent to have him under her supervision, she urged the claims of friendship, telling him he should ask permission to see her before he quit his life as a merchant.[124] Elizabeth was willing to meddle when she felt her responsibilities demanded it of her.

For those with loyalties to the British cause, the fall of 1777 brought little good news. The British campaign faltered, as General Burgoyne and his troops were forced to surrender at the Battle of Saratoga. The American victory in this confrontation changed the future of the war. Demonstrating an ability to fight and win, the Americans gained the support of the French. News of the victory contributed materially to the willingness of France to sign treaties of support and defense with the infant United States. The alliance, in turn, proved critical to the ultimate American triumph. News of Burgoyne's defeat discouraged the Murrays and their circle, who had been hoping for a speedy end to the war.

Further bad news came in September 1778 with the Act of Banishment, which targeted James Murray, among many others, by name. This Massachusetts piece of legislation declared that certain individuals were forbidden from returning to the state. Appointed earlier as an inspector for the Crown's customs, James was known to hold a royal commission.[125] That position and his flight from New England made him a political refugee. After moving his family to Halifax, James returned south, settling for a time in New York with several other refugees. There they stayed in quarters outside the city and lived "very quiet and retired, well supplied with the necessaries of Life, much more comfortably than [they] could be at Halifax," where his wife remained.[126] Over the course of the next two years, James spent time in Newport, Providence, Rhode Island, and Philadelphia before returning to Halifax for good in 1778. While his loyalties made it impossible for him to stay in Massachusetts, James was not able to find permanency or tranquillity in his later years elsewhere. His wife, like many other loyalists, found residence in Halifax unappealing. At her instigation James found himself contemplating another Atlantic crossing, a journey that would increase the distance between him and his family in Massachusetts. Margaret Murray wanted to go to Britain to join her sister. Restraining her from undertaking the voyage was her property and her husband's refusal "to accompany her until he has first had an Interview with his family in Boston."[127] He antici- pated that when the property sold, he would travel to Boston to visit his daughters and to take their "Company or Commands for En- gland."[128] His request for permission to visit Elizabeth and his daugh- ters refused, James hesitated to depart "this side of the water"; his wife continued to make plans for leaving, however.[129]

Leaving the colonies for good would be poignant and difficult for James. "For your Pa's part," he told them, "it will be with much Reluctance that he will leave America, where he has enjoy'd so many happy years."[130] In December 1780, after selling the Halifax prop- erty, they were "quite detached" from that "expensive place." He decided he would leave soon but did not know where they would settle.[131] James's loyalties — to his spouse, his sister, his children, his homeland of choice, and the nation of his youth — created layers of conflict. At various points James invited his family to join him in Halifax and also tried to go back to Boston. Hoping that he could settle in Milton without arousing any public hostility, he sought his friends' advice about a possible return to New England. James thought he could perhaps move back quietly because of his advanced age; he would not be worth the trouble of American authorities. The consensus, however, seemed to be that he could not take the chance. As one family friend put it, "If his sentiments in politicks should expose him to the rude insults of a licentious people. . . , I should much rather hear he was well & happy at N[ova] S[cotia] than run the risque of his being ill treated here."[132] James eventually agreed to put the home of his adulthood behind him. In a peaceful state, America had suited him to perfection. He also thought it "ridicu- lous" to undertake the trouble of traveling for the remainder of a "Life which he is so soon to leave."[133]

While James hesitantly prepared to leave America, Elizabeth, her husband, and her nieces continued to reside in Boston and Milton. The family's circumstances were financially difficult and physically uncomfortable. Ralph, generally at Elizabeth's side after the period of their first separation, calculated his losses at five thousand pounds sterling. During the war, their finances had been in terrible shape; they had lived on fifty pounds a year when they had spent six times that sum annually before. They had no more money because Elizabeth refused to accept paper currency for any debts due her. As soon as she could, she sold a house for hard money. Yet during the war itself, she expended very little on herself; fine dress was "needless" when she could neither entertain nor visit.[134] Despite Elizabeth and Ralph's difficulties, they looked forward hopefully to the peace. By early 1781, as the war appeared to be nearing its end, Elizabeth had sent for Polly to return from England, to resume the shopkeeping life Polly had begun and the dream that Elizabeth created, both dramatically interrupted by the Revolution.

Unlike her brother James, Elizabeth was not ready to leave America. Her attachment to the country was both emotional and political. Her life during the Revolution had demonstrated clearly that women could and had to express their loyalties and make economic choices. They were political beings, if not citizens. With members of her extended family supporting opposing sides, she had been particularly well positioned to view the conflict as one with personal repercussions and as a civil war. Faced with the complications of expressing political sentiments as a woman and torn by mixed loyalties herself — emotional attachments to patriot family and friends and the colonies, on the one hand, and political support for the Crown, on the other — Elizabeth both moved within gender constraints and manipulated them to preserve a precarious political and personal independence. As she negotiated her way during these years, she carved out a niche for herself that existed in tension with accepted as well as changing notions of feminine behavior. When the war ended, Elizabeth and Ralph returned to their ruined property in Cambridge. With her husband, nieces Betsy and Dolly, and Dolly's two younger sons, Elizabeth began to pick up the pieces of her life and to reevaluate her plans for the future.

6

The Legacy of a "Spirit of Independence"

With the war at an end, Elizabeth faced important decisions about her life and responsibilities. After several decades in America, she had developed abundant and deep ties to the new world, with three marriages, a career as a shopkeeper, and long-time residency in Boston. She had gained respect and renown, developed lasting friendships, and raised nieces who were settled nearby. Yet the Revolutionary years had shattered her peace and prosperity. She had faced privation, property loss, terrifying midnight rides, temporary imprisonment, and accusations of spying. Even more disturbing, however, were the gaps in the fabric of her personal relationships. Far away in Halifax, her brother James was preparing to return for good to Great Britain. Christian Barnes, her closest friend, had left Boston for England in 1775 and settled with her family and other loyalist exiles in Bristol.[1] Although Elizabeth had Betsy and Dolly at her side, Polly Murray, the niece for whom she had such high hopes, remained in Norwich, England, with her family. As Elizabeth took steps to bring Polly back to New England, she learned that James had changed his mind once again about undertaking another Atlantic crossing. Believing that Polly would accept Elizabeth's invitation as soon as she received it, "having severely" regretted "that ever she left America," James was equally sure he would not follow through with his own planned journey.[2] Now sixty-eight, James was growing weak. When news of his failing health arrived in Boston in the fall of 1781, Elizabeth kept it from her nieces, trying to save them from worrying. Before the year was out, James was dead. For Elizabeth, her brother's passing brought to a close a phase of her own life and prompted her to reflect on her loyalties and experiences. As she contemplated the past, she planned for the future, unaware of how little time remained to her. During her last years, criticism and conflict surrounded her personal and financial decisions. After her death, her financial legacies became a source of contention. As some of her family wrangled over her assets, others reflected more on Elizabeth's intangible, personal legacies — the ideals that emerged in her definitions of her own "spirit," her niece Polly's acknowledgment of her aunt's impact on her, and her model of womanhood.

James Murray's death plunged his whole family into mourning. For a time, Elizabeth worried that her nieces "would fall a sacrifice to grief." Dolly and Betsy would "ever regret being absent from their father."[3] Separated from his daughters and other family in Boston since he fled with other refugees in 1776, James remembered them in his will. To Dolly and Betsy he bequeathed his property in equal portions after they settled one-third on his wife. He paid particular attention to his books, giving them all to Dolly for herself and her children's use, except those which Betsy wanted "for her own Reading." James also asked his executors to settle his debts, especially those owed to his good friends Gilbert Deblois and Ame and Elizabeth Cuming. To his "beloved Sister Elizabeth" he left his gold watch "as a Small Memorial of my Affection & Gratitude to her with which I lived with which I shall Die."[4] This poetic tribute to his youngest sibling reflected the constancy and intimacy of a relationship that spanned decades.

A terrible blow to Elizabeth, James's death was the event that finally led her to contemplate migrating back to Britain. A surrogate father to her in her youth and a cherished friend in later years, James had provided the initial impetus for Elizabeth to come to America. They had shared the responsibility for raising his children and followed each other to different colonies. For the last several years of his life, they had been separated because of his status as a loyalist exile. During that time, Elizabeth had grown weary of the Revolutionary contest and the constant conflict, her earlier attachment to America weakening under the war's continual assaults on her family's happiness and circumstances. Her opinions about the struggle had changed over the course of the Revolution, as she witnessed her family and friends suffer and her own reputation come under attack in the press. Finally, after James died, Elizabeth declared her readiness to leave America permanently. Although her "attachment to this Country [had] been violent," little remained to keep her there. "These times and the Death of our much Loved Brother," she told her brother John, "has woun[de]d me in such a manner that I am anxious for the sun to rise & the wind to blow that shall clear me of this once happy shore."[5]

As she reflected on her attachment to America, Elizabeth also evaluated her life as a shopkeeper and benefactor. She did so in response to criticism from her brother John. In 1783 he insinuated that Elizabeth had to some extent ruined his daughter Polly's life. In a letter to his son Jack, which Elizabeth read, John insisted that his sister must realize that Polly had relinquished her own dreams to comply with Elizabeth's plans. Objecting to his veiled allegations, Elizabeth defended herself. "If this means business," she told him, "I am sorry the desadvantages arising from young Ladys going into business did not occur to you in time enough to prevent it." What John or Elizabeth understood by disadvantages is unclear. Perhaps John felt that his daughter's departure from England at sixteen had prevented her from marrying, or he may have come to share his daughter Anne's view of shopkeeping as an activity that a gentle-woman could not pursue without loss of status. Yet Elizabeth refused to accept any censure for her role in promoting commercial endeavor. In her mind, her plans were just. If anyone deserved blame, it was John. Elizabeth demanded that he acknowledge his culpability: "Did not you occation me to form this plan by saying what would you do with so large a family?"[6] Her attentions toward John's children stemmed directly from his requests for aid. Wealthy, widowed, and childless when she first met Polly and Anne, she had responded to her brother's needs by happily offering his offspring the benevolence and patronage she could afford. She had already helped raise her brother James's daughters and had been equally willing to involve herself with John's. Looking back on this time, Elizabeth concluded that her assistance and plan to set up her niece as a shopkeeper had been entirely appropriate and reasonable.

Rather than criticizing her earlier conduct, Elizabeth celebrated her own autonomy, initiative, and successes in commerce. How could she "be blamed for pointing out that mode of life" which had given her "the greatest advantage & satisfaction?" After coming to Boston when she was not much older than Polly had been, Elizabeth had kept a shop for over a decade and done well for herself. She felt proud of her youthful achievement, satisfied and enriched by the experience. "I rejoice that the spirit of Independence," she declared, "caused such exertions as to place me in a situation that I am content to pass the remainder of my days in." Elizabeth's triumphs had been both hard earned and fortuitous, the result in part of her own ambition and good luck. "Untaught as I was," she told John, "I am surprised & my heart overflows with gratitude at the success I have met with."[7] In short, shopkeeping had provided a young and inexperienced Elizabeth with fond memories, a store of faith in herself, and a belief that other women could replicate her good fortune. Moreover, it laid the basis for a lifetime's pursuit of independent thought and action, as she continually struggled to balance her own judgment and desire for exercising authority with the constraints that permeated her roles as a woman.

Polly echoed Elizabeth's appraisal of the transforming effect of shopkeeping. While the war may have prevented Elizabeth from seeing Polly follow her path to successful shopkeeping, her niece never rued the experience. Indeed, Polly modeled herself after her aunt in other ways as well. At one time, she proposed taking charge of younger family members, much as Elizabeth had done. "I think I won't have any children of my own," she told Dolly. She thought that when Dolly's son Bennet and her own youngest brother were old enough, and she herself "rich enough," perhaps she would claim them both as her own to raise.[8] In the early 1780s, possibly aware of her father and aunt's exchange over her fate, Polly wrote to Elizabeth and told her about how her time as a shopkeeper had affected her. "The spirit of independence you cherish'd in me is not yet extinct," she announced. Polly's experiences as a colonial retailer had apparently corrected the imbalances of her upbringing, leaving her with a legacy of industry, self-confidence, and independence that likely reassured Elizabeth. As much as she may have wished to, however, Polly could not resume her retailing career; she now spent her days caring for her aging parents.

Although Polly did not rejoin her aunt, several of Elizabeth's other nieces and nephews continued to gather near her in the 1780s. Some of Polly's younger siblings made their way to America. Anne Murray

Powell, who had married and sailed to England in 1775, was now back with her aunt, living with her in Cambridge during part of 1783 and 1784. Likewise, Dolly Murray Forbes and her younger sister Betsy remained part of Elizabeth's inner circle. In 1783 Dolly moved her family to Cambridge so that her son John could attend Harvard. Elizabeth acted as a mentor and benefactor toward Dolly's sons, promising them both substantial rewards if they graduated and behaved according to their mother's satisfaction. At some point Elizabeth considered moving from Cambridge to Boston. She went so far as to have a "favorite" house remodeled "with an Intention to live" in it and may have moved into town in the spring of 1784.[9] Despite the presence of loving nieces and a spouse, Elizabeth felt cut off from the home of her adulthood after the travails of the previous decade.

Facing life among a public whose politics left her estranged and isolated, with few of the friends who had once surrounded her, Elizabeth grew depressed. When friends went to England, Elizabeth felt envious and hoped that they would remember her. Indeed, she thought her friends across the Atlantic should feel pity for her, "a lonely Bird that endeavors to soar above melencholly."[10] In this frame of mind, Elizabeth even tried to convince some of her former neighbors to return to Boston. One of the exiles, Elizabeth Cuming, appreciated the sentiment but chose not to leave Halifax. She and her sister had continued to keep shop and receive large shipments of goods. Rather than retire or relocate, they pursued their business there, hoping that Elizabeth would commend their plan. They knew she would "approve of a life of industry."[11] While Elizabeth may have approved, she continued to miss the company of old friends. After spending over four decades away from the land of her birth, Elizabeth finally decided to return to the British Isles. By early 1785 she had begun to plan for crossing the Atlantic once more.

Before Elizabeth could put into effect her plan of leaving America, she fell ill. That spring witnessed her rapid deterioration. Falling sick at the beginning of April, she quickly grew too weak even to leave her bed. Her illness alarmed her family and friends, prompting the Cuming sisters to bemoan her poor health.[12] During Elizabeth's illness, her nieces Dolly, Betsy, and Anne attended her, acting as nurses and companions. At times they also acted as gatekeepers. Lacking the strength to sit up and entertain company, Elizabeth could bear few visitors. By restricting others' access to their aunt, the women may have given her some needed peace and quiet. Their actions and decisions, however, eventually made them the objects of suspicion directed at them by Ralph Inman and John Murray.

After she had been bedridden for a few weeks, Elizabeth began to doubt that she would recover and thus prepared herself for death. Even though she declined to see visitors, she continued to think of her friends. Elizabeth asked Anne to write a letter for her to Christian Barnes, still in Bristol. That letter, along with a ring containing a lock of Elizabeth's hair, became for Christian the last proof of a friendship that could "never be blotted from [her] remembrance."[13] As she lay dying, Elizabeth also made small personal bequests, testimonials of her attachments to a number of female friends. In late April she made presents to two women. She sent her "most affectionate regards" to one, along with a silver cup, "as a small token of her friendship and esteem." To another she sent her love and requested the woman's acceptance of a silver tankard, "perhaps as one of the last proofs of her affection" and as "a token of regard."[14]

While organizing small gifts, Elizabeth considered replacing her current will, which had been written in 1769, shortly before she sailed for England. That will was relatively brief and straightforward. Under its terms, her brother William would receive five hundred pounds sterling, her nephew John Innes Clark two hundred seventy five (which would bring his total to the same sum as William's), and her brother James an annuity of one hundred pounds sterling; she confirmed some deeds of gift (of land) to him as well. To Betsy Murray she had promised a thirty-pound annuity until she reached twenty-one; at that point she would receive one thousand pounds. The residue of her estate, both real and personal, would be managed by her executors, who would pay its annual income to her brother John and at his decease divide her personal estate among his children. Jackie Day, who headed the list of nonrelated legatees, would receive one hundred pounds sterling. To her close friend Ezekiel Goldthwait, Elizabeth promised twice that sum.[15]

Shortly before her death, Elizabeth canceled the 1769 will by writing a new one, signed on 14 May 1785, that singled out her nieces for special attention, to the detriment of Ralph. The terms of the later document confirmed some of the 1769 will's provisions and contained numerous other directions. In the new will Elizabeth named her nephews John Innes Clark and John (Jack) Murray and Edward Hutchinson Robbins (whom Betsy married later in 1785) as executors; for their trouble, they would each receive a gold ring. Her nephews would also receive the profits from the sale of a substantial piece of real estate. The nieces Elizabeth helped to raise or brought to America also received detailed notice. To Dolly and Betsy, she gave five hundred and one thousand pounds, respectively. The sisters would also receive her portraits of their father James and her, as well as her church pew and the tomb in the King's Chapel burying ground. Polly was slated to receive one thousand pounds.[16]

Elizabeth used her new will to make amends to Polly's younger sister Anne. Always unhappy with shopkeeping, Anne had shared her feelings about it only the year before. When Anne told her aunt how difficult keeping shop had been for her, Elizabeth "expressed her surprise and regret" that her niece had not told her at the time that shopkeeping was "repugnant to [her] wishes and disposition."[17] Anne could only respond that she had followed the wishes of her parents, who were much better able to decide what was best for her than she, with her own "ignorant mind," could. After learning of Anne's misery, Elizabeth apparently concluded that it had contributed to Anne's precipitate marriage to William Powell. Holding herself responsible for having promoted the match, Elizabeth considered it "a duty to make provision for its consequences." Anne had tried to dissuade her aunt from this course, sure that if Elizabeth gave her more than her siblings received that she would "be suspected of undue influence" by her family.[18] Anne's pleading had no effect. When Elizabeth rewrote her will, she devised a greater proportion of her estate to Anne than to any other legatee. Anne would receive an annuity of interest on two thousand pounds "for her own personal Use & Disposal." Once again Elizabeth acted to preserve female economic autonomy; that phrase echoes the provision in Elizabeth's own prenuptial agreement with Ralph regarding her "separate use and benefit" of a yearly dividend. With abundant experience of marriage and a deeply seated belief in the importance of women controlling their own income, Elizabeth ensured that her married niece would have that right. After Anne's death the residue of the legacy would be distributed among her children.[19]

Elizabeth also planned many other smaller bequests to those for whom she felt responsible, singling out her nieces, female friends and relations, and slaves. Together, Dolly, Betsy, and Anne would share Elizabeth's "wearing Apparell & cloaths of every kind." Prudence Middleton Whipple, who was the niece of Elizabeth's second husband and who had lived with them for some time in her youth, received a house and lot in Boston. A number of other individuals received specific small bequests. Jannette Barclay's daughter Jackie, now married and living in Ireland, would be given one hundred pounds. To Elizabeth Murray Casey, who had obviously been named in her honor, Elizabeth also bequeathed one hundred pounds. Dolly's three sons and another woman received similar gifts. Elizabeth also promised an annuity of forty pounds to her cousins Jean and Anne Bennet. This sum, as well as the annuity for her husband, Ralph, was to come from the residue of her estate, which she bequeathed to her brother John and his heirs, excluding his three oldest children, who were singled out elsewhere for special bequests. He and his heirs would also be responsible upon her death for her "two Black Servants Marlborough & Isabella," for whom her executors would have to make "suitable Provision . . . for the Necessary & comfortable Support."[20]

Although he headed the list of legatees, Elizabeth's husband Ralph stood to receive comparatively little from his wife's substantial estate. As her "much esteemed Friend," he would receive an annuity of one hundred pounds sterling. Even more insulting than this rather minor gift was a provision dictating that Ralph had to meet certain conditions before receiving any money at all. In planning her will, Elizabeth made it perfectly clear that her partner in her longest marriage should expect little. Whether the small bequest reflected his lesser need for additional income or Elizabeth's feelings became clear only later.

As May progressed, Elizabeth tried to steel herself for her imminent demise. She was "calm & serene[,] making every preparation for her disolution with as much firmness as she would have done for her intended Passage for England." Betsy thought that "the only struggle she appeared to have was her attachment to her family. 'My affections still get the better of me,' she would often say." Although Elizabeth's nieces could tell the end was near, anticipation did not alleviate the anguish of the "awful event" or enable Betsy to "fortify" her mind against it. "As the scene drew near the close," she recalled, "I was denied the satisfaction of receiving her last benedictions." On 25 May, less than two weeks after completing her new and more detailed will, Elizabeth Murray Campbell Smith Inman died.

The deathbed scenes were excruciating. Trying to describe them for Polly, she struggled to find the words. "In every attempt to address my Dear Cousin," Betsy began, "the involuntary tear will still obtrude itself & my heart throbs with the anguish . . . of our recent misfortune." The last weeks had been wrenching, she confessed. As she lay dying from an undiagnosed ailment, Elizabeth, then only fifty-eight, had undergone more than physical distress as her husband Ralph plagued her. "Our valued & beloved Aunt was not without her anxieties & perplexities," Betsy recalled. "Mr I[nman']s disposition has given her more trouble than her friends are aware of & his failings were dayly encreasing." The portrait Betsy offered of his flaws is one of thoughtlessness and pettiness. "His avarice & excesses was a source of real misfortune to her & persued her even to a bed of sickness." "Oh Polly Heaven grant that you may be long exempt from the Pangs of attending the dying bed of a friend & such a friend," Betsy prayed. Even in her extreme distress, Elizabeth had thought of Polly. "She enquired for you & the family & even our friends in Scotland with a degree of earnestness which her affectionate heart always dictated." Although there were days when Elizabeth could see company only briefly, at the last she wanted her nieces around her. Betsy described her final meeting with her aunt: "The last sentence I had from her was fraught with affection, an anxious care for my health & an earnest wish that I spend the following day with her" (figure 16). When Betsy got up to leave, Elizabeth would not let her go: "When I attempted to quit her hand, as if convinced it would be the last time, she held it fast."[21] The next day, with Dolly and Anne at her side, Elizabeth died.

Her passing made the news immediately. The next day's issue of the *Independent Chronicle, and the Universal Advertiser* carried three death notices, all of women; Elizabeth's topped the column: "Died yesterday, Mrs. Elizabeth Inman, wife of Ralph Inman, Esq." Readers learned that her funeral would be the following afternoon, "from Mrs. Minot's, at the Bank." The "friends and acquaintances of the deceased" were requested to attend.[22] Only a short distance away

16   Elizabeth (Betsy) Murray, artist unknown, ca. 1785.
Courtesy, Margaret Howe Ewing Papers, Private Collection.

from where she spent her early years in Boston, in the cemetery adjacent to King's Chapel, Elizabeth was buried. In a tomb whose inscriptions have since been destroyed by time and the elements, her earthly remains were interred next to those of her second husband. The gravestone emphasized that connection over her third marriage, reading, "To the Revered Memory of ELIZABETH the relict of James Smith Esq. who died the wife of Ralph Inman Esq."[23] Those she left behind mourned her loss. With affection and admiration, Elizabeth Cuming gratefully recalled her mentor, "the kind adviser" of her youth and "the soother" of her sorrows. She took some consolation in a friend's remarks that all people must pay this debt and that they should be happy for those "so well prepaired" for the moment.[24] Dolly and Betsy grieved for the woman who had been a second mother to them and who had suffered so much in her last days.

After Elizabeth died, Ralph grew incensed about his paltry inheritance. He created a great deal of commotion and distress for his wife's family. According to Betsy, his greed had "[hurried] him into a state of distraction." She told Polly he envied those who received more than he had. Where he should have been conscious of the gratitude he owed to one "who prolong'd his life & saved him from ruin," Ralph was angry that he had not received the whole of his wealthy wife's estate, "or such a part of it as he requested." Therefore he refused to give up the papers belonging to the estate. Declaring that his "ill conduct" had aggravated her own afflictions, Betsy nonetheless felt sorry for him. "I cannot but pity him," she wrote. "He has not a friend to take the least care of him & if any were to offer him assistance[,] he would suppose they did it with a view to plunder him." Betsy reported that although Ralph was temporarily residing in Cambridge, she doubted he would remain there; he did not have "the stability to stay in one place long."[25]

The conditions Elizabeth placed on her husband's annuity lend support to Betsy's characterization of his behavior. She began her will by emphasizing her right to make a will, her "coverture notwithstanding." Her executors would produce her authority for doing so. In providing instructions for her executors, Elizabeth dictated that Ralph's annuity would "commence from the time and As soon As he shall surrender" to them "all the Goods, Chattels & Estate" that he possessed in her right, as well as "all Writings, Papers & evidence of property of any kind." These papers would be necessary for the execution of her will, and her executors should demand them "for that purpose." Once Ralph delivered up the papers, his annuity was "to commence & have effect & not Otherwise."[26] Elizabeth apparently suspected that without this requirement, Ralph would try to keep her estate for himself. She was right to anticipate that he would make trouble. Ralph delayed relinquishing the papers in his possession for several months, finally giving them to John Innes Clark in February 1786.

Partly because of Ralph's behavior and partly because of the large bequest to Anne, the executorship of Elizabeth's estate became a sore subject, creating friction among various Murray cousins, her brother John Murray, and Ralph Inman and his family. Christian Barnes felt "grieved" that "Mr. Inman's perverseness" was causing problems for the family and hoped that Elizabeth's "good intentions [would] not be frustrated by persons undeserving any favour from her or hers."[27] While Jean and Anne Bennet pestered the executors for their annuities, they questioned their cousin Elizabeth's judgment in dividing her estate as she had. To them, it seemed that Betsy and Dolly were "scarcely put upon an equal footing" with their uncle John's children; they stood to receive less of their aunt's fortune than perhaps they ought.[28] "There are (we understand) difficulties likely to occurr from Mr Inmans claims," they wrote. The "vague reports" that had reached them were alarming. While the Bennets surmised incorrectly that their nieces would receive very little — the sisters did have claims to substantial property, including the estate at Brush Hill, not apparent in the will because of earlier deeds of gift to their father James — they were right about Inman's obstructionism.

Ralph explained his delay in discussing the settlement of his wife's estate by blaming Elizabeth's family and her executors. He told John Murray that he would have been more cooperative "had their been the least Inclination in them to encourage my continuing that Love & Harmony which subsisted in our Familys before Mrs. Inman's Death." He judged it "necessery to wait the result of their conduct" in hopes of being able to give his brother-in-law "a pleasing account of a happy reconciliation's taking place." Sounding as though he felt mistreated, Ralph declared, "It is a mortifying Reflection, to hear such representations made to you of my refusing to comply with the conditions of Mrs. Inman's Will." Ralph claimed that the executors wanted accounts before they were settled, quibbled over paying bills, and began to seize his property until he gave them ten thousand pounds security. Earnestly declaring himself the innocent and injured party "from an unjust Prosecution," Inman told John, "My Integrity I have ever held fast." No one had called it into question during his forty-eight years of residence in America; no legal action had been brought against him "until Mrs Inman's Executors served their writ" on him.[29]

As steward of his wife's estate, Ralph found himself in what he claimed was the untenable position of having to settle his wife's accounts and books, disburse funds, and collect debts while being accused of troublesome, immoral behavior by his wife's nieces. In Ralph's opinion, his wife's nieces had manipulated their aunt, abusing their acknowledged roles as caretakers and close female relations to poison her mind against both her spouse and her other Murray nieces and nephews. John Murray and his family apparently took Ralph at his word, fully convinced that the women had refused to allow Ralph to see his dying wife while they persuaded her to write a new will.

The dynamics of the encounter between Dolly, Betsy, and Ralph suggest various explanations highlighting femininity and female authority. One possible interpretation of the deathbed scene points to the role of female agency. In the private chamber, a space where women still largely ruled when it came to female experiences such as childbirth, two women acted to protect their aunt's energy, health, and peace of mind. Perhaps Elizabeth, weary of Ralph, asked or allowed her nieces to run interference for her, keeping him out of her sight for a few difficult weeks. Dolly and Betsy, in turn, played their feminine part as nurses to exert authority over the nominal head of the household to keep him out of their aunt's sickroom. He saw their behavior as conspiratorial, conniving, and controlling because he felt damaged by it, in terms of both his reputation and his financial status.

Given these conflicting accounts, puzzling together where exactly Ralph stood in his wife's graces toward the end of her life becomes very tricky. Unhappy in her marriage before the Revolution began, Elizabeth grew angry at Ralph during its early days. It would be difficult for him to make up for planning to leave Boston without her. When they married, both had been well-to-do. Their prenuptial agreement, which Ralph probably now regretted ever signing, would preserve their respective estates. Despite their marriage contract, in 1779 Ralph had asked Elizabeth to become responsible for his property and family. In a letter that reveals both his efforts to show his wife some deference and his precarious financial situation, he explained why he had not yet made appropriate plans himself. He wanted to make a will, but the disturbances and distresses of the time had postponed him "Setting about so Important a Work." Having finally done so, he showed her a copy of his will and requested her help "in making a Just Retribution of the Little Estate." Unlike the will his wife later wrote, the will that Ralph signed left everything to his spouse. He therefore needed to enlist her promise of leaving something to his family. He honeyed his request with praise, acknowledging, "Your affection towards me, & my Family, so many Instances of your Goodness, & Integrity of Heart, fills me with the High[est] Sense of Love & Gratitude, I must now Crave a Continuance of your kind Ofices." Ralph intended to leave the execution of his wishes in her hands. She should see that his son, George, receive a double portion of his property, "according to the Laws of the Land, made, & Provided for Intestates." A single portion should go to his daughter, Susannah Linzee, and her husband. Unlike Elizabeth, Ralph was indifferent as to whether a married woman ought to enjoy separate control of property; the portion he wanted his daughter to have could be given to her husband, "with or Without Restraint, according to [Elizabeth's] discretion." He also asked that she care for his brother John in his "helpless Situation." He closed this list with his regards: "With my Fervent Prayers that Heaven may Protect you, my Dear Mrs Inman, & give you that Peace which Passeth all Understanding, is the Sincere wish, of him that Loves You[.] I remain with Love & Gratitude Your most affectionate Husband Ralph Inman."[30] Clearly, Ralph expected that Elizabeth would take care of his family after his death; he was confident that she would exercise the magnanimity he solicited. Predeceasing her husband, Elizabeth never had to act on his request.

In Ralph Inman's construction of events, Dolly Murray Forbes and Betsy Murray, as well as his wife's executors, shared the blame for the acrimony and difficulties that followed Elizabeth's demise. Since her death, he explained, none of them had paid him a visit or acted to cultivate peace and harmony in their relationships. Rather, the executors persecuted him. They said they acted according to Elizabeth's written instructions but failed to produce any such orders for his perusal. Given their reticence in showing him documentation,

Ralph declared himself unwilling to believe their story "without better Proof." What made him suspicious was the conduct of Dolly and
Betsy. They "gave close attention during Mrs. Inmans Illness, so that
I impute my Situation to their Insinuations," he explained. The sisters merited special blame for behaving in a sneaky and malicious
manner. They "acted with so much Art and cunning" as to deprive
Ralph of the opportunity to see or have "any Conversation with her
from the time she was taken Ill to the time of her Dissolution." At first
he had construed their actions favorably, as stemming "from Tender-
ness and concern for their Aunt." They forbade friends' visits "as
Conversation wo[ul]d be hurtful," he recalled, and maintained this
deception until "they had accomplished their Designs of making
a new Will, w[hi]ch they got compleated to their minds." Ralph
claimed that his wife had complained one day "of her being plagued
with those two Girls, & had sent for Jack Clark to get rid of them."
Unfortunately, he said, he did not have "the opportunity to enquire
into the cause" of her unhappiness with her nieces. For his part, he
said, "it wou'd take a volume" to describe "the Particulars of their
conduct, & of my Sufferings occasion'd thereby."[31]

Trying to push his own claims and needs, Ralph did not hesitate to
malign his wife's nieces to her family in England. His accusations
found a receptive audience in John Murray's household. In expressing his opinion of the whole affair to Edward Robbins, Charles Murray conveyed his father's hope that a great part of Ralph Inman's
"Intelligence" was not true. John Murray apparently also wondered
what could have happened to change his sister's mind with regard to
assisting him and his numerous offspring; they were slighted in the
will. It was an act of injustice, if not fraud, to endeavor "to cancel a
Deed of Gift duly executed, without the consent of both Parties."
Charles questioned how his aunt could have forgotten the solemn
promise she had made to his family. Charles quoted Elizabeth's
words: "Now Brother[,] I hope I have secured you & my sister from
Want in you[r] old [age]." She promised to take care of the three
eldest and pay for the education of the rest. Charles asked plaintively,
"What have we younger children done to make her break this solemn
Promise? — What must others have done that *they* should be remembered and *we* forgotten? My Father has always acted & does he not
still act as a common Father to the whole Family ever since my p[oor]

Uncle James's Death?" Rather than characterizing John as a father to the clan, it might be more accurate to see Elizabeth as the mother; unlike John, she provided advice and income to help the younger generation. John's chief effort on behalf of his nieces centered on the loyalist reparations in England. He submitted two memorials to the loyalist commission, one on the grounds that Dolly and Betsy were the children of a suffering loyalist, another for the property lost in North Carolina.[32] Probably with this action in mind, Charles accused his female cousins of self-interested manipulations. To add further insult, Charles urged better treatment of Ralph Inman. "Please to shew Mr. Inman's Letter to Mr. Clark when you see him," he wrote, "& tell him that it is my Father's wish" that Ralph "be treated with proper Respect by her Family."[33]

In addition to complaining about Elizabeth to her family, Ralph Inman and his supporters publicly criticized her. While in a tavern, a family friend overheard a Captain Lyde say "many slighting things" about Mrs. Inman and delineate her "Ill treatment" of her husband; the friend roundly answered the man's accusations on the spot.[34] George Inman, Ralph's son, shared his father's view that something had gone wrong with the settlement of the estate, but he attributed the problems to Elizabeth rather than to her nieces. George enlisted friends' aid in trying to uncover exactly "in what State Mrs. I[nman] left her Affairs." Having had little affection or respect for his stepmother, George looked on "her as a very artful deceitful Woman."[35] According to Ralph, "the whole Town" saw him as being unjustly treated by his wife's executors; his former brother-in-law, John Rowe, tried to defend Ralph's good name and was widely applauded for his efforts.[36]

The differing accounts of Elizabeth's intentions toward her heirs, her relationship with her spouse, his behavior, and the conduct of her nieces all point to the challenge not only of reconstructing what transpired but of interpreting it as well. If Elizabeth's family and associates encountered so much difficulty in enacting her wishes and establishing her character, how can we, at the remove of over two hundred years, hope to do better? Part of Elizabeth's legacy—the bitterness and recriminations over settlement of her estate—lasted for decades. The care she attempted to show her family was seen by some as an expression of favoritism and the result of deceptive behavior on the part of Elizabeth and her nieces. Attempting to support her nieces in particular and protect their ability to have economic independence, Elizabeth acted on the lessons and values she had learned and followed over a lifetime. She cherished her own autonomy, her opportunities for independence, and had experienced the frustration of dependence. Through her exercise of benevolence, Elizabeth attempted to provide others with the same possibilities for mobility, self-direction, and economic security that she had sought in a variety of ways.

In the eighteenth century, novel consumer experiences permeated the daily lives of men and women in America and Britain. For the growing numbers of those who wanted and could afford them, new fashions were available in clothing, food, dishes, furniture, and housing. People sought out such goods and participated in the changing styles for a variety of reasons. In part, the aesthetics and convenience of manufactured textiles and fine china, for example, attracted consumers. A competitive consciousness — keeping up with one's neighbors' possessions and standard of living — motivated others. Yet goods possessed another appealing aspect. In a highly mobile society in which men and women left their communities of origin to seek their fortunes among strangers, older ways of beginning and cementing relationships — based on long familiarity, shared churchgoing, neighborhood and familial networks — could no longer suffice. Economic and social survival in new places among new people required that identity, reputation, and status had to be conveyed quickly, clearly, and easily. In such contexts, goods gained importance as explanatory symbols in an increasingly international language that needed little translation. Self-presentation through dress and manners enabled the newcomer to assert his or her status as a member of a particular social and cultural group; possessing up-to-date information about fashion and genteel behavior enabled women and men to recognize and evaluate such markers displayed by their peers.

These two aspects of consumption — display and knowledge — went hand in hand for Elizabeth Murray. For her, being a success in the world of consumption meant being an equally accomplished consumer and businesswoman. Like many contemporaries, Elizabeth decried excessive, frivolous consumption, yet did not eschew it. Rather, for her, being simultaneously a consumer and a shopkeeper was desirable. Equally accomplished at both, Elizabeth Murray helped to produce and perpetuate the genteel, material culture of Anglo-America. The roles of consumer and producer were not oppositional. Her ability to excel at both demonstrates her fulfillment of the mandates of the age. In the world of goods, she was a success, her triumphs in business based on her skills as a consumer.

As she moved from one part of the British Empire to another, Elizabeth Murray gained familiarity with and expertise in the consumer culture of the day. Each locale she experienced stood in a distinctive relationship to the world of goods centered in London, with inhabitants who aspired with varying degrees of success to the standards of living and lifestyles of the metropolis. During her early years, she was exposed to the difficulties of doing business in North Carolina, where her brother James struggled to sell goods and collect payment for them. She also had firsthand knowledge of the varieties of consumer experiences available in London, the heart of the empire, where myriad shops tempted purchasers with a seemingly infinite array of goods. When it came time for her to make her way in America, she decided to reside in Boston, a place more amenable to both consumers and shopkeepers than the newly settled Cape Fear area her brother had chosen. The Puritan capital possessed the populace and the culture to sustain the shopkeeping career she planned.

Throughout the 1750s, as she kept shop and married and was widowed for the first time, Elizabeth encountered states of dependence and independence. Always her goal, economic security was not initially based on her own resources alone but on the financial assistance of her brother. Yet she struggled to eliminate her dependence on his support. When her husband died and she found herself at odds with his family over the settling of his estate, Elizabeth experienced the complications that attended the legal constraints of marriage. In subsequent decades she acted as though she had taken the lessons of her first years in Boston very much to heart. Even while she gave up the active pursuit of commerce herself, she promoted it for other young women in search of economic self-sufficiency. And though she gained the bulk of her wealth through marrying, which brought its own kinds of dependence, she did not ever again fully relinquish the legal right to control her own income and property.

Throughout her life Elizabeth Murray endeavored to make her desires for autonomy mesh with the roles typical for women of her day. Continually, she negotiated the fine lines between dependence and independence, commitment to America and loyalty to Britain, obedience to male authority and self-determination. Elizabeth celebrated a "spirit of Independence" and directed her energies and wealth toward furthering that goal for women. As an eighteenth-century inhabitant of an Anglo-American world, Elizabeth Murray made decisions and choices that shaped her attitudes toward women and independence. At the crosscurrents of central historical developments of the period, she is at once a unique and a representative woman. As she traveled from the Scottish borderlands to the imperial hinterland of Boston, she lived in states of dependence and autonomy, marriage and widowhood. As an economic actor and political being, she found herself in the maelstrom of Revolution. Her path, at once convoluted and complicated, captures the range of a self-made woman's experiences as well as the social and political obstacles that governed an eighteenth-century woman's life and how she negotiated them. Her history—of mobility, benevolence, and loyalty toward her family and her sex—is a legacy of equal importance to the "spirit of Independence" that she cherished in herself and fostered in others.

Note on Writing Biography

In the sole essay written about Elizabeth Murray, Mary Beth Norton describes how Murray's personal independence influenced the way she raised or assisted several women and how she acted as a role model for younger women.[1] She recounts some key experiences of Murray's life: her settling in Boston alone to set up a retail business, her three marriages, and her unusual prenuptial agreements with her second and third husbands, which enabled her to act with much more freedom than the legal restrictions of marriage usually allowed. Norton offered her portrait of "admittedly an extraordinary woman" and "her beliefs and experiences" as a venue for twentieth-century individuals to learn about earlier women. Murray's life could reveal what it was like to be "a self-reliant woman in the eighteenth century, when female Americans had far fewer options than they do today and when their lives were constrained by sharp, seemingly impenetrable boundaries."[2] While Norton's brief essay pointed out important issues, it suggested to me even more powerfully how fruitful a longer study could be for exploring thoroughly the meaning and ramifications of Elizabeth Murray's life. A full biographical treatment seemed the best solution. By adopting this approach, I hope simultaneously to address the need for more in-depth studies of individual women and to examine important questions in the history of early American women.

Until relatively recently, women's lives have been largely obscured by the lack of scholarly interest. Before the 1970s, scholars had not been very concerned with recovering women's stories, particularly those of ordinary women. For the most part, only elite women — such as female monarchs or the wives of statesmen — received scholarly attention. With developments in women's history and social history transforming the field, however, interested scholars set about writing the history of the neglected majority. To great effect, sources such as sermons, advice literature, trial records, and even needlework have been analyzed to reveal the social expectations that governed women's roles.[3] At the same time, social historians, armed with computers and endless patience, have systematically probed birth and death records, newspapers, tax lists, and estate inventories to yield valuable information about the nonelite members of society. Their findings have offered important insights into standards of living, property distribution, and mortality rates, and many other aspects of the colonial experience.

Despite these advances in the practices and pursuits of historians, it continues to be extremely difficult to put enough flesh on the bare bones of statistics to bring fully alive an ordinary, or even many an extraordinary, colonist over the course of a lifetime. Thorough analyses of individual women's lives, such as that offered by Laurel Thatcher Ulrich in her award-winning study *A Midwife's Tale*, rest on the careful and creative use of somewhat fragmentary records and remain too few to capture the diversity of women's experiences. While biographies of colonial men, particularly those of the Revolutionary generation, abound, the number of eighteenth-century women whom we can envision as three-dimensional, breathing beings is limited to a handful.[4] Yet biography holds tremendous promise for transforming our vision of the past. By writing the lives of individuals, historians can more accessibly engage readers with a compelling narrative while testing established historical assumptions and offering new interpretations.

To an American woman historian writing at the end of the twentieth century, Elizabeth Murray's world seems very different in most ways, yet remarkably similar in others. Recognition of the process of comparison, of searching for the points in common, has informed my thinking about this project and about Elizabeth Murray. Like other biographers, I was drawn to a subject whose life seemed to encompass a number of important themes and questions in women's history. I also have found myself considering the connections, or lack thereof, between our lives. In discussing the process of writing about women, the editors of a collection on feminist biography described

their deep, almost inevitable sense of identifying or comparing themselves with their female subjects, as well as the biographers' compul-
sion "to sort out the connection between their lives and the personal,
political, or ideological issues" of today.[5] As I write this study, I realize
my concerns are those of both a historian striving to write a narrative
true to the life of this colonial figure and a woman reflecting on
definitions of womanhood in my time.

For women of the past, as for many women now, ambivalence
proves a key word in describing their experience of and attitudes
toward marriage, family, and work. Shifting definitions and expectations of womanhood, shaped by social, economic, political, and
religious mores, have influenced women's lives. Chronicling the
changes as well as the continuities presents a formidable challenge.
Establishing agency on the part of individual women in the past, in
either promoting or thwarting dominant ideals, can be extremely
difficult. Too often in efforts to analyze the importance of one central institution, such as that of marriage, we neglect other elements
of women's lives. A move beyond the "marriage plot" to the study
of a whole range of other meaningful moments and movements in
women's lives, including an examination of their life cycles, holds the
promise of complexifying our understanding.[6] In contemplating
"the question of woman's biography," Carolyn Heilbrun writes that
"for women, to search for a tradition of past female autonomy and
influence is to enter a problematic realm, full of anxiety and ambivalence."[7] She argues that the conflict that women continue to experience in a society that defines success and public activities as male and
therefore unfeminine causes women biographers to tread the path
of the past with care. They search for examples and predecessors, yet
prove reticent or even unwilling to claim the lives of earlier successful
women as models, either for their own day or for ours. The force of
this dilemma, according to Heilbrun, meant that "before the current
women's movement, it was difficult to find a woman's biography of an
accomplished woman that was not palpably terrified of making any
unseemly claims on behalf of the woman subject."[8]

The kind of claims that we can make on the basis of this "subject"
must emerge from the woman herself. This biographical study consti-
tutes a search for that "self," for the understanding that Elizabeth
Murray had of her life, personality, and growth. In recent years,

scholars of different theoretical persuasions have attacked the validity of various approaches to studying the past, including biography. The assumptions of deconstructionists and postmodernists seem to demand a historical orientation that focuses not on the individual but on the large-scale phenomena. In her survey of the state of women's biography, Kathleen Barry argues that there was in postmodernism "something highly suspicious about the fact that the emphasis has been placed on decentering the subject just at the time when *women's* history has made significant gains by centering on women as the subject of its study."[9]

Barry argues persuasively that a feminist-critical approach to biography has tremendous potential both for recovering women's lives and for challenging historical theories. Too often, she claims, women's subjectivity and actions have been obscured by or reduced to their sexual and reproductive functions.[10] To avoid these pitfalls, the biographer must continually test the interpretation of the subject against the evidence of how the subject understood herself—that is, ground the arguments in the "subjectivity, that which the subject is to herself," of the historical actor. The biographer, therefore, must consciously try to comprehend how the subject would have understood herself while constructing an interpretation. In writing a biography of Susan B. Anthony, Barry found the challenge "was to grasp who she was, to understand how she knew herself, and to know her as she knew herself in her interactions with others." Barry argues that the biographer must become "interactively involved with the subject through interpretation of meanings" and avoid identifying with the subject.[11] Throughout the process of writing this biography, I have tried to be critical of my relationship with Elizabeth Murray, to keep separate my own interests, and to remain grounded in her words and actions, for therein lies her subjectivity: her understanding of herself and her world.[12]

Biographical studies inevitably raise a range of methodological and historical questions about authorial bias and the representativeness of the subject. Recovering the past, regardless of the method of inquiry employed, is never an easy task. Chance and the whims of fate determine which documents survive and what pieces of information are verifiable. With luck and good archives, a biographer can sketch an individual life. But the resulting portrait may be only an outline, lacking color, features, complexity, and depth. Trying to recapture from dry pieces of paper an expression, a mentality, a full human being and the world in which she lived puts the biographer in an odd position. Given the available materials, one runs the risk of imposing an interpretation or creating a figure whom the subject might not have recognized or matched. It is the historian's everyday dilemma — the struggle between our present-minded, long-distance view of the past and the understanding of it held by contemporaries, rendered more difficult, delicate, or poignant by the intimate connection that one comes to have with the central character of the story. That person, in this case an eighteenth-century, Scottish-born woman shopkeeper in Boston, is no longer for me an abstract historical actor, a two-dimensional woman. She has become real, vivid, nuanced. And as such, her persona, or rather my imagining and interpretation of it, hovers over this manuscript, a continual touchstone in my mind as I write her story. Would she recognize herself in this account? Would she see the facets of her life to which I assign importance or historical significance in a similar light?

At times, Elizabeth Murray's movements and motivations have eluded me. She could be frustratingly self-restrained and even reticent in communications with her closest friends and family members. Often, it was the more effusive writings of her intimates that provided the most textured picture of her personality. And no matter how closely I have examined the evidence, some aspects of her life have remained permanently in shadow. There are gaps in her life that simply cannot be filled. At least with Copley's wonderful painting, I had no need to conjure up a face and figure to go with the personality I have come to know through words.

In my view a biographical approach to studying the past bears even more similarity to putting together a jigsaw puzzle than do most other forms of historical inquiry and methodology. Without the cover that shows what the final result should look like, I must follow other, less clear guidelines. And the pieces, which may make up 5 percent or maybe 85 percent of the total, have edges that are rough and worn. It can be difficult to know which piece fits where.

In her opening remarks for a symposium on the study of gender, Linda Kerber declared that it had "long since ceased to be enough to describe women's lives in terms of women's multiple roles" and that the concept of separate female and male spheres also seemed exhausted.[13] Yet Kerber and others have directed attention to the need to consider female and male spheres as linguistically and ideologically constructed, as well as spatially defined. And exploring women's multiple roles remains a useful approach to deriving the meaning from their everyday acts and extraordinary adventures. For it is in the nebulous, ill-defined terrain between the mundane and the monumental moments that the individual moves and breathes and that history excites.

NOTES

ABBREVIATIONS USED IN THE NOTES

HSP   Historical Society of Pennsylvania

JMR   James Murray Robbins Papers, MHS

LCMD   Library of Congress Manuscript Division

Letters   Nina M. Tiffany, ed., assisted by Susan I. Lesley, with a new introduction and preface by George Athan Billias, *Letters of James Murray, Loyalist* (1901; rpt., Boston: Gregg, 1972)

MHS   Massachusetts Historical Society, Boston

NYHS   New-York Historical Society, New York

WDPP   William Dummer Powell Papers, Metropolitan Library of Toronto

INTRODUCTION: AN EXTRAORDINARY ORDINARY WOMAN

1   For discussions of this issue, see Joel Perlmann and Dennis Shirley, "When Did New England Women Acquire Literacy?" *William and Mary Quarterly*, 3d ser., 48 (January 1991): 50–67, and Kathryn Kish Sklar, "The Schooling of Girls and Changing Community Values in Massachusetts Towns, 1750–1820," *History of Education Quarterly* 33 (Winter 1993): 511–42.

2   An important contribution to the body of personal papers available in print is Elaine F. Crane, ed., *The Diary of Elizabeth Drinker: The Life Cycle of an Eighteenth-Century Woman* (Boston: Northeastern University Press, 1994).

3   Linda K. Kerber et al., "Beyond Roles, Beyond Spheres: Thinking about Gender in the Early Republic," *William and Mary Quarterly*, 3d ser., 46 (July 1989): 567.

4   Patricia Cleary, " 'She Merchants' of Colonial America: Women and Commerce on the Eve of the Revolution" (Ph.D. diss., Northwestern University, 1989).

5   See Neil McKendrick, John Brewer, and J. H. Plumb, *The Birth of a Consumer Society: The Commercialization of Eighteenth-Century England* (Bloomington: Indiana University Press, 1982); T. H. Breen, " 'Baubles of Britain': The American and Consumer Revolutions of the Eighteenth Century," *Past and Present*, no. 119 (1988): 73–104, and "An Empire of Goods: The Anglicization of Colonial America, 1690–1776," *Journal of British Studies* 25 (October 1986): 467–99; Carole Shammas, *The Pre-industrial Consumer in England and America* (Oxford: Clarendon, 1990); and the

collection of essays edited by John Brewer and Roy Porter, *Consumption and the World of Goods* (New York: Routledge, 1993). Lorna Weatherill connected an expansion in women's roles as purchasers to an increase in shops in "A Possession of One's Own: Women and Consumer Behavior in England, 1660–1740," *Journal of British Studies* 25 (April 1986): 131–56.

6   For a discussion of historians' treatments of women shopkeepers, see Cleary, " 'She Merchants' of Colonial America." Earlier examinations of women's commercial activities appear in Julia Cherry Spruill, *Women's Life and Work in the Southern Colonies* (Chapel Hill: University of North Carolina Press, 1938; rpt., New York: W. W. Norton, 1972), and Elisabeth Anthony Dexter, *Colonial Women of Affairs: A Study of Women in Business and the Professions in America before 1776* (New York: Houghton Mifflin, 1924). Mary Beth Norton examines Murray's life in "A Cherished Spirit of Independence: The Life of an Eighteenth-Century Boston Businesswoman," in *Women of America: A History*, ed. Carol Ruth Berkin and Mary Beth Norton (Boston: Houghton Mifflin, 1979), 48–67.

7   Thomas Doerflinger details the evolution of and mobility with the mercantile community in *A Vigorous Spirit of Enterprise: Merchants and Economic Development in Revolutionary Philadelphia* (Chapel Hill: University of North Carolina Press for the Institute of Early American History and Culture, 1986).

8   Carol Troyen, curator for American paintings, Museum of Fine Arts, Boston, telephone interview with author, September 28, 1995. The portrait was once again in storage in July 1999 (Troyen, email communication with author, July 27, 1999).

9   Elizabeth [Murray] Smith to [Mrs. Rowe], 24 April 1770, Margaret Howe Ewing Papers, Private Collection (hereafter Ewing Papers).

1. MIGRATION AND MOBILITY

1   For several years, Spanish and French privateers had been plaguing the American coast. The British forces that sailed to Jamaica from North Carolina in November 1740 were under the command of Captain James Innes. Almost all these troops died, either in the fighting at Cartagena or from disease. Of the one hundred men who sailed from Cape Fear, only twenty-five survived. No victory accompanied such losses; by the summer of 1741 the British gave up the siege. See Lawrence Lee, *The Lower Cape Fear in Colonial Days* (Chapel Hill: University of North Carolina Press, 1965), 229; James Sprunt, ed. and comp., *Chronicles of the Cape Fear River* (1916; Spartanburg, S.C.: Reprint Company, 1973), 49, 52; and Hugh T. Lefler and William S. Powell, *Colonial North Carolina: A History* (New York: Charles Scribner's Sons, 1973), 129–32.

2   James Murray to Mrs. Bennet, 26 November 1740, in *Letters of James Murray, Loyalist*, ed. Nina M. Tiffany, assisted by Susan I. Lesley [hereafter *Letters*] (1901; Boston: Gregg Press, 1972), 48.

3   "Unthank" may have referred to useless land or soil that remained impervious to attempts to improve it. For one definition, see Alex MacBain, *Place Names Highlands and Islands of Scotland* (Stirling, Scotland: Eneas Mackay, 1922), 317.

4   Elizabeth [Murray] Smith to [unknown], 19 July 1770, Ewing Papers. I thank Mr. Stephen Busby, the current owner of Unthank, for generously allowing me to

explore the estate, including the ruins of Elizabeth Murray's home, and climb its hills on a rainy June day, 1998, and for his correspondence. He also gave Murray family history seekers Peggy and Joe Ewing my name and address, an act that led to the inclusion of the Margaret Howe Ewing Papers for this volume.

5   Francis H. Groome, ed., *Ordnance Gazetteer of Scotland: A Survey of Scottish Topography, Statistical, Biographical, and Historical*, vol. 3 (Edinburgh: Thomas C. Jack, Grange Publishing Works, 1883), 582. As the eighteenth century drew to a close, an observer noted that the population of Ewes had "for some time past, been diminishing." A 1755 report counted 392 inhabitants; four decades later, that figure had fallen to 320 people, in contrast to approximately 18,000 sheep, 120 cattle, and 40 to 50 horses. See Rev. Mr. John Laurie, "Parish of Ewes," in *The Statistical Account of Scotland*, ed. John Sinclair, 21 vols. (Edinburgh: William Creech, 1791–99), 14:468–69.

6   Laurie, "Parish of Ewes," 14:465–66.

7   Ibid., 14:466–67.

8   Dorothy Wordsworth, quoted in Groome, *Ordnance Gazetteer of Scotland*, 582.

9   Rev. Mr. William Brown, "Parish of Eskdalemuir," in *Statistical Account of Scotland*, ed. Sinclair, 12:610. Just along the sheltered Esk the climate was more temperate, relatively free from the sharp and piercing weather elsewhere that contributed to what one observer described as very common cases of rheumatism and nervous disorders (Rev. Mr. John Russell, "Parish of Canoby," in ibid., 14:412).

10 Brown, "Parish of Eskdalemuir," 12:607. The Esk ran through Eskdale's five parishes of Canoby, Langholme, Eskdalemuir, Westerkirk, and Ewes and marked part of the border with England.

11 *Letters*, 1. See also "Memoir of the Late James Murray," Murray Papers, box 7, NYHS.

12 Ned C. Landsman, *Scotland and Its First American Colony, 1683–1765* (Princeton: Princeton University Press, 1985), 21–22, 30.

13 Ibid., 45.

14 James Murray to [Andrew Bennet], 4 July 1732, Letterbooks, 1732–69, James Murray Papers, MHS [hereafter Letterbooks, 1732–69].

15 James Murray to Mrs. Murray, 6 October 1733, Letterbooks, 1732–69.

16 James Murray to Andrew Bennet, 5 October 1734, Letterbooks, 1732–69.

17 James Murray to Andrew Bennet, 5 August 1732, Letterbooks, 1732–69.

18 Ibid. On medical education in Edinburgh, see Anand C. Chitnis, "Provost Drummond and the Origins of Edinburgh Medicine," in *The Origins and Nature of the Scottish Enlightenment*, ed. R. H. Campbell and Andrew S. Skinner (Edinburgh: John Donal Publishers, 1982): 86–97, and R. G. W. Anderson and A. D. C. Simpson, eds., *The Early Years of the Edinburgh Medical School* (Edinburgh: Royal Scottish Museum, 1976).

19 Murray to Bennet, 5 August 1732.

20 Lorna Weatherill, *Consumer Behaviour and Material Culture in Britain, 1660–1760* (New York: Routledge, 1988), 169–71, 183–89. Lawrence E. Klein discusses the difficulties involved in defining such terms as *politeness* and explores the adaptive social identities Englishmen embraced in "Politeness for Plebes: Consumption and

Social Identity in Early-Eighteenth-Century England," in *The Consumption of Culture, 1600–1800: Image, Object, Text*, ed. Ann Bermingham and John Brewer (New York: Routledge, 1995), 362–82.

21 James Murray to Barbara Murray, 13 October 1734, Letterbooks, 1732–69.

22 Ibid.

23 For changes in women's roles as purchasers and consumers, see Lorna Weatherill, "A Possession of One's Own: Women and Consumer Behavior in England, 1660–1740," *Journal of British Studies* 25 (April 1986): 131–56. Women's consumerism as a dangerous phenomenon is discussed in G. J. Barker-Benfield, *The Culture of Sensibility: Sex and Society in Eighteenth-Century Britain* (Chicago: University of Chicago Press, 1992), 154–214.

24 Lorna Weatherill concludes that the impact of emulation as a primary force driving the acquisition of new goods has been overstated, ignoring both the evidence regarding possession of particular items and the multiple functions that objects filled. See *Consumer Behaviour and Material Culture*, 194–96. Others have explored this theme, finding evidence in fiction for the "poor's dangerous emulation of their betters"; see Ronald Paulson, "Emulative Consumption and Literacy: The Harlot, Moll Flanders, and Mrs. Slipslop," in *Consumption of Culture*, ed. Bermingham and Brewer, 383–400 (quotation is on 395). See also Klein, "Politeness for Plebes," 374–75.

25 James Murray to Barbara Murray, 13 October 1734, Letterbooks, 1732–69.

26 Bruce G. Trigger, ed., *Northeast*, vol. 15 of *Handbook of North American Indians*, ed. William G. Sturtevant (Washington, D.C.: Smithsonian Institution, 1978), 284. While major outbreaks of disease in 1698, 1718, and 1738 seriously weakened the Tuscarora Indians, colonists invaded their territory, desirous of the tidewater lands that Native Americans had cultivated for generations. Gary Nash, *Red, White, and Black: The Peoples of Early North America*, 3d ed. (Englewood Cliffs, N.J.: Prentice-Hall, 1992), 135.

27 Algonquian allies of the Tuscarora, devastated by disease, fell in even greater numbers. Trigger, *Northeast*, 279, 287.

28 Lee, *Lower Cape Fear*, 80, 82–83.

29 James H. Merrell, *The Indians' New World: Catawbas and Their Neighbors from European Contact through the Era of Removal* (Chapel Hill: University of North Carolina Press, 1989), 53–54; Nash, *Red, White, and Black*, 135–38; Verner Winslow Crane, *The Southern Frontier, 1670–1732* (1929; Ann Arbor: University of Michigan Press, 1959), 161.

30 E. Lawrence Lee, *Indian Wars in North Carolina, 1663–1763* (Raleigh, N.C.: Carolina Charter Tercentenary Commission, 1963), 46.

31 Marvin L. Michael Kay and Lorin Lee Cary, *Slavery in North Carolina, 1748–1775* (Chapel Hill: University of North Carolina Press, 1995), 15.

32 Ibid., 19.

33 William S. Powell, *North Carolina through Four Centuries* (Chapel Hill: University of North Carolina Press, 1989), 83–84.

34 Lee, *Lower Cape Fear*, 183–85. Three hundred and fifty Highland Scots who emigrated in September 1739 stayed in Wilmington only briefly before moving to the Northwest Cape Fear.

35   Ibid., 123–24.

36   Sprunt, *Chronicles of the Cape Fear River*, 45–46.

37   Ian Charles Cargill Graham, *Colonists from Scotland: Emigration to North America, 1707–1783* (Ithaca: Cornell University Press, 1956), 147.

38   Thomas M. Doerflinger, *A Vigorous Spirit of Enterprise: Merchants and Economic Development in Revolutionary Philadelphia* (Chapel Hill: University of North Carolina Press for the Institute of Early American History and Culture, 1986), 59–61. Frederick B. Tolles, *Meeting House and Counting House: The Quaker Merchants of Colonial Philadelphia, 1682–1763* (1948; New York: W. W. Norton, 1963).

39   Landsman, *Scotland and Its First American Colony*, 210–13.

40   James Murray to Andrew Bennet, 13 May 1735, Letterbooks, 1732–69.

41   John Brickell, *The Natural History of North Carolina* (Dublin, 1737; rpt., Murfreesboro, N.C.: Johnson Publishing, 1968), 31.

42   For the description of ships and local activities in the 1720s, see Daniel Defoe, *A Tour thro' the Whole Island of Great Britain*, 2 vols. (1724–26; New York: Augustus M. Kelley, 1968), 1:99–103 (quotation is on 101).

43   On indentured servitude see Sharon Salinger, *"To Serve Well and Faithfully": Labor and Indentured Servants in Pennsylvania, 1682–1800* (Cambridge: Cambridge University Press, 1987).

44   Lois Green Carr and Lorena S. Walsh, "The Planter's Wife: The Experience of White Women in Seventeenth-Century Maryland," *William and Mary Quarterly*, 3d ser., 34 (October 1977): 542–571.

45   Lefler and Powell, *Colonial North Carolina*, 90.

46   Harry Roy Merrens, *Colonial North Carolina in the Eighteenth Century: A Study in Historical Geography* (Chapel Hill: University of North Carolina Press, 1964), 25.

47   These figures are based on 1750 quitrent records, New Hanover tax records from 1762, and James Murray's own estimates of the value of his property in 1767. He calculated that his plantation was worth £2,000 and that he had £500 worth of mill lands, as well as property in Wilmington worth another £250 and property at Rockfish. See William S. Price Jr., " 'Men of Good Estates': Wealth among North Carolina's Royal Councillors," *North Carolina Historical Review* 49, (January 1972): 79, and *Letters*, 156 n.

48   Bernard Bailyn, *The Peopling of British North America: An Introduction* (New York: Alfred A. Knopf, 1986), 4–8.

49   Defoe, *Tour*, 2:748.

50   Landsman, *Scotland and Its First American Colony*, 6.

51   Eric Richards, "Scotland and the Uses of the Atlantic Empire," in *Strangers within the Realm: Cultural Margins of the First British Empire*, ed. Bernard Bailyn and Philip Morgan (Chapel Hill: University of North Carolina Press for the Institute of Early American History and Culture, 1991), 69, 77.

52   Ibid., 69, 76, 95.

53   For an analysis of this material, see chap. 9, " 'A Constant Intercourse of Letters': The Transatlantic Flow of Information," in David Cressy, *Coming Over: Migration and Communication between England and New England in the Seventeenth Century* (New York: Cambridge University Press, 1987).

54   For a discussion of childbirth customs and a community of women in America, see

Catherine M. Scholten, "'On the Important of the Obstetrick Art': Changing Customs of Childbirth in America, 1760 to 1825," *William and Mary Quarterly*, 3d ser. (July 1977): 426–55, and Laurel Thatcher Ulrich, *Good Wives: Image and Reality in the Lives of Women in Northern New England, 1650–1750* (New York: Oxford University Press, 1983), esp. chap. 7, "Travail," 126–45.

55 James Murray to Henry McCulloh, Brunswick, Cape Fear, 8 July 1736, in *Letters*, 33.
56 Ibid., 3 May 1736, in *Letters*, 30.
57 James Murray to [Henry McCulloh], Newton, 6 November 1736, in *Letters*, 35.
58 Kay and Cary, *Slavery in North Carolina*, 22, 24, 36, 44–45.
59 James Murray to Andrew Bennet, 14 February [1736], Letterbooks, 1732–69.
60 James Murray to Thomas Clark, 23 December 1738, Letterbooks, 1732–69.
61 For a discussion of regional variation, see Patricia Cleary, "'She Merchants' of Colonial America: Women and Commerce on the Eve of the Revolution" (Ph.D. diss., Northwestern University, 1989), 38–40.
62 James Murray to unknown, 23 December 1738, Letterbooks, 1732–69.
63 Kay and Cary, *Slavery in North Carolina*, 21.
64 Ibid., 48.
65 Elizabeth [Murray] Smith to unknown, 19 July 1770, Ewing Papers.
66 James Murray to James Rutherford, [4] September 1739, Letterbooks, 1732–69.
67 Merrens, *Colonial North Carolina in the Eighteenth Century*, 47, 86, 109, 128–29.
68 Sprunt, *Chronicles of the Cape Fear River*, 43–44.
69 The average precipitation was fifty inches (Merrens, *Colonial North Carolina in the Eighteenth Century*, 43, 45).
70 For the events leading up to this rebellion, see Peter H. Wood, *Black Majority: Negroes in Colonial South Carolina from 1670 through the Stono Uprising* (New York: Norton, 1975).
71 James Murray to Mrs. Bennet, September 1740, Letterbooks, 1732–69.
72 James Murray to James Hazel, 28 February 1744, Letterbooks, 1732–69.
73 James Murray to Mrs. Bennet, Cape Fear, September 1740, in *Letters*, 47.
74 James Murray to Henry McCulloh, 11 May 1741, in *Letters*, 63–64.
75 Quotations in this paragraph are from James Murray to Andrew Bennet, 5 September 1741, Letterbooks, 1732–69.
76 Roy Porter, *London: A Social History* (Cambridge: Harvard University Press, 1994), 131, 132, 136.
77 Peter Earle, *The World of Defoe* (New York: Atheneum, 1977), 31.
78 Porter, *London*, 134.
79 On the importance of London as a distribution and fashion center, see Hoh-cheung Mui and Lorna H. Mui, *Shops and Shopkeeping in Eighteenth-Century England* (London: Routledge, 1989), 46–72.
80 For a discussion of servants as consumers of fashion, see Neil McKendrick, "The Commercialization of Fashion," in McKendrick, John Brewer, and J. H. Plumb, *The Birth of a Consumer Society: The Commercialization of Eighteenth-Century England* (Bloomington: Indiana University Press, 1982), 34–99.
81 Elizabeth [Murray] Smith to Christian Barnes, 24 April 1770, Ewing Papers.
82 Carl Bridenbaugh, *Cities in Revolt: Urban Life in America, 1743–1776* (New York: Knopf, 1955), 29–30 (quotation is on 30), 38, 40, 41.

83 Walter Muir Whitehill, *Boston: A Topographical History*, 2d ed. (Cambridge: Harvard University Press, Belknap Press, 1968), 26–27.

84 Ibid., 41.

85 Lefler and Powell, *Colonial North Carolina*, 136–37.

86 James Murray to Jean Bennet, 24 July 1749, Letterbooks, 1732–69.

87 James Murray to John Murray, 27 July 1749, Letterbooks, 1732–69. James ultimately concluded that she was "determin'd to stay." See ibid., 7 September 1749.

88 Peter Earle, *A City Full of People: Men and Women of London, 1650–1750* (London: Methuen, 1994), 140.

89 Gary Nash, "The Failure of Female Factory Labor in Colonial Boston," in *Race, Class, and Politics: Essays on American Colonial and Revolutionary Society* (Chicago: University of Illinois Press, 1986), 120.

90 Earle, *City Full of People*, 39–40.

91 Sharon Salinger, " 'Send No More Women': Female Servants in Eighteenth-Century Philadelphia," *Pennsylvania Magazine of History and Biography* 107 (January 1983): 29–48.

92 See, for example, Merry Weisner Wood, "Paltry Peddlers or Essential Merchants? Women in the Distributive Trades in Early Modern Europe," *Sixteenth Century Journal* 12 (Summer 1981): 3–13, and Alice Clark, *Working Life of Women in the Seventeenth Century* (1919; rpt., Boston: Routledge and Kegan Paul, 1982), 198–209.

93 Elizabeth C. Sanderson, *Women and Work in Eighteenth-Century Edinburgh* (New York: St. Martin's, 1996), 16–17.

94 Ibid., 7–16.

95 Earle, *City Full of People*, 142–43.

96 For details on the experiment in linen manufacturing, see Nash, "Failure of Female Factory Labor in Colonial Boston," 119–40.

97 See Julia Cherry Spruill, *Women's Life and Work in the Southern Colonies*, with an introduction by Anne Firor Scott (Chapel Hill: University of North Carolina Press, 1938; rpt., New York: W. W. Norton , 1972), chaps. 12, 13, 14.

98 Spruill, *Women's Life and Work*, 289.

2. A "SHE MERCHANT" IN BOSTON

1 James Murray to Elizabeth Murray, 4 September 1749, Letterbooks, 1732–69.

2 "Boyle's Journal of Occurrences in Boston, 1759–1778," *New England Historical and Genealogical Register* 84 (April 1930): 157. Quick lost over one thousand pounds worth of real and personal estate in the fire of 1760 and was identified as a "rich" person; see Ms. Am. 1809 (104–105), Boston Fire Records, Boston Public Library, Boston.

3 Boston Registry Department, *Report of the Record Commissioners: Boston Town Records*. 39 vols. (Boston, 1876–1909), 17:19.

4 For a detailed discussion of women shopkeepers, see Patricia Cleary, " 'She Merchants' of Colonial America: Women and Commerce on the Eve of the Revolution" (Ph.D. diss., Northwestern University, 1989).

5 Patricia Cleary, " 'She will be in the Shop': Women's Sphere of Trade in Eigh-

teenth-Century New York and Philadelphia," *Pennsylvania Magazine of History and Biography* 119 (July 1995): 181–202.

6 Using newspapers, Elisabeth Anthony Dexter ventured that women accounted for a little less than 10 percent of colonial retailers (*Colonial Women of Affairs: A Study of Women in Business and the Professions in America before 1776* [New York: Houghton Mifflin, 1924], 38. Jean P. Jordan concluded that Dexter's figure was too high and that at most women made up 2 percent of New York's commercial community. Using a variety of sources, especially mercantile records, I found more women involved in trade in New York in the 1760s alone than Jordan did for the period 1660–1775 (Jordan, "Women Merchants in Colonial New York," *New York History* 58 [October 1977]: 436; Cleary, "She Merchants," 94–96). Another low estimate counted only ten women of business in New York between 1768 and 1775 (Robert Michael Dructor, "The New York Commercial Community: The Revolutionary Experience" [Ph.D. diss., University of Pittsburgh, 1975], 15–16). Claudia Goldin estimated that in 1791, 28 percent of all shopkeepers in Philadelphia were women ("The Economic Status of Women in the Early Republic: Quantitative Evidence," *Journal of Interdisciplinary History* 16, no. 3 (1986): 402; see also Hannah Benner Roach, "Taxables in the City of Philadelphia, 1756," *Pennsylvania Genealogical Magazine* 22, no. 1 [1961]: 3–41). The tax assessors ascribed occupations to 59 out of 184 women on the list; no women were described as merchants. The tax lists, which offer a rough sense of the proportion of shopkeepers of each sex, also show that in the 1750s and 1760s, male shopkeepers, in general, were more prosperous than their female counterparts. For a discussion of difficulties involved in using tax lists, see Thomas Doerflinger, *A Vigorous Spirit of Enterprise: Merchants and Economic Development in Revolutionary Philadelphia* (Chapel Hill: University of North Carolina Press for the Institute of Early American History and Culture, 1986), 63–67, 384–86.

7 *New York Weekly Journal*, 21 January 1733.

8 *Pennsylvania Gazette*, 19 November 1730.

9 Ibid., 3 December 1730.

10 Ronald A. Bosco, " 'He that best understands the World, least likes it': The Dark Side of Benjamin Franklin," *Pennsylvania Magazine of History and Biography* 111 (October 1987): 542.

11 James Murray to Aeneas and Hugh Mackay, 12 September 1749, Letterbooks, 1732–69.

12 Virginia Harrington, *The New York Merchant on the Eve of the Revolution* (New York: Columbia University Press, 1935), 101.

13 James Murray to Elizabeth Murray, 4 September 1749, Letterbooks, 1732–69.

14 Elizabeth Murray to James Murray, 27 May 1753, J. M. Robbins Papers, MHS (hereafter JMR). For currency values in Massachusetts and North Carolina, see John J. McCusker, *Money and Exchange in Europe and America, 1600–1775: A Handbook* (Chapel Hill: University of North Carolina Press, 1978), 133–50, 215–19.

15 Ultimately, Barbara Murray Clark paid her sister four hundred pounds for Kelso.

16 James Murray to Elizabeth Murray, 4 September 1749.

17 James Murray to Richard Oswald and Co., copy appended to James Murray to Elizabeth Murray, 15 February [1750], JMR.

18 Ibid.

19 James Murray to Elizabeth Murray, 4 September 1749.

20 James Murray to Richard Oswald and Co., 15 February [1750].

21 James Murray to Elizabeth Murray, 4 September 1749.

22 James Murray to Richard Oswald and Co., [February 1750], JMR.

23 James Murray to Bridgen and Waller, 21 June 1756, Letterbooks, 1732–69.

24 James Murray to Elizabeth Murray, 4 September 1749.

25 James Murray to Elizabeth Murray, 15 February [1750], JMR.

26 John Murray to James Murray, 28 February 1753, JMR.

27 James Murray to Mrs. Bennet, 19 September 1749, Letterbooks, 1732–69.

28 James Murray to Elizabeth Murray, 15 February [1750].

29 James Murray to John Murray (of Philipaugh), 10 November 1750, Letterbooks, 1732–69.

30 James Murray to John Murray, 31 July 1751, Letterbooks, 1732–69.

31 James Murray to Elizabeth Murray, 4 September 1749.

32 James Murray to Richard Oswald, 8 September 1750, Letterbooks, 1732–69.

33 *Boston Evening-Post*, 11 June 1750.

34 Elizabeth Murray broadside, [Cornhill, Boston, 1750], Advertising Cards, MHS. Although someone has written 1749 on the broadside, it is more probable that it dates to 1750 at the earliest, after she received her first big shipment of goods.

35 Although skilled workers in the colonies produced various kinds of cloth, imported fabrics filled much of the colonial demand. See Adrienne D. Hood, "The Material World of Cloth: Production and Use in Eighteenth-Century Rural Pennsylvania," *William and Mary Quarterly*, 3d ser., 53 (January 1996): 43–66.

36 *Oxford English Dictionary*, 2d ed. (Oxford: Clarendon, 1989), 493.

37 For a discussion of advertising changes during this period, see T. H. Breen, " 'Baubles of Britain': The American and Consumer Revolutions of the Eighteenth Century," *Past and Present*, no. 119 (1988): 73–104.

38 *Boston Evening-Post*, 21 January 1754, 5 September 1757.

39 Ibid., 11 June 1750.

40 Ibid., 20 August 1750.

41 Ibid., 28 May 1750.

42 Ibid., 25 March 1751.

43 Betty Ring, *Girlhood Embroidery: American Samplers and Pictorial Needlework, 1650–1850* (New York: Alfred A. Knopf, 1993), 2:345.

44 From 1745 to 1754, at least 33 women in Boston kept shop. That figure rose to 43 in the ten years from 1755 to 1764 and to 46 between 1765 and 1774. Overall, 41 women ran shops between 1745 and 1759 and 64 from 1760 until the Revolution (Cleary, " 'She Merchants' of Colonial America," 78, 91–95).

45 Calculations of business tenure were based on a variety of evidence from newspapers, mercantile records, correspondence, and probate documents.

46 East discovered the risks of wedlock after her husband's debts made it difficult for her to carry on business. Henrietta Maria East, Suffolk Files no. 129736, Divorces, 1760–1784, Suffolk County Court House, Boston.

47 Jane Eustis, 10 June 1760, Suffolk County Divorce Records, no. 1, Suffolk County Courthouse, Boston.

48 Letters of guardianship, 26 September 1749, Suffolk Probate Records, 43:129–33, Suffolk County Court House, Boston.

49 Whitney willed four hundred pounds lawful money each to her son, Samuel, and daughter Anna and the reside of her estate to Abigail. Ibid., Abigail Whitney, Will, 66:89–90.

50 Ibid., Hannah Newman, Will, 51:657–60.

51 *Boston Evening-Post*, 1 May 1758.

52 Elizabeth Murray to James Murray, 23 October 1753, JMR.

53 James Murray to John Murray, 31 July 1751, Letterbooks, 1732–69.

54 James Murray to Edward Bridgen, 6 August 1751, Letterbooks, 1732–69.

55 Ibid.

56 Elizabeth Murray to James Murray, 27 May 1753, JMR.

57 Louis P. Masur, ed., *The Autobiography of Benjamin Franklin* (New York: St. Martin's, Bedford Books, 1993), 77–78.

58 Elizabeth Murray to James Murray, 27 May 1753.

59 *Boston Evening-Post*, August–October 1754.

60 East, Suffolk Files no. 129736, 2–3.

61 Henrietta Maria Caine, Inventories, Suffolk Probate Records, 59:265–81, 61:48–49.

62 Elizabeth Murray to James Murray, 27 September 1754, JMR.

63 Ibid.

64 *Boston Evening-Post*, 12, 19, 26 March 1753.

65 Faith Trumbull's needlework and education are described in detail in Ring, *Girlhood Embroidery*, 1:54–59.

66 Ibid., 55. Ring cites a receipt dated 2 July 1754, Trumbull Papers, Connecticut Historical Society, and suggests that Faith Trumbull continued to study with Elizabeth Murray after Elizabeth returned from London in 1754.

67 Elizabeth Murray to James Murray, 4 December 1753, JMR.

68 Ibid.

69 Ibid.

70 Ibid.

71 Ibid., 2 April 1754.

72 Ibid.

73 Ibid.

74 Ibid., 1 November 1754.

75 Ibid., 11 April 1755.

76 James Murray to Lady Don, 14 January 1756, Letterbooks, 1732–69.

77 James Murray to John Murray, 26 January 1756, Letterbooks, 1732–69.

78 James Murray to John Murray, February 1757 [date missing from folio copy], Letterbooks, 1732–69. James's comments underline the significance of the lack of convents as a European, Catholic option for women who eschewed both marriage and business. For a survey of the importance of these contrasts, see Elaine F. Crane, *Ebb Tide in New England: Women, Seaports, and Social Change, 1630–1800* (Boston: Northeastern University Press, 1998), 27, 31–32.

79 James Murray to John Murray, 26 January 1756.

80 Ibid.

81   Barbara Murray Clark to Elizabeth [Murray] Campbell, 8 December 1757, JMR.

82   Barbara Murray Clark to Thomas Campbell, 8 December 1757, JMR.

83   Barbara Murray Clark to Elizabeth [Murray] Campbell, 8 December 1757.

84   James Murray to Bridgen and Waller, June 21, 1756, Letterbooks, 1732–69.

85   Ibid.

86   James Murray to John Murray, February 1757, Letterbooks, 1732–69.

87   See JMR for correspondence from 1756 to 1757.

88   Goldin, "Economic Status of Women," 400.

89   *Boston Evening-Post*, 31 January 1763; Boston Registry Department, *Report of the Record Commissioners*, 19:263.

90   See Kathryn Kish Sklar, "The Schooling of Girls and Changing Community Values in Massachusetts Towns, 1750–1820," *History of Education Quarterly* 33 (Winter 1993): 511–42.

91   Sklar described the situation in Sutton, Massachusetts, where public funds first supported summer schools, where girls and boys were instructed, in 1767; in Boston, similar funding appeared only in 1789, and girls were not allowed to attend regular winter schools until 1828 (ibid., 525, 537).

92   Elizabeth [Murray] Campbell to James Murray, 3 December 1756, JMR.

93   Ring, *Girlhood Embroidery*, 1:60–68.

94   *Boston Evening-Post*, 21 April 1755.

95   Elizabeth [Murray] Campbell to James Murray, 12 May 1756, JMR.

96   Elizabeth [Murray] Campbell to Barbara [Bennet] Murray, 1 August 1757, JMR.

97   Ring noted Day's Newport announcement, in the *Newport Mercury*, 8 May 1759, in *Girlhood Embroidery*, 1:59 n. 19.

98   In her 1776 will, Sarah Todd left her entire estate, "Real, personal and mixt," to her "dearly beloved friend Mary Purcell." See Sarah Todd, Will, Suffolk Probate Records, 76:593, Suffolk County Courthouse, Boston.

99   Several women shopkeepers expressed their regard by giving partial or entire estates to other women retailers. Sarah McNeal, a widowed Boston trader, left all her substantial property, including a house and land, to her "faithfull Maid Servant & Friend Ann Dearden." See Sarah McNeal, Will, Suffolk Probate Records, 58:282–84, Suffolk County Courthouse, Boston. At the time of McNeal's death in 1761, Dearden was already keeping shop.

100   *Boston Evening-Post*, 26 March 1759, 30 April 1759, 20 August 1759.

101   James Murray to John Murray, 9 February 1757, Letterbooks, 1732–69.

102   James Murray to Dolly Murray, 21 March 1758, Letterbooks, 1732–69.

103   Elizabeth Murray to James Murray, 12 May 1756, JMR.

104   Elizabeth [Murray] Campbell to James Murray, 3 December 1756, JMR.

105   Dolly could have attended a school like that advertised by William Elphinstone, who targeted "Persons of both Sexes, from 12 Years of Age to 50, who never wrote before." They could learn "to write a good legible Hand in Five Weeks," by studying one hour per day under his guidance. In addition to instructing the novice scribe, Elphinstone promised to accommodate those who sought polish and wished to acquire "a Form, which is highly approved of by those who are remarkable for a just refined Taste" (*Boston Evening-Post*, 14 July 1755).

106   Thomas Campbell to James Murray, 20 February 1758, JMR.

107   Elizabeth [Murray] Campbell to [Barbara Bennet] Murray, January 1758, JMR.
108   Ibid.
109   James Murray to John Rutherford, 3 March 1755, Letterbooks, 1732–69.
110   Tiffany listed five daughters and two sons born to the Murrays between 1745 and 1758, in *Letters*, 77.
111   James Murray to Mrs. Bennet, Cape Fear, 25 March 1758, Letterbooks, 1732–69.
112   Darret B. Rutman and Anita H. Rutman, "Of Agues and Fevers: Malaria in the Early Chesapeake," *William and Mary Quarterly*, 3d ser., 33 (January 1976): 31–60.
113   James Murray to Mrs. Bennet, 25 March 1758.
114   Rutman and Rutman, "Of Agues and Fevers," 52–53.
115   James Murray to Mrs. Bennet, 25 March 1758.
116   James Murray to Barbara [Murray] Clark, 1 April 1758, Letterbooks, 1732–69.
117   James Murray to Elizabeth [Murray] Campbell, 31 March 1758, Letterbooks, 1732–69.
118   James Murray to Barbara [Murray] Clark, 1 April 1758.
119   James Murray to John Murray, 23 January 1759, Letterbooks, 1732–69.
120   James Murray to Dolly Murray, 14 December 1753, Letterbooks, 1732–69.
121   James Murray to Thomas Campbell, 13 December 1758, Letterbooks, 1732–69.
122   John Duffy, *Epidemics in Colonial America* (Baton Rouge: Louisiana State University Press, 1953), 174–75.
123   *Boston Gazette*, 12 February 1759. I thank my brother, Tom Cleary, M.D., a specialist in pediatric infectious disease at the University of Texas–Houston Medical School, for explaining some of the properties of measles.
124   William MacKenzie to Robert Campbell, 21 October 1759, JMR.
125   Elizabeth [Murray] Campbell to James Murray, 16 January 1760, box 1, typescripts, 1732–74, JMR.
126   Ibid.
127   *Boston Gazette*, supplement, 7 May 1759.

3. THE BONDS OF MARRIAGE AND BENEVOLENCE

1   Samuel G. Drake, *The History and Antiquities of Boston, the Capital of Massachusetts and Metropolis of New England, from Its Settlement in 1630, to the Year 1770* (Boston: Luther Stevens, 1856), 649–53; *Boston Evening-Post*, 24 March 1760.
2   G. B. Warden traced the impact of the 1760 fire on Bostonians' developing efforts to communicate about their problems and make them of more than local interest; aid came from churches, legislatures, and private individuals throughout the colonies. See Warden, *Boston, 1689–1776* (Boston: Little, Brown, 1970), 150.
3   In addition to Mary Jackson, several other women retailers located in central Boston lost property in the fire. Sarah McNeal and her servant Ann Dearden, who both sold goods out of McNeal's home, reported substantial losses. Assessors described McNeal as a "rich" person with losses of £400 in real estate and personal estate losses valued at £2,005 "Lawfull Money." Dearden lost £137 in personal estate and was identified as a person of "middling" wealth. Records Commission, *A Volume of Records Relating to the Early History of Boston, Containing Miscellane-

ous Papers (Boston: Municipal Printing Office, 1900), 29:37; Ms. Am. 1809 (2), Boston Fire Records, Boston Public Library, Boston. Shopkeeper Alice Quick, identified as a "rich" person, lost over one thousand pounds of real and personal estate in the fire. See ibid., Ms. Am. 1809 (104–105). On the uses of the fire records, see William Pencak, "The Social Structure of Revolutionary Boston: Evidence from the Great Fire of 1760," *Journal of Interdisciplinary History* 10 (Autumn 1979): 267–78. These sources report different amounts of losses.

4   *Boston Evening-Post*, 31 March 1760.

5   Nancy Cott explored the constraints shaping nineteenth-century women's domestic lives and the multiple meanings of "bonds" in *The Bonds of Womanhood: "Woman's Sphere" in New England, 1780–1835* (New Haven: Yale University Press, 1977).

6   *Letters*, 107.

7   James Murray to Jean and Anne Bennet, 4 August 1760, Letterbooks, 1732–69.

8   Christian Barnes to Elizabeth [Murray] Smith, 11 June 1769, Papers of Christian Barnes, 1768–1784, Library of Congress Manuscript Division (hereafter LCMD).

9   Mary Beth Norton first wrote about Elizabeth Murray's unusual legal arrangements in "A Cherished Spirit of Independence: The Life of an Eighteenth-Century Boston Businesswoman," in *Women of America: A History*, ed. Carol Ruth Berkin and Mary Beth Norton (Boston: Houghton Mifflin, 1979), 48–67.

10 Marylynn Salmon, *Women and the Law of Property in Early America* (Chapel Hill: University of North Carolina Press, 1986), 8–9, 122.

11 Ibid.,133.

12 Mary Beth Norton, *Liberty's Daughters: The Revolutionary Experience of American Women, 1750–1800* (Boston: Little, Brown, 1980), 40–65.

13 "Indenture of James Smith to Elizabeth Campbell," 13 March 1760, JMR; Salmon, *Women and the Law of Property*, 7–8, 86, 146–47.

14 In addition to Salmon's work, see Joan R. Gundersen and Gwen Victor Gampel, "Married Women's Legal Status in Eighteenth-Century New York and Virginia," *William and Mary Quarterly*, 3d ser., 39 (January 1982): 114–34, and Cornelia Hughes Dayton, *Women before the Bar: Gender, Law, and Society in Connecticut, 1639–1789* (Chapel Hill: University of North Carolina Press, 1995).

15 Salmon, *Women and the Law of Property*, 89.

16 Such traits, celebrated attributes of women in Puritan New England, were also important on the other side of the Atlantic and widely touted in fiction that praised women for their compassion and benevolence. See Laurel Thatcher Ulrich, *Good Wives: Image and Reality in the Lives of Women in Northern New England, 1650–1750* (New York: Oxford University Press, 1982), 59–63, and G. J. Barker-Benfield, *The Culture of Sensibility: Sex and Society in Eighteenth-Century Britain* (Chicago: University of Chicago Press, 1992), 215–29.

17 James Murray to Jean and Anne Bennet, 4 August 1760.

18 James Murray to Elizabeth [Murray] Campbell, 13 May 1760, Letterbooks, 1732–69.

19 James Murray to William Murray, 4 September 1761, Letterbooks, 1732–69.

20 James Murray to [unknown], [1760], Letterbooks, 1732–69.

21 James Murray to Jean and Anne Bennet, 4 August 1760.

22   James Murray to John Murray, 18 July 1761, Letterbooks, 1732–69.

23   James Smith to James Murray, 14 November 1760, JMR.

24   James Murray to John Murray, 6 August 1760, Letterbooks, 1732–69.

25   T. H. Breen, " 'Baubles of Britain': The American and Consumer Revolutions of the Eighteenth Century," *Past and Present*, no. 119 (1988): 73–104; Richard L. Bushman, *The Refinement of America: Persons, Houses, Cities* (New York: Alfred A. Knopf, 1992), 184–85; Carole Shammas, *The Pre-industrial Consumer in England and America* (Oxford: Clarendon, 1990).

26   See Bushman, *Refinement of America*, 74–77, and Cary Carson, "The Consumer Revolution in Colonial British America: Why Demand?" in *Of Consuming Interests: The Style of Life in the Eighteenth Century*, ed. Cary Carson, Ronald Hoffman, and Peter J. Albert (Charlottesville: University Press of Virginia, 1994), 596–97, 637–39.

27   Petition signed by William Plumsted and Edward Shippen, 29 March 1751, and Overseers of the Poor, 1750–1767, Soc. Mis. Coll., box 7A, folder 1, Historical Society of Pennsylvania, Philadelphia (hereafter HSP).

28   Account of the furniture at Milton, 30 April 1770, JMR. This inventory, taken after Elizabeth had vacated the premises, does not reveal the contents of the house when she first arrived. It does, nonetheless, give a sense of the range and quality of the items the house would have contained during her period of residence.

29   Bushman, *Refinement of America*, 129–31, 185.

30   James Murray to John Murray, 6 August 1760.

31   John Murray to James Murray, 10 December 1761, box 3, Murray Papers, NYHS.

32   Ibid.

33   Paul Staiti, "Character and Class," in *John Singleton Copley in America*, ed. Carrie Rebora et al. (New York: Metropolitan Museum of Art, 1995), 60.

34   James Murray to Jean and Anne Bennet, 4 August 1760.

35   Some of his criticisms echoed those of James Burgh, who specifically attacked such components of female education as learning how to "come into a room genteelly" and "dress neatly" as "trifling and contemptible . . . serving only as ornaments or trappings." Burgh, *Thoughts on Education* (Boston, 1749), 53.

36   [Dolly Murray] account book [1763–73], Ewing Papers.

37   Elizabeth Drinker diary, 4 May 1759, 2 July 1759, 26 January 1760, typescript, HSP.

38   For a case of young women's discomfort in going out in public unaccompanied, see Carole Shammas, "The Female Social Structure of Philadelphia in 1775," *Pennsylvania Magazine of History and Biography* 107 (January 1984): 78–79.

39   J. Hector St. John de Crèvecoeur, *Letters from an America Farmer*, ed. with an introduction by Albert E. Stone (New York: Penguin, 1981), 275.

40   Mary Hooper to Dolly Murray, 18 May 1762, JMR.

41   Elizabeth [Murray] Smith to Dolly [Murray] Forbes, 22 June 1769, JMR.

42   Elizabeth [Murray] Campbell to James Murray, 16 January 1760, typescripts, JMR.

43   In November 1761, James Murray married Margaret Mackay Thompson, the widowed daughter of their family friend Mrs. Mackay, at Brush Hill.

44   Mary Hooper to Dolly Murray, 18 May 1762.

45   Elizabeth [Murray] Smith to Dolly Murray, 17 February 1762, JMR.

46   James Murray to Elizabeth [Murray] Smith, undated [1762–64], Letterbooks, 1732–69, James Murray Papers, MHS.

47   James Murray to Dolly Murray, 7 March 1764, JMR.

48   Ame Cuming to Elizabeth [Murray] Smith, November 1769, JMR.

49   Ibid.

50   *The Massachusetts Gazette and Boston News-Letter*, 15 April 1768. An embroidered coat of arms produced by Ann Grant under the Cumings' instruction is reproduced in Betty Ring, *Girlhood Embroidery: American Samplers and Pictorial Needlework, 1650–1850* (New York: Alfred A. Knopf, 1993), 1:70–71.

51   *Letters*, 152–55.

52   Edmund S. Morgan and Helen M. Morgan, *The Stamp Act Crisis: Prologue to Revolution* (Chapel Hill: University of North Carolina Press, 1953; New York: Collier, 1962), 161–69; Douglass Adair and John A. Schultz, eds., *Peter Oliver's Origin and Progress of the American Revolution: A Tory View* (Stanford: Stanford University Press, 1967), 52–54, 112.

53   For an exploration of the class elements of the mob's conduct and agenda, see Gary Nash, *The Urban Crucible: Social Change, Political Consciousness, and the Origins of the American Revolution* (Cambridge: Harvard University Press, 1979), 293–300.

54   Ibid., 273–74, 296–97.

55   Dirk Hoerder, *Crowd Action in Revolutionary Massachusetts, 1765–1780* (New York: Academic Press, 1977), 177.

56   Non-importation agreement, Boston, 1768, S. P. Savage Papers, MHS.

57   Correspondence from Bridgen and Waller to Elizabeth [Murray] Smith from early 1770 describes the orders Eustis placed. The merchants sought Elizabeth's advice as to the disposal of the goods after Eustis died while visiting London and suggested that Polly Murray could sell them (see JMR). Ultimately, Polly received a parcel of goods originally ordered by Eustis. This lot included lace, cloth, hats, women's mitts, and silk gloves. Invoice no. 5, 24 January 1771, Invoice Book, Mary Murray & Co., 1771–1775, James Murray Papers, MHS; "Non-Consumption Agreement Signed by 113 Inhabitants of Boston," 31 July 1769, Boston, Mss. L., MHS.

58   Oliver Morton Dickerson, comp., *Boston under Military Rule, 1768–1769, as Revealed in a Journal of the Times* (Boston: Chapman and Grimes, 1936; rpt., New York: Da Capo, 1970), 1 (30 September 1768).

59   Ibid., 3.

60   Ibid., 4 October 1768, 3.

61   Ibid., 26 October 1768, 11.

62   Ibid., 28 October 1768, 13.

63   Dolly Murray to Betsy Murray, 27 October 1768, Ewing Papers.

64   Hoerder, *Crowd Action in Revolutionary Massachusetts*, 192–94.

65   Dickerson, *Boston under Military Rule*, 2 December 1768, 29.

66   Jannette [Day] Barclay to Elizabeth [Murray] Smith, 19 November 1768, JMR.

67   Jannette Day to Elizabeth [Murray] Smith, 30 July 1768, JMR.

68   Jannette [Day] Barclay to Elizabeth [Murray] Smith, 19 November 1768.

69   See Carroll Smith-Rosenberg, "The Female World of Love and Ritual: Relations between Women in Nineteenth-Century America," in *Disorderly Conduct: Visions of Gender in Victorian America* (New York: Alfred A. Knopf, 1985), 53–76, esp. 60–63.

70   Jannette Day to Elizabeth [Murray] Smith, 30 July 1768.

71   Letters between friends could resemble genteel conversation, a kind of formal,

polished performance demonstrative of the writer's cultivated mind and emotions. Elizabeth's handwriting, although fluid and legible, lacked the gracefulness and uniformity of that of many in her circle, including her brothers, Edward Bridgen, Ezekiel Goldthwait, and such women as her nieces Dolly and Betsy and particularly her friend Jannette Day. Good penmanship, the result of instruction and practice, constituted an important element of genteel correspondence, a visual indicator of the writer's refinement. See Bushman, *Refinement of America*, 90–95, and Edith B. Gelles, *Portia: The World of Abigail Adams* (Bloomington: Indiana University Press, 1992), 58–59. Jannette [Day] Barclay to Elizabeth Smith, 4 February 1769, JMR.

72 Jean Bennet to Elizabeth [Murray] Smith, 26 September 1768, JMR.

73 John Rowe, *Letters and Diary of John Rowe, Boston Merchant, 1759–1762, 1764–1779*, ed. Anne Rowe Cunningham (Boston: W. B. Clarke, 1903) [hereafter Rowe, *Diary*], 183 (2 February 1769).

74 Jean Bennet to Elizabeth [Murray] Smith, 26 September 1768, JMR.

75 Elizabeth [Murray] Smith to Dolly [Murray] Forbes, 22 June 1769, JMR.

76 Jannette [Day] Barclay to Dolly [Murray] Forbes, 14 April 1769, JMR.

77 Elizabeth [Murray] Smith to Dolly [Murray] Forbes, 22 June 1769.

78 Ibid.

79 Elizabeth [Murray] Smith to Dolly Murray, [April 1768], Forbes Papers, Ms. N-49.65, MHS.

80 See Jannette Day to Elizabeth [Murray] Smith, 30 July 1768, and Jean Bennet to Elizabeth [Murray] Smith, 26 September 1768.

81 Elizabeth [Murray] Smith to Dolly [Murray] Forbes, 22 June 1769.

82 Christian Barnes to Dolly [Murray] Forbes, 11 June 1769, Papers of Christian Barnes, 1768–1784, LCMD.

83 Ibid.

84 Ibid.

85 Christian Barnes to Elizabeth [Murray] Smith, 11 June 1769, Papers of Christian Barnes, 1768–1784, LCMD.

86 Christian Barnes to Dolly [Murray] Forbes, 11 June 1769.

87 Christian Barnes to Elizabeth [Murray] Smith, 11 June 1769.

88 *Boston Evening-Post*, 7 August 1769. The *Boston Chronicle*, 9 August 1769, also noted Smith's death and funeral arrangements.

89 Mr. Burth received eighteen pounds for eighteen rings; Joseph Cooledge received six pounds for six mourning rings; Ephraim Voeax received a little over six pounds for other funeral expenses. Account, 1 September 1769, folio 107, James Murray Account Books, 1732–1781, James Murray Papers, MHS; Disbursements for Elizabeth [Murray] Smith, August 1769, James Murray Account Book, James Murray Papers, MHS.

90 According to Drake, "He was "buried from his own house at ye corner of Queen St.,' says an interleaved almanac of that year" (*History and Antiquities of Boston*, 767). John Rowe noted, "Last evening died my Friend Mr James Smith at Milton" (*Diary*, 191 [4 August 1769]).

91 [Christian] Barnes to Dolly [Murray] Forbes, 26 September [and October] 1769, Revere Family Papers, MHS; this letter was written over time.

92   Ibid.

93   James Murray to unknown, 30 September 1769, JMR.

94   *Boston Evening-Post*, 25 September 1769.

95   Christian Barnes to Elizabeth [Murray] Smith, 9 September 1769, Papers of Christian Barnes, 1768–1784, LCMD.

96   [Christian] Barnes to Dolly [Murray] Forbes, 26 September [and October] 1769.

97   Christian Barnes to Ame Cuming, 10 September 1769, Papers of Christian Barnes, 1768–1784, LCMD.

98   [Christian] Barnes to Dolly [Murray] Forbes, 26 September [and October] 1769.

99   Copley relied on such props as turbans and an assistant draper to stage his portraits. See Aileen Ribeiro, "'The Whole Art of Dress': Costume in the Work of John Singleton Copley," in *John Singleton Copley in America*, ed. Rebora et al., 105, 108. On hair scarves used to suggest the Turkish turbans popular at the time at costume parties, see Paul Staiti, "Character and Class," in ibid., 67. A good contrast to Elizabeth's dress is the dark satin *sacque*, a formal and fashionable gown in the 1760s, worn by her friend Mrs. Ezekiel Goldthwait, in Rebora et al., *John Singleton Copley in America*, 272.

100 On fruit, flowers, and female iconography in Copley's portraiture, see Theodore E. Stebbins Jr., "An American Despite Himself," in ibid., 87, and Staiti, "Character and Class," 66–67. Other 1769 portraits of women contain displays of fruit; see Copley's portraits of Mrs. Isaac Smith and Mrs. Jeremiah Lee, in *John Singleton Copley in America*, ed. Rebora et al., 255, 261.

101 There are two payments listed in James Murray's accounts: 1 September [1769], folio 107, "pd Mr Copley L20.12.—," and 23 October 1770, folio 122, "Sister Smith, pd Mr Copley for her picture 12.12.—," both in James Murray Account Books, 1732–1781, James Murray Papers, MHS.

102 On Americans' preferences for images of themselves and Copley's relationship to wealthy clients, see Margaretta M. Lovell, "Painters and Their Customers: Aspects of Art and Money in Eighteenth-Century America," in *Of Consuming Interests*, ed. Carson, Hoffman, and Albert, 285–86, 293–95.

103 Carrie Rebora, Paul Staiti, Erica E. Hirshler, Theodore E. Stebbins Jr., and Carol Troyen, *John Singleton Copley in America* (New York: Metropolitan Museum of Art, 1995), 135.

104 [Christian] Barnes to Dolly [Murray] Forbes, 26 September [and October] 1769.

105 Catherine Goldthwait to Dolly [Murray] Forbes, 23 October 1769, JMR.

106 Elizabeth Smith, Will, 30 September 1769, JMR.

107 James Murray to Elizabeth [Murray] Smith, 16 October 1769, JMR.

108 Merchant and noted diarist John Rowe, a friend of the family, skipped religious services to go to the docks to witness the departure of Captain Jacobson, who sailed for London and carried passengers Mrs. Smith and Betty Murray (*Diary*, 193 [8 October 1769]). Several friends sailed into the harbor to watch her ship until it disappeared (Nathaniel Coffin to Elizabeth [Murray] Smith, 23 October 1769, Coffin Papers, MHS).

109 [Christian] Barnes to Dolly [Murray] Forbes, 26 September [and October] 1769.

110 See "List or schedule of Mrs. Elizabeth Inman Bonds to 1785," folio C, 8 November 1770, Elizabeth Inman Estate Papers, MHS.

111   Christian Barnes to Elizabeth [Murray] Smith, 14 October 1769, in *Letters*, 121–22.

112   Elizabeth Goldthwait to Elizabeth [Murray] Smith, 12 March 1770, JMR.

113   Elizabeth [Murray] Smith to [Ezekiel] Goldthwait, 17 May 1770, JMR.

114   Christian Barnes to Elizabeth [Murray] Smith, 14 October 1769.

115   John Rowe, whose wife Hannah Speakman was the sister of the first Mrs. Inman, frequently noted gatherings in his diary that included both Elizabeth and Ralph. Dinners and parties regularly included "James Smith & wife" as well as Ralph Inman. Rowe noted six visits with the Smiths in 1766; twice he specifically named Ralph Inman as one of the company. See, for example, *Diary*, 111 (18 September 1766), 113 (23 October 1766).

116   Ibid., 18 May 1767, 132.

117   Christian Barnes to Ame Cuming, 10 September 1769.

118   *Boston Evening-Post*, 9 October 1769.

4. LEISURE AND INDUSTRY IN BRITAIN AND AMERICA

1   Elizabeth [Murray] Smith to Ezekiel Goldthwait, 17 May 1770, JMR.

2   Christian Barnes to Elizabeth [Murray] Smith, 14 October 1769, Papers of Christian Barnes, 1768–1784, LCMD.

3   Elizabeth [Murray] Smith to Christian Barnes, October 1769, in *Letters*, 124–25.

4   Ibid.

5   For a more detailed treatment of the Murray family's views of educating both sexes, see Patricia Cleary, "Making Men and Women in the 1770s: Culture, Class, and Commerce in the Anglo-American World," in *A Shared Experience: Men, Women, and the History of Gender*, ed. Laura McCall and Donald Yacovone, 98–116 (New York: New York University Press, 1998).

6   Joan R. Gundersen, *To be Useful to the World: Women in Revolutionary America, 1740–1790* (New York: Twayne, 1996), 78–82, 87.

7   Elizabeth [Murray] Smith to James Murray and Margaret Murray, 16 November 1769, JMR.

8   Elizabeth [Murray] Smith to Christian Barnes, 4 December 1769, JMR. Dressing a woman's hair could be a very complicated procedure, involving curlers, irons, powders, and the use of pads or cushions for added height. See Elisabeth McClellan, *Historic Dress in America, 1607–1800* (Philadelphia: George W. Jacobs, 1904), 217–21.

9   Elizabeth [Murray] Smith to Christian Barnes, 4 December 1769.

10   Ibid., 9 December 1769. The immediacy of this account, typical of the lengthy journals that she sent to Christian Barnes, illustrates one of the functions these letters served: to engage her friend in her emotions and experiences. For the purpose other women's journals had, see Esther Edwards Burr, *The Journal of Esther Edwards Burr, 1754–1757*, ed. Carol F. Karlsen and Laurie Crumpacker (New Haven: Yale University Press, 1984), 19–23.

11   Ibid. Waxworks were popular in eighteenth-century London. Several decades before Madam Tussaud's paraffin renderings of famous people gained renown, a

Mrs. Salmon also had a wax collection that captivated Londoners and visitors to the capital. Her Fleet Street establishment, which opened in 1711, drew many curiosity-seekers, including James Boswell, who mentioned an excursion to Mrs. Salmon's in his famous London diary (*Boswell's London Journal, 1762–1763* [New York: McGraw-Hill, 1950], 289).

12 In 1750 a privately produced amateur play at a Boston tavern incited a negative crowd reaction and led to an act "For Preventing Stage Plays and other Theatrical Entertainments"; see Samuel Eliot Morison, "Two "Signers' on Salaries and the Stage, 1789," *Proceedings of the Massachusetts Historical Society* 62 (January 1929): 56. In England, after the Crown licensed particular theaters in 1721, attendance soared; estimates for the midcentury suggest that one in twelve Londoners regularly went to the theater. See Cecil John Layton Price, *Theatre in the Age of Garrick* (Totowa, N.J.: Roman and Littlefield, 1973).

13 Lady Pennington, "An Unfortunate Mother's Advice to Her Absent Daughters," in *The Young Lady's Parental Monitor* (London: Hathaniel Patten, 1792), 84.

14 Christian Barnes to Elizabeth [Murray] Smith, 26 October 1769, Papers of Christian Barnes, 1768–1784, LCMD.

15 Elizabeth [Murray] Smith to Christian Barnes, 9 December 1769, JMR.

16 Elizabeth [Murray] Smith to N. Coffin, 28 December 1769, JMR.

17 Elizabeth [Murray] Smith to Christian Barnes, 19 December 1769, JMR.

18 Elizabeth [Murray] Smith to N. Coffin, 28 December 1769.

19 Elizabeth Goldthwait to Elizabeth [Murray] Smith, 12 March 1770, JMR. Carroll Smith-Rosenberg sees such language as indicative of the possibility of women being lovers in a sense, "emotionally if not physically," and as evidence for the acceptability of intense homosocial bonds among women ("The Female World of Love and Ritual: Relations between Women in Nineteenth-Century America," in *Disorderly Conduct: Visions of Gender in Victorian America* [New York: Alfred A. Knopf, 1985], 58).

20 Elizabeth [Murray] Smith to [Mrs. Rowe], 24 April 1770, Ewing Papers.

21 Christian Barnes to Elizabeth [Murray] Smith, 28 April 1770, Papers of Christian Barnes, 1768–1784, LCMD.

22 Elizabeth [Murray] Smith to unknown, January 1770, JMR.

23 Julia Cherry Spruill enumerated these skills in describing colonial women's education and advice literature in *Women's Life and Work in the Southern Colonies*, with an introduction by Anne Firor Scott (Chapel Hill: University of North Carolina Press, 1938; rpt., New York: W. W. Norton, 1972), 193–205, 217–23. Laurel Thatcher Ulrich explored the distinction between "pretty gentlewomen" and good housewives in *Good Wives: Image and Reality in the Lives of Women in Northern New England, 1650–1750* (New York: Oxford University Press, 1982), 68–83.

24 Mary Beth Norton explained that colonists thought industry desirable for girls because it was better than indolence, in *Liberty's Daughters: The Revolutionary Experience of American Women, 1750–1800* (Boston: Little, Brown, 1980), 98.

25 One of the most frequently cited instances of this phenomenon in the colonies involves a woman who gave a poorly attired man scraps for breakfast. Upset, the man took off his dirty cap, "pulled a linnen one out of his pocket," and put it on his

head to "look like a gentleman." Dr. Alexander Hamilton, *Gentleman's Progress: The Itinerarium of Dr. Alexander Hamilton, 1744,* ed. Carl Bridenbaugh (Chapel Hill: University of North Carolina Press for the Institute of Early American History and Culture, 1948), 14.

26 Jannette Barclay to Elizabeth [Murray] Smith, 4 January 1770, JMR.

27 *Annual Register* (1759) [from the *London Chronicle*], 424–26, excerpted in Bridget Hill, comp., *Eighteenth-Century Women: An Anthology* (Boston: Allen and Unwin, 1984), 63.

28 Elizabeth [Murray] Smith to [Mrs. Rowe], 24 April 1770.

29 Elizabeth [Murray] Smith to Mrs. Deblois, 13 April 1770, JMR.

30 Elizabeth [Murray] Smith to unknown, [February 1770], JMR.

31 Elizabeth [Murray] Smith to James Murray, 24 February 1770, JMR.

32 Elizabeth [Murray] Smith to [Mrs. Rowe], 24 April 1770.

33 Elizabeth [Murray] Smith to James Murray, 24 February 1770.

34 Elizabeth [Murray] Smith to James Murray, 26 February 1770, JMR.

35 Genteel women's trades in England, such as those of milliners, mantua-makers, and stay-makers, had appeal for middle-class seekers of advancement and had substantial capital requirements for apprenticeships, with milliners' the most costly. See Bridget Hill, *Women, Work, and Sexual Politics in Eighteenth-Century England* (Montreal: McGill-Queen's University Press, 1994), 94–96.

36 James Waller to Elizabeth [Murray] Smith, 3 February 1770, JMR.

37 Ibid.

38 Elizabeth [Murray] Smith to James Murray, 24 April 1770, JMR.

39 Elizabeth [Murray] Smith to James Murray, 26 February 1770.

40 Bridgen and Waller to Elizabeth [Murray] Smith, 15 March 1770, JMR.

41 Elizabeth [Murray] Smith to James Murray, 26 February 1770.

42 Elizabeth [Murray] Smith to James Murray, 14 April 1770, JMR.

43 Elizabeth [Murray] Smith to Mrs. Deblois, 4 April 1770, JMR.

44 Elizabeth [Murray] Smith to Mrs. Deblois, 13 April 1770.

45 After some Boston merchants signed a nonimportation agreement in March 1768, they found few supporters for the pact in either the town or the countryside. Benjamin Woods Labaree, *The Boston Tea Party* (New York: Oxford University Press, 1966), 22–25.

46 *Boston Gazette,* 6 November 1769.

47 Jn. Head to Elizabeth [Murray] Smith, 18 May 1770, JMR.

48 In the will she wrote before her departure for England, Jane Eustis directed her executors to keep her shop open for six months after her death "if so long time be found necessary for the sale" of her shop goods. Jane Eustis, Will, Suffolk Probate Records, 60:167, Suffolk County Courthouse, Boston.

49 *Boston Chronicle,* 5 October 1769. The goods, listed in the manifest of the *John Gally,* were shipped in October 1768 and arrived in February 1769. In addition to receiving cloth and haberdashery items like Eustis and the Cumings, Deblois also imported brass, stationery, and shoes. Ordered before the 1 January cutoff date, these goods did not technically violate the nonimportation agreement. Publisher John Mein was trying to draw attention to all those who imported, especially to those who claimed to oppose the Townshend duties yet continued to trade in taxed goods.

50 *Boston Gazette*, 22 January 1770; see also 12 February 1770 and 12 March 1770.

51 Christian Barnes to Elizabeth [Murray] Smith, 23 December 1769, Papers of Christian Barnes, 1768–1784, LCMD.

52 Elizabeth Cuming to Elizabeth [Murray] Smith, 20 November 1769, JMR.

53 See, for example, vote of the townspeople of Leicester, *Boston Gazette*, 5 February 1770, and vote of the townspeople of Charlestown, *Boston Gazette*, 19 February 1770.

54 Ame Cuming to Elizabeth [Murray] Smith, 27 December 1769, JMR.

55 Christian Barnes to Elizabeth [Murray] Smith, 20 November 1769, Papers of Christian Barnes, 1768–1784, LCMD.

56 Ibid., 29 November 1769.

57 Ibid.

58 Christian Barnes to Elizabeth [Murray] Smith, 20 March 1770, Ewing Papers.

59 Christian Barnes to Elizabeth [Murray] Smith, 23 December 1769, Papers of Christian Barnes, 1768–1784, LCMD.

60 Boston Registry Department, *Report of the Record Commissioners: Boston Town Records* (Boston, 1876–1909), 19:16 (19 March 1770).

61 James Murray to Elizabeth [Murray] Smith, 12 March 1770, in *Letters*, 170.

62 *Boston Gazette*, 12 March 1770. The other women shopkeepers who advertised seeds that week were Abigail Davidson, Elizabeth Greenleaf, partners Elizabeth Clark and Elizabeth Nowell, and Bethiah Oliver.

63 Elizabeth Clark, Elizabeth Nowell, and Elizabeth Greenleaf signed the 31 July 1769 nonimportation agreement (Ms. L, MHS).

64 *Boston Gazette*, 12 March 1770. A few years later Renken offered tentative support to nonimportation and nonconsumption when she signed an agreement regarding the sale of tea, subscribing her name under the column of "Those who were for quiting, providing it became general" ("A List of the Principal dealers in Tea, in this Town, lately applied to be a committee appointed for that purpose, to sign the Agreement, lately published respecting the Sale of Tea from and after the 20th of January 1774," Ms. L, MHS).

65 Abigail Adams to Mercy Warren, 5 December 1773, *Warren-Adams Letters: Being Chiefly a Correspondence among John Adams, Samuel Adams, and James Warren* (Boston: Massachusetts Historical Society, 1917; rpt., New York: AMS, 1972), 1:19.

66 Labaree, *Boston Tea Party*, 27–28.

67 Elizabeth [Murray] Smith to James Murray, 19 May 1770, JMR.

68 Elizabeth [Murray] Smith to [Christian Barnes], November [1770], JMR.

69 This vivid account of the massacre is drawn from G. B. Warden, *Boston, 1689–1776* (Boston: Little, Brown, 1970), 231–36.

70 Elizabeth [Murray] Smith to Christian Barnes, 21 April 1770, JMR.

71 Elizabeth [Murray] Smith to [Mrs. Rowe], 24 April 1770, Ewing Papers.

72 James Murray to Elizabeth [Murray] Smith, 12 March 1770, in *Letters*, 162.

73 James Murray to Colonel Dalrymple, 27 August 1770, JMR.

74 Gilbert Deblois to Elizabeth [Murray] Smith, 18 May 1770, JMR.

75 Ame Cuming to Elizabeth [Murray] Smith, 10 May 1770, JMR.

76 Elizabeth [Murray] Smith to James Murray, 19 May 1770, JMR.

77 Christian Barnes to Elizabeth [Murray] Smith, June 1770, in *Letters*, 177.

78   Ibid., 177–78.

79   Gilbert Deblois to Elizabeth [Murray] Smith, 14 June 1770, JMR.

80   Elizabeth [Murray] Smith to [Christian Barnes], [November 1770].

81   Ezekiel Goldthwait to Elizabeth [Murray] Smith, 12 June 1770, JMR.

82   James Murray to Dolly [Murray] Forbes, 14 June 1770, JMR.

83   Polly Murray to Elizabeth [Murray] Smith, [1770], JMR.

84   Christian Barnes to Elizabeth [Murray] Smith, 24 November 1770, Papers of Christian Barnes, 1768–1784, LCMD.

85   Christian Barnes to Elizabeth [Murray] Smith, 20 February 1771, Papers of Christian Barnes, 1768–1784, LCMD. Mary Beth Norton points to this exchange as evidence for women's hesitation to pursue shopkeeping, based on their lack of particular skills, in favor of other livelihoods, such as taking in boarders (*Liberty's Daughters*, 143–44).

86   Ulrich, *Good Wives*, 35–50.

87   Elizabeth [Murray] Smith to unknown, 6 September 1770, JMR.

88   John Murray to Elizabeth [Murray] Smith, 17 September 1770, box 3, Murray Papers, NYHS.

89   John Murray to Elizabeth [Murray] Smith, 11 October 1770, typescripts, JMR.

90   Dr. John Gregory, "A Father's Legacy to His Daughters," in *The Young Lady's Parental Monitor* (London: Hathaniel Patten, 1792), 13.

91   John Murray to Elizabeth [Murray] Smith, 11 October 1770.

92   Elizabeth [Murray] Smith to [unknown], 19 July 1770, Ewing Papers.

93   Elizabeth [Murray] Smith to Dolly [Murray] Forbes, [5] September 1770, JMR.

94   Elizabeth [Murray] Smith to [Christian Barnes], 5 August 1770, JMR.

95   Ibid., 2 August 1771.

96   Elizabeth [Murray] Smith to James Murray, 13 August 1770, JMR.

97   Elizabeth [Murray] Smith to Dolly [Murray] Forbes, 8 September 1770, JMR.

98   Ibid.

99   Elizabeth [Murray] Smith to Betsy Murray, 1 January 1771, JMR.

100   Elizabeth [Betsy] Murray to Elizabeth [Murray] Smith, 4 January 1771, typescripts, JMR.

101   Elizabeth Goldthwait to Elizabeth [Murray] Smith, 19 May 1770, JMR.

102   See Elizabeth [Murray] Smith to James Murray, 13 August 1770, and Hellen Stenhouse to Dolly [Murray] Forbes, 4 September 1770, typescripts, JMR.

103   Betsy Murray to Elizabeth [Murray] Smith, 29 November 1770, JMR.

104   Betsy Murray to Aunt Bennet, 7 December 1770, typescripts, JMR.

105   My thanks to Elizabeth Young, Department of English, California State University, Long Beach, for pointing out the history of this play.

106   Betsy Murray to Jean Bennet, 14 December 1770, JMR.

107   Ibid.

108   James Murray to Elizabeth [Murray] Smith, 12 November 1769.

109   Pennington, "Unfortunate Mother's Advice," 71. In letters published first in 1772, Mrs. Hester Mulson Chapone also recommended the study of history, declaring "nothing equally proper to entertain and improve at the same time" (*Letters on the Improvement of the Mind Addressed to a Young Lady* [Boston, (1782)], 195).

110   Maria Edgeworth, *Practical Education* (1798), 296–97, 332–33, excerpted in Hill, *Eighteenth-Century Women*, 60–61.

111   Elizabeth [Murray] Inman to Lady Don, [1772], JMR.

112   Paul Langford, *A Polite and Commercial People: England, 1727–1783* (New York: Oxford University Press, 1992), 464.

113   Elizabeth Hamilton, account for Elizabeth Murray, 19 February 1771, JMR.

114   Jacobina Day to [Elizabeth Smith], 13 February 1771, JMR.

115   James Murray to Dolly [Murray] Forbes, 21 June 1771, JMR.

116   James Murray to Elizabeth [Murray] Smith, 5 January 1771, JMR.

117   Edward Bridgen to [unknown, likely James Murray], 9 January 1771, JMR.

118   James Murray to Elizabeth [Murray] Smith, 2 January 1771, JMR.

119   Edward Bridgen to Elizabeth [Murray] Smith, 22 January 1771, JMR.

120   Ibid.

121   James Waller to Elizabeth [Murray] Smith, 13 February 1771, JMR.

122   Jannette [Day] Barclay to Elizabeth [Murray] Smith, 14 October 1770, JMR.

123   Elizabeth [Murray] Smith to [Christian Barnes], 25 February 1770, JMR.

124   Hellen Douglas to Elizabeth [Murray] Smith, 6 April 1771, JMR.

125   Jacobina Day to Elizabeth [Murray] Smith, 13 February 1771, JMR.

126   She also made last-minute changes to her will on the eve of her departure. "Now in the River Thames," bound for Boston, she added an annuity of twenty pounds each for her cousins Anne and Jean Bennet. Elizabeth [Murray] Smith, codicil to a will, 27 April 1771, JMR.

127   James Murray to Dolly [Murray] Forbes, 21 June 1771.

128   *Boston Gazette*, 15 July 1771.

129   James Murray to Elizabeth [Murray] Smith, 28 August 1771, JMR.

130   James Waller to Elizabeth [Murray] Smith, 31 August 1771, JMR.

131   Ibid.

132   Rowe, *Diary*, 218 (24 July and 25 July 1771). On prostitution, see Carl Bridenbaugh, *Cities in Revolt: Urban Life in America, 1743–1776* (New York: Knopf, 1955), 316–18.

133   Elizabeth [Murray] Smith to Annie [Clark] Hooper, [misfiled January 1771; must be after 11 August 1771], JMR.

134   Elizabeth [Murray] Smith to James Murray, 5 August 1771, JMR.

135   John Rowe diary, 11 August 1771, MHS. Thanks to Ed Hanson for providing this citation. He is currently preparing a new edition of the diary.

136   Alexander Barclay to Elizabeth [Murray] Smith, 30 October 1771, JMR.

137   Elizabeth [Murray] Smith to Annie [Clark] Hooper, [1771].

138   Elizabeth [Murray] Smith to [unknown], [1770], JMR.

139   Christian Barnes to Elizabeth [Murray] Smith, 5 August 1771, Papers of Christian Barnes, 1768–1784, LCMD.

140   Ibid.

141   Elizabeth [Murray] Smith to [Mrs. Rowe], 24 April 1770, Ewing Papers.

142   Elizabeth Goldthwait to Elizabeth [Murray] Smith, 19 May 1770.

143   Polly Murray to Elizabeth [Murray] Smith, 23 July 1770, Ewing Papers.

144   Elizabeth [Murray] Smith to [Christian Barnes], [August 1770], JMR.

145   Edward Bridgen to Elizabeth [Murray] Smith, 2 February 1771, JMR.

146   Hellen Douglas to Elizabeth [Murray] Inman, 26 March 1772, JMR.

147   Rowe, *Diary*, 219 (22 July 1771).

148   John Rowe diary, 16 August 1771, MHS.

149   On 1 September 1771 Rowe noted, "My Brother in Law Mr Inman was Publishd this morning to Mrs Smith at the Kings Chappell" (ibid.).

150   Ibid., 221 (26 September and 27 September 1771). Thanks to Ed Hanson for the list of guests.

151   *Boston Gazette*, 7 October 1771.

152   Rowe, *Diary*, 221 (26 September and 27 September 1771).

153   Elizabeth [Murray] Smith to John Murray, 9 October 1771 [copy of the letter, written on back of letter from Elizabeth (Murray) Smith to James Murray, 7 November 1771], JMR.

154   Bond signed by John Murray and Elizabeth Smith, 23 March 1770, Norwich, in *Letters*, 131.

155   John Murray to Elizabeth [Murray] Inman, 9 November 1771, box 3, Murray Papers, NYHS.

156   Ibid.

157   Elizabeth [Murray] Smith to John Murray, 9 October 1771.

158   She held bonds and mortgages on properties in Boston, Needham, Weston, Walpole, Dorchester, Framingham, Walden, Watertown, Braintree, Stoughton, and Milton. See "List or schedule of Mrs. Elizabeth Inman Bonds to 1785" and "A List of Mrs. Inmans Real Estate September 1771," Elizabeth Inman Estate Papers, MHS.

159   Ralph Inman signed for himself as the first party; Elizabeth Smith signed as the second party; her nephew John Innes Clark and friend Ezekiel Goldthwait jointly acted as her trustees, the third party. James Murray, who would have been a likely cosigner, was still in Britain at this time. Shopkeeper and family friend Elizabeth Cuming witnessed the agreement. Indenture tripartite, Ralph Inman and Elizabeth Smith, 24 September 1771, JMR.

160   Bond of Ralph Inman, 24 September 1771, JMR.

161   Elizabeth [Murray] Inman to John Murray, 9 October 1771.

162   Indenture tripartite, Ralph Inman and Elizabeth Smith, 24 September 1771.

163   Christian Barnes to Elizabeth [Murray] Smith, 5 August 1771, Papers of Christian Barnes, 1768–1784, LCMD.

164   Elizabeth Hamilton to Elizabeth Murray, 3 March 1772, JMR.

165   Lady Don to Elizabeth [Murray] Inman, 17 December 1771, JMR.

166   Edward Bridgen to Elizabeth [Murray] Inman, 20 January 1772, JMR.

167   Ibid. This kind of discordant marriage was at odds with the fictionalized ideals of the day, which celebrated affectionate women and sentimental domesticity; see G. J. Barker-Benfield, *The Culture of Sensibility: Sex and Society in Eighteenth-Century Britain* (Chicago: University of Chicago Press, 1992), 216.

168   Edward Bridgen to Elizabeth [Murray] Inman, 20 January 1772.

169   Elizabeth [Murray] Inman to Lady Don, [fall 1773, filed 1774], JMR.

170   Rowe, *Diary*, 231 (16 July 1772).

171   Elizabeth [Murray] Inman to Lady Don, [fall 1773, filed 1774].

172   *Boston Gazette*, 20 July 1772.

173 Bridenbaugh, *Cities in Revolt*, 336–44.

174 *Boston Gazette*, 20 July 1772.

175 Elizabeth [Murray] Inman to Lady Don, [fall 1773, filed 1774].

176 Lady Don to Elizabeth [Murray] Inman, 12 April 1773, JMR.

177 Rowe, *Diary*, 233 (1 September 1772).

178 Elizabeth [Murray] Inman to Lady Don, [fall 1773, filed 1774]. Poor diagnoses from the colonial period make it difficult to distinguish between diphtheria and severe scarlet fever. Malignant throat "distempers," especially deadly for pre-pubescent children, appeared periodically; a 1773 epidemic in Salem, Massachusetts, had high mortality. See John Duffy, *Epidemics in Colonial America* (Baton Rouge: Louisiana State University Press, 1971), 113–35. John Rowe noted his niece's death in his diary and their "Great Affliction" at her passing. After staying at the Inmans' house the night before Sally died, Rowe and his wife came back to Boston to collect other friends, the Deblois, and bring them back to Cambridge "to consult about Sallys Funeral." The burial was attended by a large number of friends, "with upwards of Forty Carriages & abundance of Spectators" (Rowe, *Diary*, 250 [14 September 1773]).

179 Elizabeth [Murray] Inman to Lady Don, [fall 1773, filed 1774].

180 Ibid.

181 Hellen Douglas to Elizabeth [Murray] Inman, 2 December 1773, JMR.

182 Elizabeth [Murray] Inman to Hellen Douglas, February 1774, JMR.

183 Labaree, *Boston Tea Party*, 84.

184 Ibid., 86–87; Warden, *Boston*, 255–69.

185 Labaree, *Boston Tea Party*, 126–45; Warden, *Boston*, 274–83.

186 Bridenbaugh, *Cities in Revolt*, 320–21.

5. Conflicting Loyalties and Fighting the Revolution

1 Elizabeth [Murray] Inman to Mrs. Hope, 24 May 1774, JMR.

2 Elizabeth [Murray] Inman to William Murray, 28 May 1774, JMR.

3 Rowe, *Diary*, 273 (31 May 1774).

4 Ibid.; see also 275–76 (14, 15, and 22 June 1774).

5 G. B. Warden, *Boston, 1689–1776* (Boston: Little, Brown, 1970), 298–99.

6 Hannah Winthrop to Mercy Warren, [April or May 1775], *Warren-Adams Letters: Being Chiefly a Correspondence among John Adams, Samuel Adams, and James Warren* (Boston: Massachusetts Historical Society, 1917; rpt., New York: AMS, 1972), 1:409.

7 The ways citizenship and political participation were understood to be gendered created all sorts of complications for Revolutionary-era Americans, particularly in the arenas of property confiscation, loyalty oaths, and treason. See Linda K. Kerber, "The Paradox of Women's Citizenship in the Early Republic: The Case of *Martin vs. Massachusetts, 1805*," *American Historical Review* 97 (April 1992): 349–78.

8 Elizabeth [Murray] Inman to [Ralph Inman], 22 April 1775, JMR.

9 The British followed the Boston-Concord route that led through Cambridge. See Robert Gross, *The Minutemen and Their World* (New York: Hill and Wang, 1976), 4.

10   Hannah Winthrop to Mercy Warren, [April or May 1775], *Warren-Adams Letters*, 1:409–11.
11   Elizabeth [Murray] Inman to [Ralph Inman], 22 April 1775.
12   Polly Murray to Betsy Murray, 20 July 1775, Ewing Papers.
13   Stephen Greenblatt analyzes the experience of the marvelous, the way outsiders viewed unknown individuals and unprecedented behaviors as "wonders," and the many meanings of wonder. He writes that "the expression of wonder stands for all that cannot be understood, that can scarcely be believed," in *Marvelous Possessions: The Wonder of the New World* (Chicago: University of Chicago Press, 1991), 20.
14   Elizabeth [Murray] Inman to [Ralph Inman], 22 April 1775, JMR.
15   Linda K. Kerber, " 'History Can Do It No Justice': Women and the Reinterpretation of the American Revolution," in *Women in the Age of the American Revolution*, ed. Ronald Hoffman and Peter J. Albert (Charlottesville: University Press of Virginia, 1989), 41.
16   Elizabeth [Murray] Inman to [Ralph Inman], 22 April 1775.
17   See E. Alfred Jones, *The Loyalists of Massachusetts: Their Memorials, Petitions, and Claims* (London: Saint Catherine Press, 1930), 216; *Letters*, 160–67.
18   E. Alfred Jones cites a 1783 letter from Ralph Inman to his son that carried the complaint that the father had been harmed by his son's action (A.O. 13/75); see Jones, *Loyalists of Massachusetts*, 177–78.
19   John Richard Alden, *General Gage in America* (Baton Rouge: Louisiana State University Press, 1948), 240. Linzee's previous command was of the warship *Beaver*. Linzee's arrival on 16 April enabled him to participate in the battles that spring. See Rowe, *Diary*, 291 (16 April 1775), 291–92 (19 April 1775).
20   Christian Barnes to Elizabeth [Murray] Inman, [late April 1775], in *Letters*, 187.
21   Ibid.
22   Elizabeth [Murray] Inman to Christian Barnes, [March or April 1775], JMR.
23   Christian Barnes to Elizabeth [Murray] Inman, 29 April 1775, in *Letters*, 188.
24   Elizabeth [Murray] Inman to [Ralph Inman], 22 April 1775, JMR.
25   Ralph Inman to Elizabeth [Murray] Inman, [May or June] 1775, JMR.
26   Elizabeth [Murray] Inman to Ralph Inman, 27 April 1775, JMR.
27   Elizabeth [Murray] Inman to Ralph Inman, 30 April and 1 May 1775, JMR.
28   Elizabeth [Murray] Inman to Ralph Inman, 6 May 1775, JMR.
29   Ibid.
30   Elizabeth [Murray] Inman to Ralph Inman, 12 June 1775, JMR.
31   Elizabeth [Murray] Inman to Ralph Inman, 6 May [1775], JMR.
32   For example, see entries for 19 May and 29 May 1775 in "Paul Lunt's Book," *Proceedings of the Massachusetts Historical Society*, 1st ser., 12 (February 1872): 193–94, and entries for 26 April and 19 June 1775, in "Orderly Book of Col. William Henshaw," *Proceedings of the Massachusetts Historical Society*, 1st. ser., 15 (October 1876): 92, 109.
33   Daniel Putnam, quoted in William Farrand Livingston, *Israel Putnam: Pioneer, Ranger, and Major-General, 1718–1790* (New York: G. P. Putnam's Sons, 1901), 213.
34   Elizabeth [Murray] Inman to Ralph Inman, 6 May 1775.
35   James Murray to Elizabeth [Murray] Inman, 17 May 1775, JMR.
36   On loyalist women, see Mary Beth Norton, *The British-Americans: The Loyalist Exiles in*

England, 1774–1789 (London: Constable, 1974), and *Liberty's Daughters: The Revolutionary Experience of American Women, 1750–1800* (Boston: Little, Brown, 1980); on the legal status of women, see Marylynn Salmon, *Women and the Law of Property in Early America* (Chapel Hill: University of North Carolina Press, 1986).

37 Ralph Inman to Elizabeth [Murray] Inman, 18 May 1775, JMR.

38 Elizabeth [Murray] Inman to Ralph Inman, 20 May 1775, JMR.

39 James Murray to Elizabeth [Murray] Inman, 23 May 1775, JMR.

40 Elizabeth [Murray] Inman to Ralph Inman, 29–30 May 1775, JMR.

41 Dolly [Murray] Forbes to Ralph Inman, [30] May, 1775, JMR.

42 Elizabeth [Murray] Inman to Ralph Inman, 12 June 1775, JMR.

43 Laurel Thatcher Ulrich, *Good Wives: Image and Reality in the Lives of Women in Northern New England, 1650–1750* (New York: Oxford University Press, 1982), 35–50. Although separation caused by war is a more extreme situation that those which typically required women to act as "deputy husbands," the actions that Elizabeth took did not undermine gender roles.

44 Elizabeth [Murray] Inman to Ralph Inman, 12 June 1775, JMR.

45 Ralph Inman to Elizabeth [Murray] Inman, 13 June 1775, JMR.

46 Norton, *British-Americans*, 29.

47 Ralph Inman to Elizabeth [Murray] Inman, 13 June 1775.

48 Elizabeth [Murray] Inman to Ralph Inman, 14 June 1775, JMR.

49 Ibid.

50 Livingston, *Israel Putnam*, 216.

51 Ibid., 239.

52 Ibid., 254; see also Samuel Adams Drake, *Historic Mansions and Highways around Boston* (Boston: Little, Brown, 1899).

53 *An Historic Guide to Cambridge*, comp. Hannah Winthrop Chapter, Daughters of the American Revolution, 2d ed. (Cambridge, Mass., 1907), 175.

54 A six-week silence in the correspondence makes it impossible to determine the course of their relationship between mid-June and late July 1775.

55 Elizabeth [Murray] Inman to Ralph Inman, 30 July 1775, JMR.

56 Ibid.

57 Ibid.

58 Samuel Adams to James Warren, 28 June 1775, *Warren-Adams Letters*, 1:70.

59 Elizabeth [Murray] Inman to Ralph Inman, 30 July 1775.

60 James Murray to Dolly [Murray] Forbes, 10 September 1775, in *Letters*, 219.

61 James Murray to Elizabeth [Murray] Inman, 26 July 1775, Forbes Papers, MHS.

62 James Murray to Elizabeth [Murray] Inman, 28 August 1775, JMR.

63 Elizabeth [Murray] Inman to James Murray, September 1775, JMR.

64 James Murray to Dolly [Murray] Forbes, 10 September 1775, JMR.

65 Ibid.

66 James Murray to Elizabeth [Murray] Inman, 28 August 1775.

67 Bridgen and Waller to Elizabeth [Murray] Smith, October 1771, JMR.

68 A ledger book for "Mary Murray & Co." reveals the merchandise the young women offered for sale, all of it ordered initially by Elizabeth. The first order lists a variety of cloth as well as specific clothing items, all of which came from Bridgen and Waller. The invoice included articles of apparel for both sexes, such as six dozen

men's hose and three dozen women's cotton double heels, for a bill totaling several hundred pounds. Trimming, silk gloves, handkerchiefs, and satin hats filled out the shop stock. Invoice Book Mary Murray & Co., 1771–1775, James Murray Papers, MHS.

69   Bridgen and Waller to Elizabeth [Murray] Inman, 25 June 1773, JMR.
70   Christian Barnes to Elizabeth [Murray] Smith, 6 March 1774, Papers of Christian Barnes, 1768–1784, LCMD.
71   Linda Kerber, *Women of the Republic: Intellect and Ideology in Revolutionary America* (Chapel Hill: University of North Carolina Press, 1980; rpt., with new preface, New York: W. W. Norton, 1986).
72   Elizabeth [Murray] Inman to Hellen Douglas, February 1774, JMR.
73   Polly Murray to James Murray, 8 January 1775, typescripts, Murray Papers, NYHS.
74   Anne Murray to Betsy Murray, 13 August 1774, JMR.
75   Anne [Murray] Powell to George Murray, 2 January 1840, William Dummer Powell Papers, Metropolitan Library of Toronto [hereafter MLT].
76   Anne [Murray] Powell to George Murray, 1 August 1838, William Dummer Powell Papers, MLT.
77   Anne [Murray] Powell to George Murray, 2 January 1840, William Dummer Powell Papers, MLT.
78   John Murray to Elizabeth [Murray] Inman, 12 July 1773, JMR.
79   Anne [Murray] Powell to George Murray, 2 January 1840.
80   Ralph Inman to Elizabeth [Murray] Inman, 13 June 1775, JMR.
81   James Murray to Elizabeth [Murray] Inman, 12 July 1775, JMR.
82   Ibid., 23 August 1775.
83   Ibid., 28 August 1775.
84   Ralph Inman to Elizabeth [Murray] Inman, 13 June 1775.
85   Elizabeth [Murray] Inman to James Murray, September 1775, JMR.
86   Anne Murray to Betsy Murray and Dolly [Murray] Forbes, 3 October 1775, JMR.
87   William Powell to Elizabeth [Murray] Inman, 30 September 1775, JMR.
88   William Powell to Elizabeth [Murray] Inman, 28 January 1776, JMR. The criticism she encountered perhaps stemmed as much from the fact of the "elopement" as a socially unsanctioned act as from Powell's loyalty; after some time in England, the Powells joined the loyalist exile community in Canada. For a detailed examination of Anne Murray Powell's life, see Katherine M. J. McKenna, *A Life of Propriety: Anne Murray Powell and Her Family, 1755–1849* (Buffalo: McGill-Queen's University Press, 1994).
89   Elizabeth [Murray] Inman to Dolly [Murray] Forbes, 3 November 1775, in *Letters*, 225–26.
90   Dolly [Murray] Forbes, "Memorial to the Honorable Council and House of Representatives," 12 December 1775, in *Letters*, 229.
91   Kerber, *Women of the Republic*, 127.
92   Ibid., 125.
93   Dolly [Murray] Forbes, "Memorial," 229–30.
94   James Murray to Dorothy [Murray] Forbes and Elizabeth Murray, 10 January 1776, in *Letters*, 233.

95   James Murray to Dolly Forbes and Betsy Murray, 14 February 1776, JMR.

96   Warden, *Boston*, 328–30.

97   "List of Refugees from Boston in 1776," *Proceedings of the Massachusetts Historical Society*, 1st ser., 18 (December 1880): 266.

98   Elizabeth [Betsy] Murray to James Murray, 14 May 1780, typescripts, JMR; Gilbert Deblois to James Murray, 14 September 1776, and Gilbert Deblois to Elizabeth [Murray] Inman, 30 September 1776, JMR.

99   The week after the evacuation, John Rowe reported dining "at home with Genl Putnam, Genl Greene, Mr Inman, Mrs Inman, Mrs Forbes, Mrs Rowe & Jack" (*Letters and Diary of John Rowe*, March 22, 1776, 305).

100 Samuel Adams Drake, *Historic Mansions and Highways*, 189.

101 E. F. to Christian Barnes, 17 April 1776, in *Letters*, 245–46.

102 Ibid.

103 Drake, *Historic Guide to Cambridge*, 176.

104 E. F. to Christian Barnes, 17 May 1776, in *Letters*, 249.

105 E. F. to Christian Barnes, 16 June 1776, in *Letters*, 251.

106 Betsy Murray to Caty [Goldthwait], 12 August 1776, Ewing Papers.

107 Ibid.

108 On 17 June 1776, John Rowe noted the capture of two ships with "Highlanders taken by the Privateers, among them is Colo. Campbell" *Letters and Diary of John Rowe*, 311.

109 Archibald Campbell to General Howe, 14 February 1777, JMR. Campbell spent time imprisoned in Concord and Reading.

110 Archibald Campbell to General Heath, 17 April 1777, JMR.

111 Archibald Campbell to Elizabeth [Murray] Inman, 17 July 1777, JMR.

112 *Independent Chronicle, and the Universal Advertiser*, 31 July 1777.

113 Ruth H. Bloch, "The Gendered Meanings of Virtue in Revolutionary America," *Signs* 13, no. 1 (1987): 38.

114 Archibald Campbell to Elizabeth [Murray] Inman, 8 August 1777, JMR.

115 *Independent Chronicle, and the Universal Advertiser*, 7 August 1777.

116 Kerber, *Women of the Republic*, 123.

117 Contemporaries saw treason as a crime both sexes could commit. A Massachusetts statute of 1777 dictated hanging as the punishment for all persons, "male or female," found guilty of treason. See Kerber, "Paradox of Women's Citizenship," 358.

118 *Independent Chronicle, and the Universal Advertiser*, 7 August 1777.

119 James Murray to Sir Henry Clinton, 15 May 1778, JMR.

120 Elizabeth [Murray] Inman to John Innes Clark, 4 January 1777, JMR.

121 Ibid.

122 Jean Bennet to James Murray, 13 August 1776, Ewing Papers.

123 When James Murray, temporarily in Philadelphia in 1778, wrote a letter describing himself and his family to Sir Henry Clinton, he mentioned his nephew Thomas Clark, "a Colonel in Mr Washingtons Army." James Murray to Sir Henry Clinton, 15 May 1778.

124 Elizabeth [Murray] Inman to John [Jack] Murray, 4 January 1777, JMR. How

Elizabeth Murray considered the end of this affair is difficult to determine. John Innes Clark maintained his loyalty to the land of his birth, that is, America, whereas his cousin persisted in his attachment to the colonies.

125 General Howe ordered the deputy paymaster general of British forces to pay James Murray £50 sterling as an "allowance for his Service to Government & for his Sufferings, commencing the 1ˢᵗ July and ending the 31ˢᵗ December 1777" (General William Howe to Thomas Barrow, 10 February 1778, Ewing Papers).

126 James Murray to Elizabeth [Murray] Inman and his daughters, 7 November 1776, JMR.

127 James Murray to Dolly [Murray] Forbes and Betsy Murray, 28 March 1780, JMR.

128 Ibid., 11 April 1780.

129 James Murray to Betsy Murray, 2 August 1780, JMR.

130 James Murray to Dolly [Murray] Forbes and Betsy Murray, 11 April 1780.

131 Ibid., 11 December 1780.

132 Unknown to Betsy Murray, [January 1779], JMR. For James's views, see James Murray to John Innes Clark, 28 December 1778, in *Letters*, 272–74.

133 James Murray to Dolly [Murray] Forbes and Betsy Murray, 11 April 1780, JMR.

134 Elizabeth [Murray] Inman to John Murray, 18 September 1783, JMR.

6. The Legacy of a "Spirit of Independence"

1 After London, American loyalists in England settled in Bristol most commonly. On the loyalist community in Bristol, see Mary Beth Norton, *The British-Americans: The Loyalist Exiles in England, 1774–1789* (London: Constable, 1974), 100–102.

2 James Murray to Dorothy [Murray] Forbes and Elizabeth Murray, 17 February 1781, in *Letters*, 285.

3 Elizabeth [Murray] Inman to John Murray, 22 July 1782, JMR.

4 James Murray, Will, 5 October 1781, Ms. L, MHS.

5 Elizabeth [Murray] Inman to John Murray, 22 July 1782.

6 Elizabeth [Murray] Inman to John Murray, 18 September 1783, JMR..

7 Ibid.

8 Polly Murray to Dolly [Murray] Forbes, 7 May 1775, Ewing Papers.

9 Elizabeth Murray to James Forbes, [undated; filed 1784], JMR. For the cost of repairing the house, see Ralph Inman to John Murray, 10 June 1787, Ms. N-79.43, MHS. See also Elizabeth Murray to Dolly [Murray] Forbes, 29 March 1784, JMR.

10 Elizabeth [Murray] Inman to Mrs. Belcher, 17 November 1782, JMR.

11 Elizabeth Cuming to Elizabeth [Murray] Inman, 5 May 1784, JMR.

12 Elizabeth Cuming to Mary or Catherine Byles, 24 March and 30 May 1785, ms. N-38, Byles Family Papers, MHS.

13 [Christian Barnes to unknown], 1 April 1786, Ewing Papers.

14 Bequests of Mrs. Inman, 29 April 1785, JMR.

15 Elizabeth Inman, Will, 14 May 1785, box 3, Murray Papers, NYHS.

16 Ibid.

17 Anne [Murray] Powell to George Murray, 2 January 1840, William Dummer Powell Papers, MLT.

18 Ibid., 16 October 1838.

19   Elizabeth Inman, Will.

20   Ibid. Estate papers from 1791 show the maintenance of another man, likely a servant, as well. The rents of three Boston houses, which were eventually to become the property of Betsy and Polly, were being used to pay the annuities of the Bennet sisters and "the Maintenance of a certain blind Negro named Jack during his life." Elizabeth Inman's Estate, 25 May 1791, JMR.

21   All quotations in this paragraph come from Elizabeth [Betsy] Murray to Mary [Polly] Murray, 26 June 1785, JMR.

22   *Independent Chronicle, and the Universal Advertiser*, 26 May 1785.

23   Thomas Bridgman, *Memorials of the Dead in Boston; Containing Exact Transcripts of Inscriptions on the Sepulchral Monuments in the King's Chapel Burial Ground, in the City of Boston* (Boston: Benjamin B. Mussey, 1853), 82.

24   Elizabeth Cuming to Mary or Catherine Byles, 7 October 1785, ms. N-38, Byles Family Papers, MHS.

25   All quotations in this paragraph come from Elizabeth [Betsy] Murray to Mary [Polly] Murray, 26 June 1785.

26   Elizabeth Inman, Will.

27   [Christian Barnes to unknown], 1 April 1786.

28   [Bennet sisters] to Elizabeth [Betsy] Murray, 27 February 1786, JMR.

29   All quotations in this paragraph come from [Ralph Inman to John Murray], 10 June 1787, copied in Charles Murray to Edward H. Robbins, 2 September 1787, Ms. N-49.43, MHS.

30   Ralph Inman to Elizabeth [Murray] Inman, 25 January 1779, JMR. Ralph did not go abroad, staying in New England instead and living throughout much of the war in the sugarhouse in Boston. See Elizabeth [Murray] Inman to John Murray, 18 September 1783, JMR.

31   All quotations in this paragraph come from [Ralph Inman to John Murray], 10 June 1787, copied in Charles Murray to Edward H. Robbins, 2 September 1787.

32   John Murray to Elizabeth Murray, June 1784, JMR.

33   All quotations in this paragraph come from Charles Murray to Edward H. Robbins, 2 September 1787, Ms. N-49.43, MHS.

34   E. Belcher to Elizabeth [Betsy Murray] Robbins, 24 May 1786, JMR.

35   Thomas Aston Coffin to Mary Coffin, 5 February 1786, Coffin Papers, MHS. My thanks to Ed Hanson, MHS, for bringing this reference to my attention.

36   [Ralph Inman to John Murray], 10 June 1787, copied in Charles Murray to Edward H. Robbins, 2 September 1787.

NOTE ON WRITING BIOGRAPHY

1   Mary Beth Norton, "A Cherished Spirit of Independence": The Life of an Eighteenth-Century Boston Businesswoman," in *Women of America: A History*, ed. Carol Ruth Berkin and Mary Beth Norton (Boston: Houghton Mifflin, 1979), 48–67.

2   Ibid., 60, 49.

3   See, for example, Laurel Thatcher Ulrich, *Good Wives: Image and Reality in the Lives of Women in Northern New England, 1650–1750* (New York: Alfred A. Knopf, 1982),

and Cornelia Hughes Dayton, *Women before the Bar: Gender, Law, and Society in Connecticut, 1639–1789* (Chapel Hill: University of North Carolina Press, 1995).

4   See Laurel Thatcher Ulrich, *A Midwife's Tale: The Life of Martha Ballard, Based on Her Diary, 1785–1812* (New York: Alfred A. Knopf, 1990), and Joy Day Buel and Richard Buel Jr., *The Way of Duty: A Woman and Her Family in Revolutionary America* (New York: W. W. Norton, 1984).

5   Sara Alpern et al., eds., *The Challenge of Feminist Biography: Writing the Lives of Modern American Women* (Chicago: University of Illinois Press, 1992), 3.

6   Alpern et al. aver the importance of the female life cycle as another important aspect of feminist biography, crediting Carolyn Heilbrun for her description of "reinventing the narrative of women's lives" (ibid., 9). See Heilbrun, *Reinventing Womanhood* (New York: W. W. Norton, 1979), and *Writing a Woman's Life* (New York: Ballantine, 1988).

7   Carolyn G. Heilbrun, "Margaret Mead and the Question of Woman's Biography," in *Hamlet's Mother and Other Women* (New York: Columbia University Press, 1990), 23. See also Heilbrun, *Writing a Woman's Life*, esp. 11–31.

8   Heilbrun, "Margaret Mead," 25.

9   She asserts that the "deconstruction of the male/female binary opposition in favor of the generic Subject, the familiar generic He, [returns] feminist theory to the man-the-model standard." See Kathleen Barry, "The New Historical Syntheses: Women's Biography," *Journal of Women's History* 1 (Winter 1990): 93, 94.

10   Ibid., 76.

11   Ibid., 77, 76, 78–79.

12   For discussions of the need for biographers to be self-consciously critical and the process of separation from the subject, see Dee Garrison, "Two Roads Taken: Writing the Biography of Mary Heaton Vorse," 68, and Sara Alpern, "In Search of Freda Kirchwey: From Identification to Separation," 175, in Alpern et al., *Challenge of Feminist Biography*.

13   Linda Kerber et al., "Beyond Roles, Beyond Spheres: Thinking about Gender in the Early Republic," *William and Mary Quarterly*, 3d ser., 46 (July 1989): 565.

BIBLIOGRAPHY

UNPUBLISHED PRIMARY SOURCES AND MANUSCRIPT COLLECTIONS

Canada

Toronto
  Metropolitan Library of Toronto
    William Dummer Powell Papers
  Public Archives of Ontario
    Jarvis-Peters Papers

United States

Boston
  Boston Public Library
    Boston Fire Records
  Massachusetts Historical Society
    Advertising Cards
    Byles Family Papers
    Coffin Papers
    Forbes Papers
    Dorothy Murray Forbes Papers, 1768–1811
    Elizabeth Inman Estate Papers
    James Murray Papers
    Revere Family Papers
    J. M. Robbins Papers
    John Rowe Diary
    S. P. Savage Papers
    Thwing Collection
  Suffolk County Courthouse
    Suffolk County Divorce Records
    Divorces, 1760–1784
    Suffolk Probate Records

Cambridge
  Houghton Library, Harvard University
    George Inman's Diary
New York
  New-York Historical Society
    Murray Papers
Pennsylvania
  Margaret Howe Ewing Papers, Private Collection
Philadelphia
  Historical Society of Pennsylvania
    Overseers of the Poor, 1750–1767
Washington, D.C.
  Library of Congress Manuscript Division
    Papers of Christian Barnes, 1768–1784

PUBLISHED PRIMARY SOURCES

Acts and Resolves of Massachusetts, 1775–1800. Boston: Wright and Potter Printing, 1890–1918.

Adair, Douglass, and John A. Schultz, eds., *Peter Oliver's Origin and Progress of the American Revolution: A Tory View.* Stanford: Stanford University Press, 1967.

Boston Chronicle.

Boston Evening-Post.

Boston Gazette.

Boston Registry Department. *Report of the Record Commissioners: Boston Town Records.* 39 vols. Boston, 1876–1909.

Boswell, James. *Boswell's London Journal, 1762–1763.* With an introduction by Frederick A. Pottle. New York: McGraw-Hill, 1950.

———. *A View of the Edinburgh Theatre during the Summer Season, 1759.* Los Angeles: William Andrews Clark Memorial Library, 1976.

Brickell, John. *The Natural History of North Carolina.* Dublin, 1737; rpt., Murfreesboro, N.C.: Johnson Publishing, 1968.

Burgh, James. *Thoughts on Education.* Boston, 1749.

Burr, Esther Edwards. *The Journal of Esther Edwards Burr, 1754–1757.* Ed. with an introduction by Carol F. Karlsen and Laurie Crumpacker. New Haven: Yale University Press, 1984.

Chapone, Hester Mulson. *Letters on the Improvement of the Mind Addressed to a Young Lady.* Boston, [1782].

Defoe, Daniel. *A Tour thro' the Whole Island of Great Britain.* 2 vols. 1724–26. New York: Augustus M. Kelley, 1968.

Dickerson, Oliver Morton, comp. *Boston under Military Rule, 1768–1769, as Revealed in a Journal of the Times.* Boston: Chapman and Grimes, 1936; rpt., New York: Da Capo, 1970.

Drinker, Elizabeth. *The Diary of Elizabeth Drinker: The Life Cycle of an Eighteenth-Century Woman.* Edited by Elaine F. Crane. Boston: Northeastern University Press, 1994.

Franklin, Benjamin. *The Autobiography of Benjamin Franklin.* Ed. Louis P. Masur. New York: St. Martin's, Bedford Books, 1993.

Gregory, Dr. John. "A Father's Legacy to His Daughters." In *The Young Lady's Parental Monitor.* London: Hathaniel Patten, 1792.

Hamilton, Alexander. *Gentleman's Progress: The Itinerarium of Dr. Alexander Hamilton, 1744.* Ed. Carl Bridenbaugh. Chapel Hill: University of North Carolina Press for the Institute of Early American History and Culture, 1948.

Hutchinson, Thomas. "Letters from Thos. Hutchinson to James Murray." *Proceedings of the Massachusetts Historical Society,* 2d ser., 5 (January 1862): 360–64.

Independent Chronicle, and the Universal Advertiser.

"List of Refugees from Boston in 1776." *Proceedings of the Massachusetts Historical Society,* 1st ser., 18 (December 1880): 265–68.

Massachusetts Gazette and Boston News-Letter.

Murray, James. *Letters of James Murray, Loyalist.* Ed. Nina M. Tiffany, assisted by Susan I. Lesley, with a new introduction and preface by George Athan Billias. 1901. Rpt., Boston: Gregg Press, 1972.

New York Weekly Journal.

"Orderly Book of Col. William Henshaw." *Proceedings of the Massachusetts Historical Society,* 1st ser., 15 (October 1876): 75–160.

"Paul Lunt's Book." *Proceedings of the Massachusetts Historical Society,* 1st. ser., 12 (February 1872): 192–207.

Pennington, Lady. "An Unfortunate Mother's Advice to Her Absent Daughters." In *The Young Lady's Parental Monitor.* London: Hathaniel Patten, 1792.

Pennsylvania Gazette

Rowe, John. "Diary of John Rowe." *Proceedings of the Massachusetts Historical Society,* 2d ser., 10 (1896): 11–108.

———. *Letters and Diary of John Rowe, Boston Merchant, 1759–1762, 1764–1779.* Ed. Anne Rowe Cunningham. Boston: W. B. Clarke, 1903.

St. John de Crèvecoeur, J. Hector. *Letters from an American Farmer.* Ed. with an introduction by Albert E. Stone. New York: Penguin, 1981.

Sinclair, John, ed. *The Statistical Account of Scotland.* 21 vols. Edinburgh: William Creech, 1791–99.

Warren-Adams Letters: Being Chiefly a Correspondence among John Adams, Samuel Adams, and James Warren. 2 vols. Boston: Massachusetts Historical Society, 1917; rpt., New York: AMS, 1972.

SECONDARY SOURCES

Alden, John Richard. *General Gage in America.* Baton Rouge: Louisiana State University Press, 1948.

Alpern, Sara, Joyce Antler, Elisabeth Israels Perry, and Ingrid Winther Scobie. *The Challenge of Feminist Biography: Writing the Lives of American Women.* Chicago: University of Illinois Press, 1992.

Anderson, R. G. W., and A. D. C. Simpson, eds. *The Early Years of the Edinburgh Medical School.* Edinburgh: Royal Scottish Museum, 1976.

Armstrong, Nancy, and Leonard Tennenhouse, eds. *The Ideology of Conduct: Essays on Literature and the History of Sexuality*. New York: Methuen, 1987.

Bailyn, Bernard. *The Peopling of British North America: An Introduction*. New York: Alfred A. Knopf, 1986.

Bailyn, Bernard, and Philip Morgan, eds. *Strangers within the Realm: Cultural Margins of the First British Empire*. Chapel Hill: University of North Carolina Press for the Institute of Early American History and Culture, 1991.

Barker-Benfield, G. J. *The Culture of Sensibility: Sex and Society in Eighteenth-Century Britain*. Chicago: University of Chicago Press, 1992.

Barry, Kathleen. "The New Historical Syntheses: Women's Biography." *Journal of Women's History* 1 (Winter 1990): 75–105.

Batchelder, Samuel F. "Burgoyne and His Officers in Cambridge, 1777–1778." Cambridge Historical Society, *Publications*. Vol. 13. *Proceedings for the Year 1918* (1925): 17–79.

Bloch, Ruth H. "The Gendered Meanings of Virtue in Revolutionary America." *Signs* 13, no. 1 (1987): 37–58.

Bosco, Ronald A. " 'He that best understands the World, least likes it': The Dark Side of Benjamin Franklin," *Pennsylvania Magazine of History and Biography* 111 (October 1987): 525–54.

Boydston, Jeanne. *Home and Work: Household, Wages, and the Ideology of Labor in the Early Republic*. New York: Oxford University Press, 1990.

Breen, T. H. " 'Baubles of Britain': The American and Consumer Revolutions of the Eighteenth Century." *Past and Present*, no. 119 (1988): 73–104.

———. "An Empire of Goods: The Anglicization of Colonial America, 1690–1776." *Journal of British Studies* 25 (October 1986): 467–99.

Brewer, John, and Roy Porter, eds. *Consumption and the World of Goods*. New York: Routledge, 1993.

Bridenbaugh, Carl. *Cities in Revolt: Urban Life in America, 1743–1776*. New York: Knopf, 1955.

Bridgman, Thomas. *Memorials of the Dead in Boston; Containing Exact Transcripts of Inscriptions on the Sepulchral Monuments in the King's Chapel Burial Ground, in the City of Boston*. Boston: Benjamin B. Mussey, 1853.

Buel, Joy Day, and Richard Buel Jr. *The Way of Duty: A Woman and Her Family in Revolutionary America*. New York: W. W. Norton, 1984.

Bushman, Richard L. "American High-Style and Vernacular Cultures." In *Colonial British America: Essays in the New History of the Early Modern Era*, ed. Jack P. Greence and J. R. Pole, 345–83. Baltimore: Johns Hopkins University Press, 1984.

———. *The Refinement of America: Persons, Houses, Cities*. New York: Alfred A. Knopf, 1992.

Calvert, Karin. "The Function of Fashion in Eighteenth-Century America." In *Of Consuming Interests: The Style of Life in the Eighteenth Century*, ed. Cary Carson, Ronald Hoffman, and Peter J. Albert, 252–83. Charlottesville: University Press of Virginia, 1994.

Carr, Lois Green, and Lorena S. Walsh. "The Planter's Wife: The Experience of White Women in Seventeenth-Century Maryland." *William and Mary Quarterly*, 3d ser., 34 (October 1977): 542–71.

Carson, Cary, Ronald Hoffman, and Peter J. Albert, eds. *Of Consuming Interests: The Style of Life in the Eighteenth Century.* Charlottesville: University Press of Virginia, 1994.

Chitnis, Anand C. "Provost Drummond and the Origins of Edinburgh Medicine." In *The Origins and Nature of the Scottish Enlightenment*, ed. R. H. Campbell and Andrew S. Skinner, 86–97. Edinburgh: John Donal Publishers, 1982.

Clark, Alice. *Working Life of Women in the Seventeenth Century.* 1919. Rpt., Boston: Routledge and Kegan Paul, 1982.

Cleary, Patricia. "Making Men and Women in the 1770s: Culture, Class, and Commerce in the Anglo-American World." In *A Shared Experience: Men, Women, and the History of Gender*, ed. Laura McCall and Donald Yacovone, 98–116. New York: New York University Press, 1998.

———. " 'She Merchants' of Colonial America: Women and Commerce on the Eve of the Revolution." Ph.D. diss., Northwestern University, 1989.

———. " 'She will be in the Shop': Women's Sphere of Trade in Eighteenth-Century New York and Philadelphia." *Pennsylvania Magazine of History and Biography* 119 (July 1995): 181–202.

———. " 'Who shall say we have not equal abilitys with the Men when Girls of 18 years of Age discover such great capacitys?': Women of Commerce in Boston, 1750–1776." In *Entrepreneurs: The Boston Business Community, 1700–1850*, ed. Conrad E. Wright and Katheryn P. Viens, 39–61. Boston: Massachusetts Historical Society, 1997.

Cott, Nancy. *The Bonds of Womanhood: "Woman's Sphere" in New England, 1780–1835.* New Haven: Yale University Press, 1977.

Crane, Elaine F. *Ebb Tide in New England: Women, Seaports, and Social Change, 1630–1800.* Boston: Northeastern University Press, 1998.

Crane, Verner Winslow. *The Southern Frontier, 1670–1732.* 1929. Ann Arbor: University of Michigan Press, 1959.

Cressy, David. *Coming Over: Migration and Communication between England and New England in the Seventeenth Century.* New York: Cambridge University Press, 1987.

Crowley, J. E. *This Sheba, Self: The Conceptualization of Economic Life in Eighteenth-Century America.* Johns Hopkins University Studies in Historical and Political Science, 92d ser., no. 2. Baltimore: Johns Hopkins University Press, 1974.

Davidoff, Leonore, and Catherine Hall. *Family Fortunes: Men and Women of the English Middle Class, 1780–1850.* London: Hutchinson, 1987.

Dayton, Cornelia Hughes. *Women before the Bar: Gender, Law, and Society in Connecticut, 1639–1789.* Chapel Hill: University of North Carolina Press, 1995.

Dexter, Elisabeth Anthony. *Colonial Women of Affairs: A Study of Women in Business and the Professions in America before 1776.* New York: Houghton Mifflin, 1924.

Doerflinger, Thomas. *A Vigorous Spirit of Enterprise: Merchants and Economic Development in Revolutionary Philadelphia.* Chapel Hill: University of North Carolina Press for the Institute of Early American History and Culture, 1986.

Drake, Samuel Adams. *Historic Mansions and Highways around Boston.* Boston: Little, Brown, 1899.

Drake, Samuel G. *The History and Antiquities of Boston, the Capital of Massachusetts and Metropolis of New England, from Its Settlement in 1630, to the Year 1770.* Boston: Luther Stevens, 1856.

Dructor, Robert Michael. "The New York Commercial Community: The Revolutionary Experience." Ph.D. diss., University of Pittsburgh, 1975.

Duffy, John. *Epidemics in Colonial America*. Baton Rouge: Louisiana State University Press, 1971.

Dunn, Richard S. "Servants and Slaves: The Recruitment and Employment of Labor." In *Colonial British America*, ed. Jack P. Greene and J. R. Pole. Baltimore: Johns Hopkins University Press, 1984.

Dwyer, John. *Virtuous Discourse: Sensibility and Community in Late-Eighteenth-Century Scotland*. Edinburgh: John Donald Publishers, 1987.

Earle, Peter. *A City Full of People: Men and Women of London, 1650–1750*. London: Methuen, 1994.

———. *The World of Defoe*. New York: Atheneum, 1977.

Fischer, David Hackett. *Paul Revere's Ride*. New York: Oxford University Press, 1994.

Gelles, Edith B. *Portia: The World of Abigail Adams*. Bloomington: Indiana University Press, 1992.

Goldin, Claudia. "The Economic Status of Women in the Early Republic: Quantitative Evidence." *Journal of Interdisciplinary History* 16, no. 3 (1986): 375–404.

Graham, Ian Charles Cargill. *Colonists from Scotland: Emigration to North America, 1707–1783*. Ithaca: Cornell University Press, 1956.

Greenblatt, Stephen. *Marvelous Possessions: The Wonder of the New World*. Chicago: University of Chicago Press, 1991.

Groome, Francis H., ed., *Ordnance Gazetteer of Scotland: A Survey of Scottish Topography, Statistical, Biographical, and Historical*. Vol. 3. Edinburgh: Thomas C. Jack, Grange Publishing Works, 1883.

Gross, Robert. *The Minutemen and Their World*. New York: Hill and Wang, 1976.

Gundersen, Joan R. "Independence, Citizenship, and the American Revolution." *Signs* 13, no. 1 (1987): 59–77.

———. *To be Useful to the World: Women in Revolutionary America, 1740–1790*. New York: Twayne Publishers, 1996.

Gundersen, Joan R., and Gwen Victor Gampel. "Married Women's Legal Status in Eighteenth-Century New York and Virginia." *William and Mary Quarterly*, 3d ser., 39 (January 1982): 114–34.

Heilbrun, Carolyn G. *Hamlet's Mother and Other Women*. New York: Columbia University Press, 1990.

———. *Reinventing Womanhood*. New York: W. W. Norton, 1979.

———. *Writing a Woman's Life*. New York: Ballantine, 1988.

Hill, Bridget, comp. *Eighteenth-Century Women: An Anthology*. Boston: Allen and Unwin, 1984.

———. *Women, Work, and Sexual Politics in Eighteenth-Century England*. Montreal: McGill-Queen's University Press, 1994.

An Historic Guide to Cambridge. Comp. Hannah Winthrop Chapter, Daughters of the American Revolution. 2d ed. Cambridge, Mass., 1907.

Hoerder, Dirk. *Crowd Action in Revolutionary Massachusetts, 1765–1780*. New York: Academic Press, 1977.

Hoffman, Ronald, and Peter J. Albert, eds. *Women in the Age of the American Revolution*. Charlottesville: University Press of Virginia, 1989.

Hood, Adrienne. "The Material World of Cloth: Production and Use in Eighteenth-Century Rural Pennsylvania." *William and Mary Quarterly*, 3d ser., 53 (January 1996): 43–66.

Jones, Alice Hanson. *Wealth of a Nation to Be: The American Colonies on the Eve of the Revolution*. New York: Columbia University Press, 1980.

Jones, E. Alfred. *The Loyalists of Massachusetts: Their Memorials, Petitions, and Claims*. London: Saint Catherine Press, 1930.

Jordan, Jean P. "Women Merchants in Colonial New York." *New York History* 58 (October 1977): 412–39.

Kay, Marvin L. Michael, and Lorin Lee Cary. *Slavery in North Carolina, 1748–1775*. Chapel Hill: University of North Carolina Press, 1995.

Kellock, Katharine A. "London Merchants and the Pre-1776 American Debts." *Guildhall Studies in London History* 1 (October 1974): 109–49.

Kerber, Linda K. " 'History Can Do It No Justice': Women and the Reinterpretation of the American Revolution." In *Women in the Age of the American Revolution*, ed. Ronald Hoffman and Peter J. Albert, 3–42. Charlottesville: University Press of Virginia, 1989.

——. "The Paradox of Women's Citizenship in the Early Republic: The Case of *Martin vs. Massachusetts, 1805*." *American Historical Review* 97 (April 1992): 349–78.

——. *Women of the Republic: Intellect and Ideology in Revolutionary America*. Chapel Hill: University of North Carolina Press, 1980; rpt., with new preface, New York: W. W. Norton, 1986.

Kerber, Linda K., Nancy F. Cott, Robert Gross, Lynn Hunt, Carroll Smith-Rosenberg, and Christine M. Stansell. "Beyond Roles, Beyond Spheres: Thinking about Gender in the Early Republic." *William and Mary Quarterly*, 3d ser., 46 (July 1989): 565–85.

Keyssar, Alexander. "Widowhood in Eighteenth-Century Massachusetts: A Problem in the History of the Family." *Perspectives in American History* 8 (1974): 83–119.

Klein, Lawrence E. "Politeness for Plebes: Consumption and Social Identity in Early-Eighteenth-Century England." In *The Consumption of Culture, 1600–1800: Image, Object, Text*, ed. Ann Bermingham and John Brewer, 362–82. New York: Routledge, 1995.

Labaree, Benjamin Woods. *The Boston Tea Party*. New York: Oxford University Press, 1966.

Landsman, Ned C. *Scotland and Its First American Colony, 1683–1765*. Princeton: Princeton University Press, 1985.

Langford, Paul. *A Polite and Commercial People: England, 1727–1783*. New York: Oxford University Press, 1992.

Lebsock, Suzanne. *Free Women of Petersburg: Status and Culture in a Southern Town, 1784–1860*. New York: Norton, 1984.

Lee, E. Lawrence. *Indian Wars in North Carolina, 1663–1763*. Raleigh, N.C.: Carolina Charter Tercentenary Commission, 1963.

——. *The Lower Cape Fear in Colonial Days*. Chapel Hill: University of North Carolina Press, 1965.

Lefler, Hugh T., and William S. Powell. *Colonial North Carolina: A History*. New York: Charles Scribner's Sons, 1973.

Lemire, Beverly. "Consumerism in Preindustrial and Early Industrial England: The Trade in Secondhand Clothes." *Journal of British Studies* 27 (January 1988): 1–24.

Lesley, Susan I. *Recollections of My Mother, Mrs. Anne Jean Lyman, of Northampton.* Boston: Houghton, Mifflin, 1899.

Lewis, Jan. "The Republican Wife: Virtue and Seduction in the Early Republic." *William and Mary Quarterly,* 3d ser., 44 (October 1987): 689–721.

Livingston, William Farrand. *Israel Putnam: Pioneer, Ranger, and Major-General, 1718–1790.* New York: G. P. Putnam's Sons, 1901.

Lovell, Margaretta M. "Painters and Their Customers: Aspects of Art and Money in Eighteenth-Century America." In *Of Consuming Interests: The Style of Life in the Eighteenth Century,* ed. Cary Carson, Ronald Hoffman, and Peter J. Albert, 284–306. Carlottesville: University Press of Virginia, 1994.

MacBain, Alex. *Place Names Highlands and Islands of Scotland.* Stirling, Scotland: Eneas Mackay, 1922.

Maier, Pauline. *From Resistance to Revolution: Colonial Radicals and the Development of American Opposition to Britain, 1765–1776.* New York: Knopf, 1972.

McClellan, Elisabeth. *Historic Dress in America, 1607–1800.* Philadelphia: George W. Jacobs, 1904.

McCusker, John J. *Money and Exchange in Europe and America, 1600–1775: A Handbook.* Chapel Hill: University of North Carolina Press, 1978.

McCusker, John J., and Russell R. Menard. *The Economy of British America, 1607–1789.* Chapel Hill: University of North Carolina Press, 1985.

McKendrick, Neil, John Brewer, and J. H. Plumb. *The Birth of a Consumer Society: The Commercialization of Eighteenth-Century England.* Bloomington: Indiana University Press, 1982.

McKenna, Katherine M. J. *A Life of Propriety: Anne Murray Powell and Her Family, 1755–1849.* Buffalo: McGill-Queen's University Press, 1994.

Merrell, James H. *The Indians' New World: Catawbas and Their Neighbors from European Contact through the Era of Removal.* Chapel Hill: University of North Carolina Press, 1989.

Merrens, Harry Roy. *Colonial North Carolina in the Eighteenth Century: A Study in Historical Geography.* Chapel Hill: University of North Carolina Press, 1964.

Morgan, Edmund S., and Helen M. Morgan. *The Stamp Act Crisis: Prologue to Revolution.* Chapel Hill: University of North Carolina Press, 1953; rpt., New York: Collier, 1962.

Morison, Samuel Eliot. "Two 'Signers' on Salaries and the Stage, 1789." *Proceedings of the Massachusetts Historical Society* 62 (January 1929): 55–63.

Mui, Hoh-cheung, and Lorna H. Mui. *Shops and Shopkeeping in Eighteenth-Century England.* London: Routledge, 1989.

Nash, Gary. "The Failure of Female Factory Labor in Colonial Boston." In *Race, Class, and Politics: Essays on American Colonial and Revolutionary Society,* 119–40. Chicago: University of Illinois Press, 1986.

———. *Red, White, and Black: The Peoples of Early North America.* 3d ed. Englewood Cliffs, N.J.: Prentice-Hall, 1992.

———. *The Urban Crucible: Social Change, Political Consciousness, and the Origins of the American Revolution.* Cambridge: Harvard University Press, 1979.

Norton, Mary Beth. *The British-Americans: The Loyalist Exiles in England, 1774–1789.* London: Constable, 1974.

———. "A Cherished Spirit of Independence: The Life of an Eighteenth-Century Boston Businesswoman." In *Women of America: A History*, ed. Carol Ruth Berkin and Mary Beth Norton, 48–67. Boston: Houghton Mifflin, 1979.

———. "The Evolution of White Women's Experience in Early America." *American Historical Review* 89 (June 1984): 593–629.

———. *Liberty's Daughters: The Revolutionary Experience of American Women, 1750–1800.* Boston: Little, Brown, 1980.

Paulson, Ronald. "Emulative Consumption and Literacy: The Harlot, Moll Flanders, and Mrs. Slipslop." In *The Consumption of Culture, 1600–1800: Image, Object, Text*, ed. Ann Bermingham and John Brewer, 383–400. New York: Routledge, 1995.

Pencak, William. "The Social Structure of Revolutionary Boston: Evidence from the Great Fire of 1760." *Journal of Interdisciplinary History* 10 (Autumn 1979): 267–78.

Perlmann, Joel, and Dennis Shirley. "When Did New England Women Acquire Literacy?" *William and Mary Quarterly*, 3d ser., 48 (January 1991): 50–67.

Porter, Roy. *London: A Social History.* Cambridge: Harvard University Press, 1994.

Powell, William S. *North Carolina through Four Centuries.* Chapel Hill: University of North Carolina Press, 1989.

Price, Cecil John Layton. *Theatre in the Age of Garrick.* Totowa, N.J.: Roman and Littlefield, 1973.

Price, William S., Jr., " 'Men of Good Estates': Wealth among North Carolina's Royal Councillors," *North Carolina Historical Review* 49 (January 1972): 72–82.

Rebora, Carrie, Paul Staiti, Erica E. Hirshler, Theodore E. Stebbins Jr., and Carol Troyen. *John Singleton Copley in America.* New York: Metropolitan Museum of Art, 1995.

Ring, Betty. *Girlhood Embroidery: American Samplers and Pictorial Needlework, 1650–1850.* 2 vols., New York: Alfred A. Knopf, 1993.

Roach, Hannah Benner. "Taxables in the City of Philadelphia, 1756." *Pennsylvania Genealogical Magazine* 22, no. 1 (1961): 3–41.

Robbins, James M. *Address Delivered before the Inhabitants of the Town of Milton, on the 200th Anniversary of the Incorporation of the Town, June 11, 1862.* Boston: David Clapp, Printer, 1862.

Rutman, Darret B., and Anita H. Rutman. "Of Agues and Fevers: Malaria in the Early Chesapeake." *William and Mary Quarterly*, 3d ser., 33 (January 1976): 31–60.

Salinger, Sharon. " 'Send No More Women': Female Servants in Eighteenth-Century Philadelphia." *Pennsylvania Magazine of History and Biography* 107 (January 1983): 29–48.

———. *"To Serve Well and Faithfully": Labor and Indentured Servants in Pennsylvania, 1682–1800.* Cambridge: Cambridge University Press, 1987.

Salmon, Marylynn. *Women and the Law of Property in Early America.* Chapel Hill: University of North Carolina Press, 1986.

Sanderson, Elizabeth C. *Women and Work in Eighteenth-Century Edinburgh.* New York: St. Martin's, 1996.

Scholten, Catherine M. " 'On the Importance of the Obstetrick Art': Changing Customs of Childbirth in America, 1760 to 1825." *William and Mary Quarterly*, 3d ser., 34 (July 1977): 426–55.

Scott, Ann Firor. "What, Then, Is the American: This New Woman?" *Journal of American History* 65 (December 1978): 679–703.

Shammas, Carole. "The Female Social Structure of Philadelphia in 1775." *Pennsylvania Magazine of History and Biography* 107 (January 1984): 78–79.

———. *The Pre-industrial Consumer in England and America.* Oxford: Clarendon, 1990.

Shammas, Carole, and Michel Dalin. *Inheritance in America: From Colonial Times to the Present.* New Brunswick: Rutgers University Press, 1987.

Sklar, Kathryn Kish. "The Schooling of Girls and Changing Community Values in Massachusetts Towns, 1750–1820." *History of Education Quarterly* 33 (Winter 1993): 511–42.

Smith-Rosenberg, Carroll. "The Female World of Love and Ritual: Relations between Women in Nineteenth-Century America." In *Disorderly Conduct: Visions of Gender in Victorian America*, 53–73. New York: Alfred A. Knopf, 1985.

Soderlund, Jean R. "Women in Eighteenth-Century Pennsylvania: Toward a Model of Diversity." *Pennsylvania Magazine of History and Biography* 115 (April 1991): 163–83.

Spruill, Julia Cherry. *Women's Life and Work in the Southern Colonies.* Introduction by Anne Firor Scott. Chapel Hill: University of North Carolina Press, 1938; rpt., New York: W. W. Norton, 1972.

Sprunt, James, ed. and comp. *Chronicles of the Cape Fear River.* 1916. Spartanburg, S.C.: Reprint Company, 1973.

Stone, George Winchester, Jr., ed. *The London Stage, 1660–1800: A Calendar of Plays, Entertainments, and Afterpieces together with Casts, Box Receipts, and Contemporary Comment. Part 4: 1747–1776.* Carbondale: Southern Illinois University Press, 1962.

Sturtevant, William G., ed. *Handbook of North American Indians.* Washington, D.C.: Smithsonian Institution, 1978.

Tolles, Frederick B. *Meeting House and Counting House: The Quaker Merchants of Colonial Philadelphia, 1682–1763.* 1948. New York: W. W. Norton, 1963.

Tyler, John W. *Smugglers and Patriots: Boston Merchants and the Advent of the American Revolution.* Boston: Northeastern University Press, 1986.

Ulrich, Laurel Thatcher. *Good Wives: Image and Reality in the Lives of Women in Northern New England, 1650–1750.* New York: Oxford University Press, 1983.

———. *A Midwife's Tale: The Life of Martha Ballard, Based on Her Diary, 1785–1812.* New York: Alfred A. Knopf, 1990.

Wall, Helena M. *Fierce Communion: Family and Community in Early America.* Cambridge: Harvard University Press, 1990.

Warden, G. B. *Boston, 1689–1776.* Boston: Little, Brown, 1970.

Weatherill, Lorna. *Consumer Behaviour and Material Culture in Britain, 1660–1760.* New York: Routledge, 1988.

———. "A Possession of One's Own: Women and Consumer Behavior in England, 1660–1740." *Journal of British Studies* 25 (April 1986): 131–56.

Whitehill, Walter Muir. *Boston: A Topographical History.* 2d ed. Cambridge: Harvard University Press, Belknap Press, 1968.

Wood, Merry Weisner. "Paltry Peddlers or Essential Merchants? Women in the Distributive Trades in Early Modern Europe." *Sixteenth Century Journal* 12 (Summer 1981): 3–13.

Wood, Peter H. *Black Majority: Negroes in Colonial South Carolina from 1670 through the Stono Uprising.* New York: Norton, 1975.

Index